DISAPPEARING ROOMS

Dissident Acts

A series edited by Macarena Gómez-Barris and Diana Taylor

Disappearing Rooms

The Hidden

Michelle Castañeda

Theaters of

Immigration Law

WITH ILLUSTRATIONS BY MOLLY CRABAPPLE

Duke University Press · Durham and London · 2023

Printed in the United States of America on acid-free paper ∞
Project Editor: Lisa Lawley
Designed by Matthew Tauch
Typeset in Arno Pro by Westchester Publishing Services

Library of Congress Cataloging-in-Publication Data
Names: Castañeda, Michelle, [date] author. | Crabapple, Molly,
illustrator.
Title: Disappearing rooms : the hidden theaters of immigration law /
Michelle Castañeda ; with illustrations by Molly Crabapple.
Other titles: Dissident acts.
Description: Durham : Duke University Press, 2023. | Series: Dis-
sident acts | Includes bibliographical references and index.
Identifiers: LCCN 2022040979 (print)
LCCN 2022040980 (ebook)
ISBN 9781478019633 (paperback)
ISBN 9781478016991 (hardcover)
ISBN 9781478024262 (ebook)
ISBN 9781478093565 (ebook other)
Subjects: LCSH: Emigration and immigration law—United States. |
Hispanic Americans—Legal status, laws, etc. | Discrimination in
justice administration—United States. | Performative (Philosophy) |
BISAC: SOCIAL SCIENCE / Ethnic Studies / American / Hispanic
American Studies | SOCIAL SCIENCE / Sociology / General
Classification: LCC KF4819 .C37 2023 (print) | LCC KF4819 (ebook) |
DDC 342.7308/2—dc23/eng/20221215
LC record available at https://lccn.loc.gov/2022040979
LC ebook record available at https://lccn.loc.gov/2022040980

Cover art: The trailer-courtroom in Dilley, Texas. Illustration
by Molly Crabapple.

This book is freely available in an open access edition thanks
to TOME (Toward an Open Monograph Ecosystem)—a
collaboration of the Association of American Universities,
the Association of University Presses, and the Association of
Research Libraries—and the generous support of New York
University. Learn more at the TOME website, which can be
found at the following web address: openmonographs.org.

Publication of this book is supported by Duke University
Press's Scholars of Color First Book Fund.

Para ti, Patricia, y la sabiduría de tu silencio

CONTENTS

ACKNOWLEDGMENTS

Thanks to Molly Crabapple for producing the illustrations for *Disappearing Rooms*. It was such a privilege to think through ideas with you, and even more so to see what you created. I am amazed by your talent.

Thanks to the Department of Performance Studies at New York University for providing a supportive community. Thanks to Diana Taylor, for recommending my project for this book series and for her solidarity; Fred Moten, for steering me toward musical accompaniment and for accompanying me through grief; Barbara Browning, for lending her careful eye and her famous red pen; Hentyle Yapp, for his brilliant suggestions regarding this book's introduction; and Alexandra Vasquez, André Lepecki, Ann Pellegrini, and Malik Gaines, for their camaraderie and mentorship. Thanks to Paula Chakravartty, Nora Hansen, and Gianpaolo Baiocchi, for treating everyone like family. Thanks to Marcial Godoy, for giving me a leg up at an early stage of this project and for showing me that it is possible to effect radical politics in the institution. At the New School, Alexandra Délano Alonso, Anne McNevin, and Abou Farman allowed me to introduce this book in their class and gave me inspiration for the coda. Deep thanks to them.

During my time at Brown University, I was lucky enough to work with Rebecca Schneider, Patricia Ybarra, and Paja Faudree. They each move through the academic world with tenacity, accountability to real people, and a sense of humor. They guided many iterations of my research, kept me focused on the political stakes, and encouraged unorthodox methods. I am grateful to have them as role models. Thanks to the Department of Theater and Performance at Brown for nourishing such a vibrant intellectual community. I am grateful to have shared so much with my extended cohort in Providence: Elizabeth Gray, Lilian Mengesha, Stefanie Miller, Lakshmi Padmanabhan, and Brian Torrey Scott. Thanks as well to many other advisers along the way: Alexandra Dufresne, for spurring my interest in immigration law years ago; Emily Coates, for carving out a space at Yale for performance studies; Martin Hargreaves and Eirini Kartsaki, for keeping pleasure at the center of performance studies; and Peter Goodrich, for giving me opportunities to share my work at Cardozo Law School.

My project would not have been possible without the friendship of many people in the immigration justice and sanctuary movements who brought me into the fold. Claire Thomas of New York Law School and Heather Axford of Central American Legal Assistance allowed me to participate in their work and ask questions about the law. Claire and I visited a detention center together, and it was our attempt to process that difficult experience that led me to the idea of a *disappearing room*. I would not have established contacts in the field had it not been for Jeffrey Solomon, Emily Weiner, and their theater company Houses on the Moon. Thanks for allowing me to tag along to productions of *De Novo* in New York and Texas. Sara Gozalo invited me to my first New Sanctuary Coalition meeting and taught me the meaning of accompaniment. Sam Sundius made illustrations for an earlier version of *Disappearing Rooms*, and I am grateful for her artistic collaboration, her friendship, and her political vision. Thanks to Myrna Lazcano and Juan Carlos Ruiz, from whom I learned to make time for listening, for healing, and for friendship. *Vamos lento, porque vamos lejos.* When I think of the transformational power of community organizing, these are some of the faces I see: Amanda, Anahí, Angeles, Astha, Babak, César, Cinthya, Colette, Joan, Juan Pablo, Judith, Katie, Kyle, Marco, María, Mauricio, Megan, Natalie, Nathan, Raquel, Savitri, Susana, Sylver, and Tammy. *Y cuando pienso en la valentía, pienso en Abela, Alex, Antonio, Christian, Cristina, Elizabeth, Erick, Flor, Gladys, Juan, Kimberly, Lupita, Marco, Marco Antonio, Martín, Melisa, Miguel, Ricardo, Rocío, y Sandy.*

At Duke University Press, thank you to Gisela Fosado and Alejandra Mejía for their kindness and commitment to this work. I am grateful also to the two anonymous readers whose suggestions pushed the project much farther than I imagined.

Thanks to my siblings, who, as I write this, are conspiring to take some very large things off my plate so that I can finish the book. What a gift it is to be on your team.

Thanks to you, Pedro, *el máximo acompañante*. You were there at every stage, thinking through ideas with me. That gift, invaluable as it was, is just a fraction of the daily ways your kindness buoys my spirit.

Thanks to my parents and stepparents: Anna, Ricardo, Ana Lucia, and Neil. It is not really possible to acknowledge what a parent does for a child. Every day I understand a little more of the work it entails, and one day I'll see the whole picture.

My dad died of COVID-19 while I was finishing this book, so he became my ghost writer. He added lots of adjectives; he took his Magic Marker and drew pictures of birds; he replaced the commas with drumrolls and the periods with exclamation marks. He reminded me that *Para las estrellas, somos nosotros los fugaces.* Thanks, Papi, for making me smile.

Introduction

When Spanish conquerors arrived in the Western Hemisphere, they took the bizarre step of presenting a formal argument to Indigenous people about the legal legitimacy of colonization. In a ritual that repeated itself across the Americas, the conquistadors stood in front of people they planned to colonize and recited the text of a document known as the *Requerimiento*. The first part of this text established the moral authority of colonization in grand, universal terms, tracing Spain's authority in the New World through a chain of authorized ventriloquists all the way back to God. The second part of the text promised "love and charity" to Native peoples who converted to Christianity and recognized the authority of the Spanish Crown. The final part of the text threatened elimination, enslavement, and gratuitous violence to all those who refused to accept these terms ("[We] shall do you all the mischief and damage that we can"). The audience witnessing this ritual was then encouraged to ponder this information and provide consent.

Disappearing Rooms: The Hidden Theaters of Immigration Law studies contemporary scenes in immigration courtrooms in the United States. This book is based on the years I spent participating in the immigration justice movement in various roles: as a community organizer, Spanish-English interpreter, and member of a program that accompanies criminalized (im)migrants into immigration court.[1] In these various roles, I spent time in the bureaucratic offices and courtrooms where decisions about (im)migrants' lives are made. As someone who studies performance, I thought about how these rooms function as little theaters. I thought about the arrangement of architectural features, lighting, images, sounds, timing, and movement in those spaces—the totality of expressive elements that filmmakers and theater producers call *mise-en-scène*. Immigration courtrooms are often hidden spaces that are either inaccessible to the public or simply unknown. But just because these spaces are hidden does not mean the law is not putting on a show. The purpose of this book is to study the kinds of shows the law produces in hidden spaces. If the phrase *hidden theaters* seems like a contradiction in terms, it provides an initial sense of the paradoxical dynamics of showing and hiding, appearing and disappearing, described in this book. As I sat in these strange corners of the state, these back alleys of government, I thought: If people understood what goes on in these rooms, they would never see immigration law the same way again.

What is it about the mise-en-scène of the immigration courtroom that is so radicalizing? Improbable as it may sound, perhaps the best way to grasp the staging of an immigration courtroom is to think back to that legal ritual that took place five hundred years ago. As a defining feature of Spanish colonialism, the Requerimiento has been invoked to teach many lessons about the nature of coloniality. Among these lessons is that when the law is founded on hopeless contradictions, its theatrical presentation becomes strange. The text of the Requerimiento ends with a formal request for the Indigenous audience to ponder their options and signal their consent. Yet much of the time, the Requerimiento was staged in a way that made Native people's consent, comprehension, and even physical presence superfluous to the scene.[2] Sometimes the colonists assembled Native people and recited the text in Latin without translation. Other times the colonists did not bother to assemble an audience at all. They read the document to trees; they read it from their boats before arriving onshore; they read it to the backs of people as they ran away. Bartolomé de Las Casas, who witnessed some of these scenes, called the Requerimiento an "unjust, impious, scandalous, irrational, and absurd" document that made him unsure whether to "laugh, or, better, to cry" (Faudree 2012, 183).

When we picture the law, we generally do not imagine such a twisted scene. Instead, we picture some combination of solemn ritual and systematic rules. Yet the Requerimiento was indeed parodic, nonsensical, and absurd. It was not only cruel but also strange, and the strangeness and cruelty were intertwined. Its strange cruelty and cruel strangeness reflected the fundamental incoherence of the colonial project. The text of the Requerimiento called for Indigenous people's consent, but who in the world would consent to their own colonization? The document claims that political authority rests in the Vatican, yet it conveniently announces jurisdiction over the entire world. The document treats Indigenous people as interlocutors, yet the notion of a divine mandate leaves little room for dialogue. The document addresses Indigenous people as potential members of the legal community yet simultaneously treats them as enemies of law itself. The document asks them to believe in a promise of salvation yet enforces that promise with violent threats.

When European law arrived on American shores and made a show of itself, these contradictions had not been worked out. And so, not only the text of the Requerimiento but also its mise-en-scène aired and exposed those contradictory premises. The colonists did not call off the show just because their mission made no sense. Instead, they turned the Requerimiento into a show of a different kind—a display of nonsense itself. Would the orator reciting the text look up periodically at the trees as one might look up at a human audience? Would he acknowledge the absurdity of his own performance and let a sentence trail off? Any manner of interpreting that performance would have thickened the gap between meaning and its negation. Law, in its colonial mode, is cruel and strange theater. It is force compensating for fragility; it is the fraudulence of consent; it is the idiocy of authority and the institutionalization of the absurd; it is the fundamental delirium that ensues when one announces salvation and elimination in a single breath.

In this book, disappearing rooms are places where the old jurisprudential question "What is the status of the colonized person before the law?" continues to show up in the theatricality of immigration courtrooms where legal officials are unsure how to proceed with their own show. US immigration law, like the Requerimiento, is wrought with contradiction. Since its founding in the Chinese Exclusion Acts of 1882, this legal system has consistently been used to manufacture an exploited, racialized workforce. In doing so, it extends the legacies of slavery and settler colonialism, facilitating a process that immigration historian Mae Ngai calls "imported colonialism" (2013, 13).[3] Yet, immigration agencies never come clean about the fact that their policies maintain a racialized economic order. Instead, the steady unraveling of the law's genocidal effects is treated as the merely administrative consequence of individual violations of the law. Like the Requerimiento, then, there is an enormous gulf between what the law is prepared to say about itself and what the law actually enacts. And like the Requerimiento, immigration law has a fundamentally split character, enveloping promises of salvation and recognition within an atmosphere of violence. Since the emergence of the international human rights regime following World War II, US immigration law has taken on an increasing number of commitments toward asylum seekers and other (im)migrants who are deemed exceptionally vulnerable or exceptionally virtuous. But this business of protecting, rescuing, and recognizing vulnerable individuals has never been functionally disentangled from the racial and economic injustice of imported colonialism. Instead, humanitarian recognition and imported colonialism are deeply entwined in ways that none of the dominant narratives about migration are prepared to acknowledge.[4]

Disappearing Rooms studies how these deep contradictions add up to a profound crisis of meaning and how this crisis, in turn, manifests as mise-en-scène. In the courtrooms I describe in this book, immigration officials never recited texts to trees. Yet, they found other ways to treat people as though they did not exist. They found other ways to dramatize their own confusion and invert their own rituals. In the scenes I depict, legal officials did not know whether to make a show of authority or its absence, of meaning or its negation, of recognition or disappearance. Thus, the scenes involved a delirious mixture of all these elements. This book traces the courtroom experiences of racialized (im)migrants—primarily but not exclusively of Central American origin—whose lives are shaped by multiple overlapping colonial systems.[5] The courtrooms that I call disappearing rooms are theatrical microcosms—rooms in which the accumulated incoherence that is inherent to the colonial project resounds like a silent scream in the mise-en-scène.

The premise of this book is that if we were to listen to that scream, it might change some of our habitual modes of perceiving immigration law. The mise-en-scène of immigration courtrooms puts the moral value of individual recognition into crisis. And it raises the possibility of a decolonial perspective inherent in (im)migrants' freedom of movement. The chapters that follow explore these two issues in detail, while the rest of this introduction elaborates the problem of coloniality in the immigration justice movement and this book's method of scenographic analysis.

The Immigration Justice Movement and the Coloniality of Recognition

During the years I participated in the immigration justice movement, I developed a small sense of the deep hypocrisy of a state that threatens to kill and promises to save. I was personally involved in this movement between 2013 and 2019, during the administrations of Barack Obama and Donald Trump. These years witnessed an almost constant increase in criminalization, detention, deportation, and raids. To many people, these policies appeared shockingly new, but the Obama and Trump years only accelerated patterns that had been developing since at least the 1980s. Since that time, the budgets and physical infrastructures of immigration enforcement agencies steadily increased, concurrent with a proliferation of policies that reduced (im)migrants' legal rights.[6] Since the 1980s these trends, combined with the deliberate policy of funneling (im)migrants into physically dangerous migration routes, have vastly increased the number of (im)migrants whose lives and livelihoods are threatened by the state.[7] In response to their criminalization, many racialized (im)migrants sought relief through various legal avenues of humanitarian recognition such as political asylum, special visas for young people, visas for victims of torture and trafficking, and stays of deportation. When these avenues were not applicable, (im)migrant rights organizations also pursued public pressure campaigns to convince immigration authorities to exercise their discretion in favor of certain individuals. During the time I was involved with various (im)migrant rights organizations, we carried out campaigns to convince government officials, lawyers, and the public to grant individual (im)migrants legal status, free them from detention, or halt their deportation. Some percentage of the time, these efforts worked. Yet, it was clear that we were fighting a war of attrition. Larger and larger sectors of the (im)migrant community were getting caught up in criminalizing nets. The redemption of individuals did not seem to dampen the population-based machinery of criminalization. Instead, recognition for so-called good immigrants often went hand in hand with criminalization of so-called bad immigrants—a deeply entrenched historical pattern that immigration activists term the "good/bad immigrant binary."[8] Indeed, the youth-led movement that became the center of (im)migrant organizing in the 2010s learned hard lessons about the good/bad immigrant binary and the limitations of recognition-based politics.[9] Not only was the nature of the work impossible and exhausting, but it also embroiled (im)migrant activists in a false discourse. We were sometimes able to say, *Help us free everyone because no one should be caged.* We were sometimes able to say, *Abolish the border, abolish the police, abolish the prison, and abolish Immigration and Customs Enforcement* (ICE). But more often we were compelled to say, *Save this person because he or she is special.* In order to drum up support for individual (im)migrants, we enumerated the moral, economic, and spiritual details we hoped might convince a judge to favor our friend, our loved one, or our client. We tried to make government officials see what we saw in people. Thus, and rather queasily, we offered love itself up to judgment. We mixed the actual love we felt for people with the recognition offered by the court—a type of love that, because it is backed up by the threat of deportation, feels more like hatred.

If you do this kind of work long enough, you might get sick—sick of the judge; sick of telling him stories; sick of the stories themselves; sick, even, of the idea of the individual that is the supposed subject of recognition and rights.[10] If you spend enough time trying to convince the state that everyone it criminalizes is special, you might become persuaded that no one is special or that everyone is. More to the point, you will dream of a world in which criminalization has come to an end and everyone's relative specialness is beside the point.

Frustrated with the limits of state-based recognition, diverse sectors of the immigration justice movement have started to use a kind of "inside-outside" strategy. While criminalization makes it all but necessary for (im)migrant organizations to participate in the work of seeking individual recognition, many simultaneously advance broader visions of decolonization, abolition, and freedom of movement.[11] During the years I participated in the movement, Mexican and Central American (im)migrants did this by powerfully asserting their transnational realities. Indeed, many Mexican and Central American nationals participate in forms of circular migration, some of which (as in the case of certain Indigenous communities) predates the founding of the modern nation-state (Carmack 1981, cited in N. Rodríguez and Menjívar 2009). Their politics is not about an exclusive relation to one nation-state but about the freedom to participate in the economic, cultural, and political life of multiple nations without criminalization (Camacho 2008). These groups thus claimed their right to belong *aquí y allá* (here and there), or, in the words of one Arizona-based organization, to "live, love, and work wherever we please."[12] A distinct but related vision of decolonization was articulated by Black-led immigration justice groups, many of which argued that justice for immigrants is impossible without dismantling the larger police and prison systems. The Black Alliance for Just Immigration and the UndocuBlack Network were among the most influential organizations active during the period of my research. They worked to situate immigration politics within longer histories of racial capitalism that implicate both citizens and noncitizens of color (Morgan-Trostle, Zheng, and Lipscombe 2018). They called for a type of "transformational solidarity" between Black US citizens and (im)migrant organizations that would reframe immigration as an issue of racial justice, address anti-Blackness in the immigration justice movement, and develop inclusive platforms to dismantle all forms of criminalization at their root (Palmer 2017, 99). And finally, decolonial visions were coming from Native groups in the US Southwest that forcefully opposed border militarization on their lands. Members of the Tohono O'odham nation, the Ndé Lipan Apache, and many other Indigenous communities have drawn a straight line between the contemporary violence of immigration enforcement and the violence of settler colonialism.[13] In doing so, they remind us that the land immigration law appoints itself to defend remains actively contested territory and that resistance to border militarization is part of a historical decolonial struggle.

Although I had the opportunity to participate in some, but not all, of these movements, *Disappearing Rooms* is not an account of the immigration justice movement per se. Instead, inspired by the decolonial and abolitionist currents described above, *Disappearing Rooms* is a study of the immigration courtroom as a space where the coloniality of immigration law—and thus the urgency of decolonization—is intensely felt. (Im)migrant activists have been working toward a world in which no one has to be special in order to be free. They seek a form of liberation that does not depend on any assertion of purity, innocence, or exceptionality but rather accepts that undocumented and transnational people, like everyone else, inhabit a "contaminated reality" (Ticktin 2017, 588). Such a political vision conceptually decouples innocence and exceptionality from freedom of movement. If that vision represents the macroscopic call articulated by a range of contemporary social movements, then this book offers a microscopic contribution by putting forward the individual room of immigration law as a scene within which we can attend to the minor register and practice the flexibility of our perceptions.

Mise-en-Scène as Method

One day, some members of our New York immigration justice organization arrived at the office in a bad state. They had just accompanied a man (call him Ernesto) to his deportation hearing. During the hearing, Ernesto's hands were cuffed behind his back. The judge told him to raise his right hand and swear to tell the truth, but no one bothered to remove his handcuffs.

The people who told me this story were shocked and appalled for a lot of reasons, not least because Ernesto was deported that day. But they were also shocked by the seemingly gratuitous cruelty of making a handcuffed man struggle to raise his right hand. As they told the story, they reenacted the scene using their own bodies—this "swearing to tell the whole truth" ritual associated with legal personhood and the state of being handcuffed, which makes the gesture impossible to perform. As the members of the accompaniment team reenacted this moment, it struck me that what they were doing was important. They were taking the strange and cruel rituals that abound in clandestine rooms and circulating them in the outside world. In doing so, the ritual was transformed from something imposed in a sealed environment of punishment into something examined in a shared space of struggle. The impulse to reenact the gesture came from the desire to get inside it. By reexperiencing it in their own bodies, the members of the accompaniment team were trying not only to understand its significance but also to break its power. By reenacting the gesture together, they underwent a collective process of accompaniment, transformation, and repair.

Anyone familiar with theater and performance would recognize this activity. When we create a performance—whether a play, a dance, or a work of performance art—we experiment with the gestures, postures, spatial arrangements, sounds, lighting designs, and myriad other details that collectively compose the scene. In a traditional theatrical play, these details are present as stage directions—for instance, an instruction that "the chairs should be arranged in a loose circle." In this example, you can sense, even if you cannot articulate, why the scene would be totally transformed if the chairs were placed in another arrangement—for instance, in a tight circle or a square. At times, the objective of such experimentation is to achieve what theater director Bertolt Brecht called *gestus*, meaning a scenographic detail so precise and so evocative that it seems to distill an entire historical moment or social issue (1964, 104–6). In this case, the scenographic detail has a clarifying function. It helps amorphous or abstract phenomena become visible, audible, and concrete. At other times, the objective of scenographic experimentation may be to achieve social change. In the devised performance practice known as theater of the oppressed, for instance, the scenes that compose the performance present an ongoing, unresolved social problem (Boal 2008). Performers and spectators alike are then asked to return to certain details of a scene in order to investigate how it would unfold differently through a particular intervention, such as a longer pause, a deeper shadow, or a shifted gaze. Over and above these individual experiments, the process awakens a sense of the plasticity of lived experience, an awareness of latent potentials within everyday reality and the capacity of subtle changes to activate them. The assumption is that participants have faced and will continue to face related scenes of oppression, and thus the particular interventions elaborated in a rehearsal space become tools that can be employed in the real world. The method of mise-en-scène that I pursue in this book essentially follows the same process. I identify, analyze, and *play with* (like the experimental play of a rehearsal process) the scenographic details of the legal scenes I witnessed.

In order to pursue this method, I collaborated with Molly Crabapple, a renowned journalist, activist, and artist. Molly has accompanied people into immigration courtrooms and detention centers, and she has a keen understanding of the type of colonial theater that takes place in those rooms. I sent her my descriptions of the scenes I witnessed, which she used in combination with her own memories of similar scenes to produce illustrations for this book. Our complementary practices of writing and illustration work in the manner of scenographic experimentation described above. That is, they exist halfway between documentary and speculative realms. One of their goals is to document the details of what I witnessed in immigration courtrooms: record them, get inside them, and analyze their emotional and political significance. The other aim, like a stage direction, is to project the kernel of each scenographic detail into unforeseen spaces of reinterpretation and transformation. In this way, Molly's images and my words attempt to distill what really happened, while recognizing that what really happened remains alive in the present and available for experimentation and change.

To get a better sense of mise-en-scène as method, we can return to the example of the gesture described at the beginning of this section. At his deportation hearing, Ernesto was told to raise his right hand and swear to tell the truth, yet he was physically inhibited from doing so because his hands were cuffed behind his back. I attempted to reenact the handcuffed-hand-raise gesture with my own body and sent Molly the following description: "I could feel how my whole body had to get involved to poorly approximate what should be the province of one hand. I leaned my torso down and to the right. I arched the fingers of my right hand up. Even without the handcuffs, I could feel that it was a corporeal riddle. I could feel what a strange and groping journey it was for my tissues."

When you look at the illustration Molly created (figure I.1), it might be helpful to remember that the facial features, clothing, and props are the

Figure I.1: Ernesto seen from the judge's perspective.

product of Molly's imagination. Molly was not an eyewitness to this scene or to any of the other scenes described in this book. Therefore, we cannot treat Molly's illustrations in a forensic manner (i.e., as facts ascertained by an impartial observer meant to establish some kind of objective truth). Instead, they are more akin to Brecht's description of *gestus*—the ability of a scenographic detail to express something deeper about the whole event. The feeling you get when navigating the hidden rooms of immigration law is that the law wants you to lose your mind. It is the feeling that the room itself has gone crazy, but that is not something you can talk about without sounding crazy yourself. The feeling of colonial legality is painfully present but elusive. And yet there are moments, like Ernesto's attempt to raise his shackled hand, that boil down an ambient feeling into something we can look at, reenact, and name. In this case, the handcuffed-hand-raise gesture concretizes the ambivalence of immigration law. The gesture gives us a physical and visual representation of what it means to be cast as both a *supplicant* and an *enemy* of the state. If those two positions are impossible to resolve, then the gesture symbolizes impossibility itself. Its puzzle-like quality captures the paradox of a system that wants Ernesto to strive for the love of a system that excludes him.

Legal processes are rich in scenographic details because institutions tend to dramatize their own authority.[14] In performance studies terms, we call this *showing doing*.[15] In other words, as legal officials do something—in this case, ordering that Ernesto be deported—they may simultaneously make a show of what they are doing and create a little scene that elaborates deportation's ugly logic. What is the reason for the show? What does the show tell us? Performance theorists argue that when we pay attention to law's mise-en-scène, it is no longer possible to perceive the law as a coherent and self-assured entity. Instead, we see the law's "fragile and volatile nature," the ongoing attempt by legal officials to manage contradictions.[16] In their minds, Spanish colonists had reached the edge of civilization: no one here but Indigenous people and trees. In their minds, immigration officials operate at the edge of civilization: no one here but racialized (im)migrants behind closed doors. The same racist map activates both scenes, turning somebodies into nobodies and turning the law into a microtheater of impunity.[17] This combination of terror and idiocy, of force compensating for fragility, must have been apparent to audiences of the Requerimiento. It would have been apparent to the trees. And it continues to be apparent to racialized (im)migrants who encounter the law in its petty colonizing displays. How can you look at someone like Ernesto, who is right there in the room, standing next to his family, breathing the same air you breathe, and convince yourself that, from a legal standpoint, he never really arrived and can therefore be simply "removed"?[18] In the absence of easy answers, the judge at Ernesto's hearing engineers a spectacle of humiliation for which the judge himself is the prime audience. And through this recursive loop, the judge convinces himself that Ernesto's deportation is necessary or inevitable because he has already found a way to put Ernesto's degraded status on display.

Yet, even as this show ridicules Ernesto, it also reveals the law's dependence on Ernesto to collaborate in his own exclusion. Theater is a participatory medium. Ernesto is asked to exercise the creative action of his own body to make sense of deportation. Ernesto's very muscles have been contracted to resolve the irresolvable contradictions of colonial rule. And this participation means that the judge has already lost control of the event. As Ernesto goes through the motions, the scene changes. The room tilts. You cannot make a mockery of legal subjects without making a mockery of the law.

While figure I.1 shows the handcuffed-hand-raise gesture from the judge's perspective, in figure I.2 Molly reimagines that same moment from Ernesto's point of view.

Imagine that Ernesto was not handcuffed when he was asked to raise his right hand. He would have stood upright and sworn to tell the truth in the traditional way. He would have looked up at the vertical pomposity of empire: the floating head of the judge, the elevated bench, and the predatory flight of the eagle that reads "Department of Homeland Security." But because he had to lean his torso over in order to raise his hand, Ernesto ends up gazing upon these symbols of law from a slanted view.

Molly's second drawing teaches us that although the law's colonial show is powerful, it is never the only thing happening in the room. There are always infinite angles of the same scene. In the act of attempting to humiliate Ernesto, the judge unwittingly inaugurates a novel perspective, one that frames his own obsolescence. At the very moment Ernesto swears to tell the truth, he is looking at the judge from an angle at which that particular petty sovereign on his paltry throne is already askew.

Figure I.2: The judge seen from Ernesto's perspective.

It is a surprising but frequent observation made by criminalized, deported, and imprisoned people that at the very moment the state mobilizes massive arms to make them feel small, they suddenly experience a sense of inner wholeness relative to the spiritual poverty of a racist law.[19] Another reason I focus on mise-en-scène in this book is to draw our awareness toward dimensions of the room that exceed the law's comprehension and control. The judge may have classified Ernesto's past, but the judge does not know what Ernesto has been through. The judge may cast Ernesto as a supplicant, but he has no access to Ernesto's heart. The judge may disorganize the muscles of Ernesto's right hand yet unwittingly sharpen Ernesto's view. The judge may deport Ernesto, but he cannot map Ernesto's future.

The "room" of this project might be a rehearsal room, a space in which to sound out and play with possibilities that are latent in the room and might be reactivated through scene study. Now that the handcuffed-hand-raise gesture is circulating among us, the possibilities are in our hands.[20] If we were all participating in a rehearsal process, what would we do? Perhaps we would use our bodies to duplicate Ernesto's experience. We would tilt down and to the right, multiplying the handcuffed-hand-raise gesture, multiplying the number of those who possess a slanted perspective on the room. And then suddenly the calculus of humiliation would change. Suddenly it is no longer Ernesto isolated by that painful posture but the judge isolated by his singular exclusion from the slanted view. Perhaps, as we collectively linger in this posture, we are no longer asking, what does the law see in Ernesto? How can we make a system that is fundamentally hostile to racialized noncitizens care about and appreciate this particular man? Instead, we might be thinking that whatever this judge determines, Ernesto will have his freedom—whether through an upright appeal to the law's meager offerings of sanctioned humanity or at a slant to those categories and their hypocrisy. Maybe he will go around the law this time, like he already has.

Mise-en-scène is rooted in concrete observations, yet it aims to illuminate the multiplicity, indeterminacy, and plasticity of lived experience. How might this sensibility contribute to decolonial and abolitionist movements? As I explain in chapter 2, many attempts to dismantle the carceral system and the deportation machine struggle with problems of representation. Communities and scholars working in these areas identify twin issues of *invisibility* and *hypervisibility*. Either the realities produced by those systems remain "in the shadows" and invisible, or they become *hypervisible* (i.e., culturally saturated to such a degree that they begin to seem inevitable and impossible to change).

While invisibility and hypervisibility seem like opposite problems, they both stem from a similar scenographic predicament. They both imply a world in which our subject-object relations are stuck. Some people are watching and others are being watched. Some people are affected by these systems and others are assumed to be unaffected. Some people are inside and others are outside. All of these assumptions contribute to the sense that we are trapped in a fixed social order. In contrast, the process of scenographic experimentation that takes place in performance rehearsals often involves quite different assumptions. When one dancer continuously repeats the same movement, or when one actor plays multiple roles, or when a sound technician projects a performer's voice from a point in space far away from the performer's physical body, these acts imply that social positions and embodied actions are not the exclusive property of *that* moment or *that* person. Instead, scenographic experimentation treats reality as a set of spatial and temporal relations that can be lifted from their context, rearranged, and cast over and over again onto new people and objects.[21] First we try the scene facing upstage and then we try it facing downstage, or first we have a performer whisper a line alone and then we have a small group shout it as a chorus. This experimental sensibility might be a useful tool in decolonial and abolitionist struggles because it invites us to resist the isolating effects of social violence and treat those effects, instead, as the dispersed material of a predicament that is ongoing and shared. By doing so, we might break down barriers between the affected and the supposedly unaffected, the subject and the object, the inside and the outside.

The Rooms

Disappearing Rooms is organized as a journey through several immigration courtrooms. Each room was chosen because it encapsulates a particular contradiction in the staging of immigration law.

Chapter 1 focuses on a place ominously called the *Removal Room*. At the time of my participation in an accompaniment program, the Removal Room occupied one floor of a crowded multipurpose government building in Manhattan. In this room, (im)migrants were expected to "check in" with ICE officials. Those who appeared at check-ins were sometimes detained and deported, but the room was designed to shield the event of deportation from view. The central contradiction examined in chapter 1 is that the work of "removing" people requires putting on a show. I analyze the scenographic design of the room as a theater of disappearance, a nauseating type of state theater that aims not only to remove people but also, paradoxically, to make their removability visible. The first half of the chapter examines how this complex combination of appearance and disappearance manifests in the scenographic details of that room.

The second half of the chapter retraces some of my journeys through the Removal Room during the time I participated in an accompaniment program run by the New Sanctuary Coalition of New York. Volunteers accompanied (im)migrants as a form of moral support and as a way to signal our stance against deportation. Accompaniment involved the difficult work of apparently doing nothing: holding still, holding silent, and holding oneself back from any unplanned action. Analyzing the evolution of the accompaniment program in 2017, this section describes the collective scenographic experimentation we undertook in an effort to shift the dynamics of the room.

The prison abolition movement has long argued that reformers' attempts to make prison more humane, gender-sensitive, and participatory tend not to diminish the institution but to expand it (Kaba 2014; Murakawa 2014). This contradiction has been especially pronounced in the type of immigration imprisonment known as family detention, where humanitarian reforms spurred what some call an "immigration detention improvement complex" (Morris 2017, 51). In chapter 2 I examine the cycles of resistance and reform that took place in the institution of family detention in the post-9/11 period.

These cycles of resistance and reform led not only to the expansion of family detention but also to the creation of blurred spaces in which humanitarian and eliminatory impulses coincide. The second half of chapter 2 documents my experience at the South Texas Family Residential Center, where I volunteered as a Spanish-English interpreter helping detained women apply for a preliminary form of political asylum. I analyze the mise-en-scène of an immigration courtroom built inside the detention center: a retrofitted trailer where the immigration judge was broadcast on a screen. The judge, in this instance, was literally a no-show—absent from the courtroom over which he supposedly presided. This scene testifies to the bizarre theater that ensues when the seemingly benevolent act of refuge offered by asylum law is nested inside a detention center built on a history of racial elimination. Like the Requerimiento, these two projects cannot coexist without undoing each other. They cannot coexist without breaking the room.

The final contradiction I explore in this book is that while the immigration courtroom treats (im)migrants as suppliants dependent on the state's recognition, many of the people seeking legal recognition in immigration courtrooms arrive in the United States through their own acts of unsanctioned, autonomous movement.[22] Chapter 3 conducts a kind of rehearsal process that pays attention to the freedom of movement and freedom of conscience that, though suppressed, are always present in the room. In order to conduct this thought experiment, the chapter changes our perspective on the scene. While the first two chapters study these rooms from the perspective of (im)migrants, translators, and accompaniment teams, chapter 3 studies the asylum office from the perspective of asylum officers tasked with interviewing asylum seekers and determining whether to grant asylum. The premise of such interviews is that some people have legitimate claims to asylum and others do not, that some people are credible and others are not, and—although this is unlikely to be stipulated in any official handbook—that some people are special and others are not. The scene of the asylum interview thus gives us an entry point into the good/bad immigrant binary—the moral distinctions between people to whom the state grants protection and those from whom the state supposedly protects itself. Chapter 3 examines the range of familiar cultural formulas used by these officials to make sense of their work: the liberal plot of a special individual rising above his or her society, the melodramatic trope that good can be thoroughly wrested from evil, and the forensic appetite to sift truth from lies.

While these basic plotlines dominate the asylum interview, they do not represent the totality of the scene. Rather, the term *mise-en-scène* points to the fact that the sense of a scene is a product of the constant interplay between background and foreground, onstage and offstage, what happened and what might have happened.[23] Even if the framing of a scene aims to exclude certain realities, those realities persist—or "insist," in Gilles Deleuze's terms (1983, 17). Chapter 3 applies this sort of scenographic sensibility in order to sustain a double feeling, a flicker between the official drama of the asylum interview and the suppressed presence of all it excludes. Alongside the apparently urgent work of classifying (im)migrants into categories of good and bad and real and fake, immigration remains a heterogeneous, unpredictable, and unruly phenomenon. As we imagine sitting in the asylum officer's chair, we ask what it would mean to hold on to the *autonomy* of mobility: the fact that racialized (im)migrants move in unpredictable ways, for their own reasons, according to a transnational consciousness that the state can neither understand nor control. What would it take to make this unspecial, unknown terrain of human mobility more compelling than the drama of individual recognition? What would it feel like to offer refuge from recognition, rather than recognition as refuge? What would it mean to shelter the unknowability of the refugee?

Finally, in the coda, this book leaves the confines of the courtroom altogether and also leaves behind geometric space and linear time. We return to the question of accompaniment, but this time as part of a wider geography of (im)migrant disappearance. In accompaniment, physical presence is not a metaphor. Accompanying another person means sharing space with them, moving with them wherever their journey leads. But what if we cannot share space with another person because we cannot find that person on any map? What if we cannot move with them because we do not know whether they are in motion? The coda tells the story of a woman who disappeared while crossing the US-Mexico border and her family's search for answers. Drawing from musical ideas of accompaniment, it ponders how the searchers and the searched for accompany one another outside space and time.

....

As I sat in these strange corners of the state, these back alleys of government, I thought: If people outside knew what goes on in these rooms, the rooms themselves would change. Just by exposing the contents of these rooms, the law has already lost its power to seal a colonial microcosm behind closed doors. As we move to chapter 1, we enter the terrorizing design of the Removal Room, but by doing so together, we open a window.

ONE

Removal Room
Disappearance and the Practice of Accompaniment

That is how we talk about it: "the ninth floor." There are many floors in this New York office building filled with a range of governmental purposes, which means that many people in the building are laughing, drinking coffee, texting on their phones, or discussing meetings. The ninth floor, or its silence, starts in the elevator on the way up; it is like a chill that other people bound for more benign floors might not catch. The ninth floor has only one destination: the Removal Room.

In the spring of 2017 I took part in an accompaniment program, which involves taking people up to the ninth floor, when that is the last thing they want to do, and spending the day there with them. They present themselves to this room knowing they might not come out—or, rather, they might not come out the way they went in. They might not retrace their steps through the main elevators and the main entrance. Instead, they might exit through the back elevators, shackled, and be taken somewhere and "held" for an indeterminate time; taken somewhere else and "held" there, not allowed to call their loved ones, then allowed, then not allowed; "transferred" somewhere, shackled, and put on a plane. They might enter this building and never see their homes again.

Yet to miss an appointment for an "ICE check-in" in the Removal Room is to be ordered deported in absentia, to potentially become the subject of a raid, and to lose grounds for any legal avenues of appeal. Thus, to resist the room is to make any sphere of existence a potential Removal Room. The room is simultaneously localized in space and expansive. It coerces people to enter only by threatening to grow larger and engulf their homes, workplaces, safety, sleep. The Removal Room thus participates in what political geographer Nancy Hiemstra has termed the "everywhere-ness of the immigration bureaucracy," the quality of unpredictable and generalized threat that defines "removable" noncitizens' experience of both public and private space (2014, 574).

Everywhereness. Hidden elevators. Localized in space, yet expansive. When we talk about the Removal Room, we are not talking about the fixed proportions of a geometric cube. This chapter analyzes the expe-rience of repeatedly entering a room whose strange spatial parameters are part of its violence. It theorizes a set of scenographic distortions that include, as mentioned above, the sensation that the room grows larger than itself. But to focus on such distortions does not imply that the Re-moval Room is a wholly subjective phenomenon. It is not a figment of the imagination. Rather, the Removal Room is a real place with real, objec-tive properties. Its dimensions, its blocked sightlines, the images that hang on the walls—these objective elements are the basic materials with which "removal" is executed as a simultaneously physical and perceptual project. To talk about this room, then, we need a concept of mise-en-scène, where space is neither wholly objective nor wholly subjective, but rather a dy-namic interaction of both.[1] In this chapter, I analyze how the room's spatial arrangement contributes to a particular paradigm of state violence known as *disappearance*. But I do not undertake this analysis from the perspective of a neutral observer. Instead, I do so as a participant in the accompani-ment program, where our job is to remain by the side of people attending ICE check-ins and sit with them for a seemingly eternal duration until we find out whether they will be "removed." Accompaniment conditions the path-way through which our bodies enter the room, the amount of time we spend there, and the commitment we feel. Accompaniment amplifies the stakes and thickens the air. For reasons I will elaborate in this chapter, the embod-ied practice of accompaniment can heighten awareness of mise-en-scène at the same time that it meaningfully transforms the room.

Ravi Ragbir, one of the New Sanctuary Coalition's cofounders, devel-oped the accompaniment program in concert with his personal refusal to be "hunted in his own home." He joins many others, including those taking physical sanctuary in houses of worship across the country, in publicly refusing the condition of fugitivity and psychological terrorization of deportable life. The accompaniment program functions as part of a strategy to prevent deportations in New York City. This strategy requires a constant reassessment of risks. At the time of this writing in 2017, the individual decision to appear at an ICE check-in in the Removal Room, when supported by an extended community movement, continues to be less risky than missing the appointment. Yet, as Ravi reminds accompaniment trainees, that risk assessment does nothing to reduce the terror of entering the ninth floor. When your life has been transformed into "perpetual traumatic stress disorder," as he calls it, the reasoning of calculated risk feels more abstract the closer you get to the building. Sara Gozalo, the program's coordinator, explained that many people become physically ill and disoriented during the train journey to an ICE check-in. One woman I accompanied told me, *"Tengo el estómago revuelto, la cabeza revuelta. Tengo todo revuelto."* Her articulation of a body *revuelto*—scrambled, queasy, and (a more distant definition) in revolt—distills the sensation of entering the Removal Room. How can one not feel *revuelto* when one has to coerce the body to enter this building against the body's better judgment?

The check-in is an ICE process for individuals who have been released from detention under an order of release on recognizance or an order of supervision. It can apply to people who have been ordered removed but the state has been unable to deport, stateless people who cannot be deported to any country, people living in the United States who were arrested and released on bond, and people who turned themselves in at the border requesting asylum and were then "paroled" into the United States. The check-in is thus a kind of extended probation for those with pending immigration cases that ICE has placed on its "nondetained docket." Such (im)migrants are supposed to report regularly to ICE, obtain travel documents to prepare for the possibility of future deportation, keep ICE informed of their whereabouts, and generally demonstrate their "compliance" (Rutgers School of Law 2012, 6).

"Absolute power," as Nicholas De Genova writes, "is the power to make oneself unpredictable and deny other people any reasonable anticipation, to place them in total uncertainty" (2016a, 7). In the case of those subject to ICE check-ins, the state exacerbates this uncertainty, producing a kind of extended, sadistic play. Most of the time, ICE officers do not detain those checking in. Based on factors unknown to us—and absent from any transparent norm—these officers dispense a quantity of time until those checking in must check in again.[2] I once tried to comfort someone I had accompanied by saying, "Six months? Not so bad! I'm glad they didn't give you one month like last time." And to that ignorant comment, I received an important correction: "I still can't breathe." To me, six months meant five extra months outside the room. But that is because my time is not spent imagining the room. We habitually postpone breathing until after the crisis ends; we habitually say we will deal with the crisis after we "catch our breath" and can "actually breathe." For the woman I accompanied, the moment after her check-in was a restart of the countdown to a decision that would most likely be *Now, await the next indecision.* Who is to say that six months are better than one? Who is to say that time outside the room is time outside the room?

According to Sara, participation in the accompaniment program changes people. "Once accompaniers have been to the Removal Room," she told me, "they never believe any false narratives about immigration law again. They will never listen to an elected official say, 'We're just going to deport the criminals,' and be fooled. Now they know who the supposed criminals are. Once people see the violence of the room they can see the system for how it is and become part of the movement for change." When Sara cites the familiar refrain, "We're just going to deport the criminals," she names the liberal law-and-order discourse that sustains the good/bad immigrant binary: on one side, the "deserving" (im)migrant, and on the other, the "criminal alien." As abolitionist scholar and activist Angela Davis notes, individuals break laws, but regimes of punishment work through a population-based logic to constitute criminals "as a class, and, indeed, a class of human beings undeserving of the civil and human rights accorded to others" (2011, 112). To be considered criminal goes far beyond individual acts that violate the law. Instead, it involves larger material and ideological processes that turn some people "permanently, rather than temporarily (during an unfortunate period in their lives)," into a social enemy (Gilmore and Loyd 2012, 49). These processes can shift the rules of the game to the point where it becomes "all but impossible for [criminalized people] to be law-abiding" (Cacho 2012, 6).

Yet according to Sara, participation in the accompaniment program appears to work against these powerful processes. Having visited the Removal Room, participants find that they can no longer take the term *criminal* at face value. Somehow, the embodied journey of accompaniment has the potential to sidestep the concept of criminality that normalizes and justifies the deportation regime. What does it mean to sidestep criminality? When you accompany someone into the Removal Room, you are physically immersed in the environment of punishment. You accompany that individual through security procedures, dismissive gestures, barked orders, barriers inhibiting movement, blocked sightlines, gratuitous prohibitions against eating, impositions of uncertainty, and threats of separation. You thus witness a multifaceted theater of criminalization at work. But you do not do so as a spectator watching from an external position. Rather, you witness a theater of criminalization while standing to the side of the one criminalized, walking as her shadow, taking her steps, sidestepping. Thus, you realize that you did not meet a "criminal immigrant" when you met the particular person you accompanied that day; in fact, you will never meet one if "criminal immigrant" names the kind of person whose behavior somehow triggered the array of ambient insults taking place in that room. Standing to the side of the supposed criminal, you see the array of insults but not the criminal behavior. You see criminalization but not criminals. You see the scenographic devices that attempt to frame the criminal, but you never see the criminal framed.[3]

This chapter begins with a brief history of the policies since the 1980s that expanded the class of "removable" people and helped produce the figure of the "criminal immigrant." It then mirrors the practice of accompaniment by retracing a journey into the mise-en-scène of the Removal Room. Here, I analyze how the architectural and aesthetic elements of the room convey the logic of disappearance. If that section analyzes the scene from the accompanier's perspective, the next section flips the perspective and asks how accompaniers, in turn, transform what they observe. I examine how an embodied practice based on silence, stillness, and self-restraint manages to change the dynamics of the room.

Crimmigration

When the Trump administration took office, it started detaining and deporting people during their routine check-ins, as described in the following newspaper article:

> Across the U.S., judges have issued final removal orders for more than 900,000 people in the country illegally. Many remain as long as they check in regularly with ICE.

Under the Obama administration, they were not considered priorities for deportation because they had clean criminal records or strong ties to their communities. The Trump administration, however, is taking a more aggressive enforcement stance.

President Trump signed executive orders that broadly expanded the number of people who are priorities for deportation. That category now includes many immigrants whose only offense may be entering or staying in the country illegally. (Robbins 2017)

From this article, it is clear that even introducing the idea of the Removal Room embroils us in a discourse that measures the violence of the system based on the perceived criminality or innocence of the (im)migrants it targets. This discourse encourages us to account for the current escalation of state violence by arguing, effectively, that they are *taking the wrong people.* The article implies that, prior to Trump, ICE targeted only serious criminals rather than those with family ties who dutifully showed up at check-ins. This creates the impression that it is possible to maintain a system of removal so long as that system distinguishes between law-abiding individuals and criminals. The assumption here is that incarceration and banishment can proceed in a fair, unbiased way. The problems with this analysis are both conceptual and historical. On a conceptual level, the practice of deportation is founded in white supremacy, and the idea of fairly administering white supremacy is a contradiction in terms.[4] On a historical level, the analysis errs because it implies that criminalization began with the Trump presidency. In fact, current processes of criminalization began much earlier with the advent of a set of policies collectively termed "crimmigration."

Starting in the 1980s, a wave of new policies inaugurated what abolitionist scholar Ruth Wilson Gilmore calls a "criminal-law production frenzy" and dramatically expanded the population in both prisons and detention centers (2007, 110). In the criminal system, such policies included racial profiling, mandatory sentencing guidelines, antidrug laws, three-strikes policies, gang databases, and sentencing enhancements, as well as "broken windows" policing practices that target low-level "crimes of poverty" such as shoplifting, loitering, and jumping turnstiles (Vitale 2017). In the immigration system, new policies ensured that those (im)migrants convicted in the criminal system would also suffer severe immigration consequences. These laws established the concept of the "aggravated felony," a list of actions that trigger detention and deportation without due process. The list began in 1988 with a limited number of relatively serious offenses and then steadily expanded to include not only trivial activities such as writing a bad check but also "undocumented entry following deportation" (Coleman and Kocher 2011). In other words, the legal invention of the aggravated felony criminalized actions by noncitizens that would not count as aggravated felonies if committed by citizens. And at the same time, it deftly began to blur undocumented status and crime, rendering the term *criminal immigrant* conceptually redundant in ways that mapped onto and fortified long-standing constructions of Latinxs as natural criminals (Gonzales 2013). As a result of these laws, (im)migrants, including legal permanent residents (LPRs), could serve sentences in the criminal legal system and then immediately be transferred to immigration detention, thus experiencing what in other circumstances we would call double jeopardy.[5] (Im)migrants could also be detained and deported for old or juvenile convictions, including cases in which the charges were eventually dismissed, or in which the defendant had pled guilty or no contest to avoid the expense of a trial (Cacho 2012, 94). The number of people deported since passage of the main crimmigration law in 1996 is double the total of all deportations that occurred prior to 1997, demonstrating the immense effect crimmigration has had on the immigration system (Golash-Boza 2015).

Crimmigration also implies increased communication and data sharing among law enforcement agencies, turning the criminal legal system into a giant funnel for immigration enforcement. This funnel effect disproportionately affects Black (im)migrants, who are far more likely than other groups to be deported for criminal convictions (Morgan-Trostle, Zheng, and Lipscombe 2018). Although the deportation of LPRs used to be very rare (Stumpf 2006), many Black and Latinx LPRs are now deported following instances of racial profiling by state and local police (Golash-Boza 2010a, 2010b). The effects of crimmigration are not limited to Black and Latinx (im)migrants, however. Rather, the apparatus of the criminal legal system amplifies the scope of immigration enforcement generally. Thus, the immigration system builds off the large arsenal of surveillance technologies available to law enforcement agencies, their enormous budgets and personnel, and, crucially, the histories that established a disproportionate police presence in poor Black and brown neighborhoods.[6]

As a result of three decades of crimmigration policies, we now have a situation in which the two systems have effectively merged. As immigration scholar David Hernández notes, "these two forms of governmental authority are good neighbors," feeding information and resources to each other and "filling each other's open beds" (2019, 79). Above, I described how the criminal legal system expands the reach of the immigration system, and the reverse is also true. Immigration law expands the reach of the criminal system because it can bypass the procedural safeguards associated with conventional concepts of crime and punishment.[7] Noncitizens are typically not granted the same array of constitutional protections as citizens. And some activities, such as deportation, apply only to noncitizens, and may not activate the same degree of due process protections because they are not technically considered punishment.[8] In truth, immigration law is continuously confronted with constitutional challenges and international human rights standards, and yet the political marginalization of racialized (im)migrants reinforces the impression of a cordoned-off legal realm. Historically, immigration law has insulated its operations by pursuing what philosopher Nasser Hussain calls "administrative legality," a style of government where administrative categorizations can "unleash immediate and terrible consequences," such as indefinite detention and deportation, yet they "do not belong to a normative system"—that is, they "draw on no norm nor are they capable of generating one" (2007, 749). In this way, immigration law routinely produces conditions of rightlessness that are shrouded in layers of mystery and euphemism. Terms like "detention" and "check-in," for instance, create the impression that nothing serious is happening—as if it were just some automatic administrative response or passive event over which no one has control.[9]

For some Latin American (im)migrants, this combination of persecution and untruth is the hallmark of a paradigm of state violence known as disappearance. Indeed, many observers of current US immigration policy draw connections to the range of tactics deployed by military dictatorships in the so-called dirty wars of the previous century (see, e.g., Bernstein 2017; C. Hernández 2013; Loyd, Mitchelson, and Burridge 2012; Lykes et al. 2015): unmarked vans kidnapping people in the middle of the night, people being held captive at unknown locations, fear of inquiring about a relative's whereabouts lest one come to the attention of the authorities, and the official obfuscation of deaths in detention centers and on the US-Mexico border. When someone says a detained relative was "disappeared," it indicates a system of state kidnapping under conditions of extortion and invisibility that echoes and extends deeper histories of colonial and neocolonial violence. Indeed, some Central American (im)migrants who experienced the disappearance of relatives during the era of US-sponsored military dictatorships speak of contemporary US immigration enforcement practices as a "second war" that makes the wounds of that generation "burn anew"

(Lykes et al. 2015, 207). Taking this insight seriously means heeding the lessons of these histories as they relate to the current operations of immigration law. After all, "disappearance" was not a condition that magically befell thousands of people in the Americas living under military dictatorships; rather, it was a condition planned, executed, and arranged to appear as though nothing had been planned, executed, or arranged. When relatives of the disappeared invoked that term, they meant to indicate precisely that their family members had not, in fact, disappeared but had been taken to a particular place, by particular people, at a particular time, and under particular orders that included the steps required to create the impression that these people had simply vanished. The invocation of that term, in its very inaccuracy, calls out the systematic production of false reality. Disappearance thus involves a kind of make-believe, a theatrical condition of turning facts into fiction and fiction into fact. As Diana Taylor (1997) argues, "disappearance" must then be understood as a particularly hideous form of state theater that compounds the loss of life and liberty with the loss of reality.

In the next section, we turn to the physical environment of the Removal Room to investigate how disappearance is manifest as mise-en-scène.

The Room

Before an accompaniment, you meet at a coffee shop with the individual who will be checking in on the ninth floor. You are introduced to each other as "friends," and you walk together into the building, through security procedures, and up the elevator to the ninth floor. When you emerge from the elevators and approach the room, you see rows of miserable, mostly silent people facing you. If it were a typical waiting room, it might have a more circular, conversational arrangement. Instead, the chairs are arranged in rows facing the glass wall of the entrance to the room (figure 1.1). Behind them, against the back wall, you see the window of the clerk's office, which is partially covered with masking tape and butcher paper so you can only partially see into the office. Your instructions for accompaniment are roughly as follows:

> Walk with your friend to the clerk and hand in their papers with them. Sit down. Be prepared to sit for three hours or more. Once your friend gets called, stand with them until they are taken in to

Figure 1.1: The Removal Room.

meet with an officer. Sit back down and wait. One of three things can happen: they can be told immediately when to come back, they can be called into an office to talk to the deportation officer and then be told when to come back, or they can be called into the office, told they are being detained, and not come out.

Sometimes you wait the entire day before your friend is called. Eating is prohibited. Even though silence is not enforced, there is very little conversation in the room. It does not feel entirely safe to speak. The individual offices of the ICE officers line the side walls. On the yellow doors to these offices, unpainted white rectangles bear four pieces of black adhesive. It looks as if nametags had been affixed and then removed, or perhaps someone thought about labeling the doors and then changed their mind. You never know which door will open. A journalist visiting the ninth floor captured this sense of danger darting around the perimeter of the room: "From one of the four unmarked doors—no one knew where to look—an ICE officer would emerge and call a name" (Robbins 2017). I cannot describe the architecture of the offices that lie behind the unmarked doors because I have never been allowed inside. First, I had imagined that the offices were separated. Then I saw an officer go in one door and come out a door on the other side. I still don't know how to make sense of that invisible traffic around the perimeter. Are the offices connected? Is there a circular hallway behind them? I have sat in that waiting room for so long, with nothing to do besides try to track these movements and form an image of what I cannot see.

This reflects the spatial logic of what some have called "silent raids" in the middle of a busy city (America's Voice 2017). They have created a graduated series of prohibitions where successively fewer and fewer people are allowed deeper and deeper into the office space (the deepest point being the most isolated, the most invisible). Undocumented family members often do not accompany their loved ones into the building because to do so would invite the attention of ICE. Accompaniment teams, for the most part, can accompany their friends into the Removal Room, but ICE has persistently denied accompaniment teams access to the offices. Those allowed into the offices (primarily lawyers, but sometimes faith leaders and individual family members) are prohibited from entering the back area of the ninth floor behind the offices if their friend is detained. The back area thus takes on even more mysterious proportions. It is a space that only those who have been detained can picture. To the extent that spatial and social isolation coincide, this graduated series of prohibitions threatens a step-by-step removal not only from one's social world but also from sociality in a more basic sense.

Noncitizen relatives are quite reasonably afraid to enter the building, lest they come to the attention of ICE officers. Many would deem this separation from family members unintentional or collateral, but from the perspective of those checking in, it functions as a kind of threatened rehearsal for a more permanent estrangement from their relations. Indeed, the separation of families inside the Removal Room is continuous with the assault on family within immigration enforcement policies in general (see Abrego and Menjívar 2012). It is inside these spaces of enforcement that such underlying dynamics become more explicit. During one of my first accompaniments, for instance, we watched as ICE officers prevented a woman from saying goodbye to her husband. She stood in the Removal Room crying when she heard that he would be deported. He was just behind one of the office doors, no more than ten feet away from her. She requested two minutes to give him one last hug. The officers refused. All those in the waiting room looked back and forth between the woman and the door; her husband was only feet away, but the barrier suddenly seemed like a fortress. The denial of her request, in the view of everyone in the room, broadcast the scenographic demarcation of disappearance: *Once behind these doors*, the officers seemed to warn, *you belong to no one but us.* In the Removal Room, this status is scenographically arranged. The room's design charts a graduated passage from a world in which people can maintain meaningful social relations to one in which people are separated from their families and subject to the direct control of what Judith Butler might term "petty sovereigns" (2004, 65). As we watched that particular petty sovereign refuse the woman's request to say goodbye to her husband, we were asked to treat the nondescript yellow door as if it radiated the entire might of the US government. We were asked to bow to a personal power that was simultaneously terrifying and idiotic: terrifying because of the violence it enacted, and idiotic because there was no reason to prevent the couple's hug except for a brute display of domination. When the officer separated that woman from her husband, he relied on the arbitrariness of a particular prop—the door—to enforce an *open illusion*, as if the door straddled a geographic fault line beyond which the detained man had been swallowed up.

On another occasion, the accompaniment team spent several hours moving through space as if we were one being, aligning our intentions and our movements to a common purpose. In the Removal Room, I sat next to the woman checking in, inhaling and exhaling along with her to calm her nerves and pass the time. When her name was called, she and several faith leaders went into the office, but when they returned without her, it was clear she was being detained. A priest in the group emerged absolutely pale and explained, "We were in there trying to get some information about where she would be taken, and the officer suddenly stood up and said, 'Let's move the body.' She was right there and the officer said, 'Let's move the body,' like she was dead." Calling an undocumented person "the body" is apparently a common rhetorical practice by ICE (Hiemstra 2014). In this case, uttered behind the magic line of the office door as part of a sequence of events that would lead to our friend's incarceration, the ICE officer's comment clarified how linguistic removal facilitates the task of physical removal, rhetorically rendering her lifeless in advance of that removal process.

When they extricated this woman from the group and spoke of her as a nonbeing, they also turned the other people present into conduits of intimidation. The priest's shocked transmission of the ICE officer's language catalyzed a rumor of things said behind closed doors, a rumor that would circulate in community meetings as people learned about the woman's detention and prepared to write the letters of support for the campaign that would secure her release months later. But before that happened, the community that had accompanied her internalized its terror as guilt: we had many conversations about our inability to stop her detention, wondering what we could have done, wondering where they took her and whether we could have intervened. Talking about these experiences can become a kind of infection, magnifying terror through the proxy work that asks us to conduct fear and rumor on ICE's behalf. Indeed, it is difficult to tell this story without adding a kind of mystical power to the open illusion that ICE stages, an illusion that is, after all, both terrifying and stupid. The power is real, but it is also a compendium of theatrical elements: a room, a magic line, the word *removal*, a yellow door, and the game of making people wait.

During another accompaniment, Sara and I sat together in the Removal Room, waiting for our friend to finish her check-in. Then Sara looked at me with alarm and asked: "Wait, what happened to that woman and her daughters? The one with the braids? Didn't they go in a few hours ago? Did you see them come out?" I was horrified, not only because I didn't know the answer but also because, until that moment, I had not fully understood the room's design. My attention had been entirely focused on the one person we accompanied. Entering the room to "bear witness," I realized that what I had witnessed was given to be hidden rather than given to be seen. You could spend all day in the Removal Room, and unless you meticulously tracked all entrances and exits into the ICE offices, you would not know whether anyone had been detained. I was seemingly "right there," yet I did not know whether that family disappeared from an ICE office into a detention center or whether they simply exited the room and went home with instructions to return at a later date.

Whether you and I are in the room or elsewhere, we are equal in our sensation of powerlessness because neither one of us can reconstruct the event. If, in Sara's words, "there is no way of understanding the violence of the system until you've been in the room," this is true partially because, on any given day, it can be difficult to know whether anyone has been removed. As we continually bear witness to possible nonevents, the event of removal recedes from objectivity and becomes more and more a product of our own imagination. It turns into the generic sensation that we cannot perceive the violence happening immediately around us. In *Disappearing Acts*, Taylor describes the effect of invisible operations as follows:

> It is important to realize that dealing in disappearance and making the visible invisible are also profoundly theatrical. Only in the theatre can the audience believe that those who walk offstage have vanished into limbo. So the theatricality of torture and terror, capable of inverting and fictionalizing the world, does not necessarily lie in its visibility, but rather in its potential to transform, to recreate, to make the visible invisible, the real unreal. Perhaps the fact that we know what is going on and yet cannot see it makes the entire process more frightening, riveting, and resistant to eradication. (1997, 132)

The combination of knowing what happened and not being able to see it produces a dissonance between the visual and the factual that denatures both. Disappearance relies on us distrusting what we see and what we know, which ultimately undermines our sense of reality. Michael Taussig writes that the state project of disappearance seeks to "fix" memories in the "fear-numbing and crazy-making fastness of the individual mind" (1992, 28). By making the event of disappearance into a nonevent, the state moves incarceration and banishment from the seeming objectivity of a collective reality to the seeming fantasy of an internal reality. While "fastness" describes a kind of imprisonment within the mind, "crazy-making" refers to the imagination's ability to supply content to the withheld invisible scene. Invisibility has no content. Invisibility requires you to produce that content, making your imagination work. Then, because you are imagining terror, the terror in your head appears to have originated there. You feel like you are going crazy. "It's in the room!" you want to claim. "It's not in my head." But it's both. In the Removal Room, terror is arranged scenographically. We sit in the visible part of the room frantically imagining what has taken place, what might have taken place, or what will take place in the invisible parts. Everyone can sit together feeling individually crazy because the introjection of objective fear is part of the design.

One day, Sara reported to a group of accompaniers a puzzling interaction she had with a security guard in the Removal Room. (The security guards work for the building, rather than ICE, and monitor who enters the room.) "The other day," she said, "we were on the ninth floor and a woman was crying because her husband had just been detained. The security guard asked us why she was crying and I explained. Then he asked, 'Wait, people get detained here?'" How could the security guards working on the ninth floor every day be unaware of what happened in the ICE offices? How did we know more about the room than those policing the room? I had been imagining a coordinated state apparatus administering "silent raids." But that image of absolute power began to peel back when I realized that at least some of those involved did not know about the "removals" happening ten feet away from them. The design renders such ignorance possible. Unless you monitor every entrance and exit into the offices, you might not know that people disappear down the back elevators. The event of disappearance is designed to be a nonevent.

Perhaps the term *disappearance* in this context seems like a historical erasure or a dangerous stretch. Deportation is not murder, although it can be. Incarceration is not torture, although it can be. The comparison between the deportation regime and dictatorial regimes of disappearance is meant not to elide historical differences but to underscore what is shared: namely, a type of theatricality in which the state compounds the loss of life with the loss of reality. Disappearance, as a state project, refers not only to the disappearance of individuals from their world; it also refers to the attempted destruction of the factuality of the event. This can involve removing the means of getting at the truth (destruction of records, clandestine sites), as well as requiring society to perform as if the event had not occurred (Taylor 1997, 119–39). True to this pattern, the Removal Room seeks not only to remove a human being in the physical sense but also to remove that event's reverberation—rendering it invisible, inaudible, uncounted.

One day, as I am sitting in the waiting room waiting, I notice a poster next to the window of the clerk's office. I approach to get a better look, while trying not to be obvious. It is labeled "New York Field Office Enforcement and Removal Operations." It contains a familiar panoramic shot of the New York City skyline. Above the buildings, in the night sky, are the backs of three men who seem to be floating away from the city. The two on the outside wear blue uniforms labeled "I.C.E.," and the man in the middle wears a plain white T-shirt. The two officers are grabbing the third man's elbows, as if "escorting" him somewhere. Given that this scene takes place far above the skyline, the implication is that they are escorting him out of the city (and, by extension, out of the national consciousness). These three figures are headless, their necks blurring into the indigo sky. With very little visible skin, this depiction appears to be racially ambiguous. In other words, the image depicts a genocidal fantasy while leaving the racial identity of its target invisible, rendering that fantasy flexible and generic. Below these figures, symmetry: the skyline is perfectly reflected in the water. Once this figure is gone, we are meant to understand, all will be in balance again. He will be taken away in the night, a removal as painless as the night is indigo, as nameless as these figures are headless.

Who is this poster's intended audience? As a depiction of the imagined peace after removal of the Other, it seems directed toward the future citizen of the nation once all the Others have been removed. The image appeals to a fascist notion of a longed-for white nation as envisioned in the discourse of "homeland security" (Kaplan 2003). However, this imagined white supremacist citizenry is not actually present in the room. The only citizens in the waiting room are people accompanying and advocating for noncitizens. A fantasy of nocturnal disappearance has thus been directed primarily toward an assembled group of noncitizens facing the check-in process. And yet, those assembled noncitizens are treated as if they are not even there—which is, oddly, a theatrical scene. They are treated as if they are not spectators. Somehow, (im)migrants are shown a spectacle that voids the very fact of their presence in the room. Stuck to the wall of the Removal Room, the poster calls an absent white supremacist citizenry into being while operating on a tangent line to the very existence of the people present. Because the message is not *Hide, we will find you*, or *Don't try to resist, we are stronger*. The message does not take their existence into account, and not taking their existence into account is the message.

The poster's flexible genocidal fantasy reminds us that there is a concept of the enemy and an infrastructure to capture him before law enforcement agencies know exactly who the enemy is. We can recall the origin of the Department of Homeland Security (DHS), inaugurated after the events of September 11, 2001. The department responded to a historical event by instituting a "continual state of emergency" (Kaplan 2003, 90). The term *security* combined with the fascist-identified term *homeland* implies an anxiously threatened ethno-nation. This logic commits the department to a permanent mission of discovering enemies, and unless it continually regenerates the image of the enemy as a source of insecurity, it has no purpose. The department must continually rediscover the retroactive reason why we are supposed to feel so insecure.

There is a parallel example in the origins of the US Border Patrol, as traced by immigration historian Kelly Lytle Hernández (2010). Combing through accounts of the Border Patrol's first officers, Hernández shows how they generated the practices that gave meaning to the idea of the "illegal immigrant." Many classes of people were officially excludable in the 1920s—prostitutes, anarchists, those with communicable diseases, and all Asians, among other groups. The Border Patrol, Hernández argues, could have interpreted its broad mandate in a number of ways: it could have patrolled brothels, political unions, or Asian neighborhoods; it could have stationed officers along the geographic border between the United States and Mexico or the United States and Canada (K. Hernández 2010, 43). Instead, the Border Patrol built on existing practices of racial hunting—including those of the Texas Rangers, who were some of the agency's first recruits—to develop a set of practices that dramatically narrowed its broad mandate. Border Patrol agents focused their activities on policing the mobility of brown-skinned Mexicanos in the interior of the country, some of whom were US citizens, and generally enforced a racial order that served agribusiness (for instance, by deporting Mexican laborers who had left their worksites in search of better wages).[10] Thus the Border Patrol "Mexicanized" the concept of illegality in a way that would echo throughout the twentieth century and beyond.

Here, we see how law enforcement agencies gradually develop an image of the enemy through their geographic and racial choices and the alliances they build with particular sectors of society. These choices, in turn, flesh out the enemy figure, giving it an embodied form (Ahmed 2000, 3). Racializing practices help law enforcement make practical sense of an activity that might otherwise be overly broad or abstract. Such is the case for the DHS, whose purported sources of insecurity are multiple and contradictory (De Genova 2007). Although its original referent was primarily Arab and

Islamic, the DHS used its new powers to detain, disenfranchise, and deport Mexican and other Latin American individuals.[11] The overlapping of Islamophobic and anti-Latino discourses brought wildly diverse world cultures together based on a generic suspicion of brown bodies. And as the DHS coordinated with police agencies to ensnare more and more people in the net of immigration enforcement, the particularly anti-Black character of police departments disproportionately funneled Afro-diasporic peoples into the category of removability, even though they did not fit the primary image of illegality and anti-immigrant sentiment (Palmer 2017). Like the early Border Patrol, the infrastructures of policing preceded the identification of their targets. The DHS depicts its enemy in the form of a racially unmarked figure in the poster hanging in the Removal Room. Rather than targeting one particular group, this image establishes a flexible structure for evolving racist projects.

During one of my first accompaniments, I watched heavily armed officers suddenly force a group of women to line up along a wall. Names were called—Morales, Gonzalez, Ruiz—as the officers pushed the women up against the wall, separating them from their children and anyone else who accompanied them. The whole room was watching. Bits of conversations I heard in English focused on how this scene caused the onlookers to recollect other images. One lawyer said it looked like a "firing squad." A member of an accompaniment team called it a "chain gang." Conversations I overheard in Spanish were about family groups making plans to reconnect, because no one was sure how they would find one another again. The women being lined up had all been fitted with ankle monitors upon their release from immigration detention, and they were required to report periodically to another nearby building. They were asking strangers to take care of their children and meet them outside later. For some reason, the process of moving these women from one building to another had to include lining them up against the wall, forcibly separating them from their children, and marching them single file, led by armed guards, across the snowy Manhattan street.

These women suddenly became a category apart from others in the Removal Room, thanks to the spectacle of separating them from the larger group and making them move through public space as a single condemned body. Race is an effect of that spectacle, but the spectacle makes it seem like a cause. The guard calls "Morales, Gonzalez, Ruiz," and the commonality of a Central American background becomes visible retroactively, as if it were the answer to the question of why they are being lined up. *Why must they do it this way?* we routinely ask. Why, if they are just carrying out a bureaucratic procedure, must the ICE officers also stage a scene of humiliation?

Even as it hides its own operations, ICE seems concerned about showing the face of the enemy, to dramatize, through the recursive loop of its own violence, that the people assembled deserve to be disappeared. To select a group of removable people and display them in a row is a theatrical attempt to demonstrate that there is a reason for this room.

This racial production of removability demonstrates a central paradox in the staging of disappearance. Performance theory holds that institutional arrangements of bodies in space work to concretize otherwise abstract social processes, making those processes visible and available to common perception and social transmission. For instance, a sporting event might be arranged so that people with more money sit in special boxes close to the field, thus rendering visible the configuration of social status. This kind of staging is reflexive: we are both the subjects and spectators of those arrangements. These arrangements are thus a means of "showing ourselves to ourselves," in Barbara Myerhoff's phrase (1982, 105), the means by which societies hold their own value systems up for observation. What, in this sense, does the Removal Room show to itself? Immigration and Customs Enforcement asks people to "check in"—that is, to "appear," as one would appear in court—only to signal that they may be disappeared and, at a perceptual level, at least, have already been removed. This perversion of what it means to appear before the law surely aims to demonstrate that those present are condemned and thus deserve disappearance. Yet, by showing ourselves disappearance, disappearance also becomes, as Taylor (1997) theorized, dependent on spectacles. While individual instances of detention and deportation may occur in the shadows, the disappearing state also acquires public consent for and participation in that violence by announcing its agenda: publicly broadcasting the extrication of demonized populations. In this sense, those threatened with removal are paradoxically made to participate in racialized scenes of criminalization—that is, they are put on display—even as they are perceptually and physically removed.

These scenes are racializing, not racial.[12] They conscript the pretense of biology to give apparent self-evidence to evolving atrocities-in-question. In the Removal Room, many people check in, but only some are removed. The Removal Room waits for race and requires race to relieve the decision makers of the complexity of their task. How else are they going to decide among the removable? This is not simply a case of the officers disproportionately selecting people to remove based on their nationalities or phenotypic traits. Rather, in choosing to remove particular people, the room itself works to produce racial meaning or even to create its own race: the "removed."[13] New participants in the accompaniment program are often surprised to see that many security guards, deportation officers, judges, and others who work in the building are people of color. There is an assumption that white supremacy is necessarily carried out by white people. Instead, the racial line is drawn not through a color line of white officials and Black and brown (im)migrants but through the ongoing work of the mise-en-scène to draw and redraw boundaries between the in-group and the enemy, between the homeland and its phantasms of insecurity.

The attempt to make the mythic figure of the criminal immigrant land on particular people exposes profound contradictions: ICE claims to remove those who somehow threaten the nation, yet quite clearly it is ICE behaving in a threatening manner. Although ICE attempts to make those it targets look degraded, it can do so only through its own brutality. It claims to punish those who have supposedly broken the law, yet it erects a shadow zone of law insulated from accountability and devoid of normativity. All such contradictions simmer perpetually in the Removal Room. They are constantly below the surface, poised to erupt.

Following is an excerpt from field notes taken during an accompaniment: "I was accompanying a family in the Removal Room who were whispering back and forth because the little girl wanted some potato chips but her mom told her she had to wait, otherwise the guards would get angry. 'What if I do it like this?' she whispered and, peering around like a spy, folded herself behind the door where there were no official sight lines. Then, with exaggerated pantomime, she took her hand out of an imaginary bag of chips and began noiselessly savoring each one." In an instant, the room became elastic (figure 1.2). Her gesture registered the staging of disappearance, the need to make herself invisible. But invisibility, at that moment, became something she used to sneak around, outsmart, and solve. She hid behind the door where the officers could not see her and pretended to eat potato chips. She showed her awareness of the scenographic nature of disappearance, calculating the room's sight lines and revealing its blind spots. Her gesture mocked the criminality the Removal Room needed her to embody. It mocked that need. And in doing so, her gesture held a mirror to the panicked idiocy of ICE's authority. Only the most insecure, totalitarian forms of authority would prohibit children from eating snacks. In such moments, the work of criminalization and disappearance reveals its fundamental fragility.

Figure 1.2: Girl pretending to eat chips.

In a newspaper article about the Removal Room, a lawyer representing (im)migrant clients reported the following encounter. During a check-in, an ICE officer apparently told the lawyer: "It's a whole new world, Counselor. . . . I'm sorry, I'm getting pressure because my title is deportation officer—my job is to deport people" (Robbins 2017). Her title is deportation officer and that is her job. So someone must be deported. After she has chosen that person, her decision will be the law. Her predicament mirrors the kind of legality that Walter Benjamin (1978) calls "the police." The police operate in a blurry zone that defies the distinction between "applying" and "enacting" the law. The police "intervene 'for security reasons' in countless cases where no clear legal situation exists," thus extending legal power into new domains without the need to draw from an existing norm or to formally institute a new one (Benjamin 1978, 287). The law of ICE becomes real—we learn what it consists of—only at the moment when ICE officers make a decision about what it means, this time, to do their jobs.

In the very confusion of the officer's "I'm sorry," there is an opportunity for the community to say, *If you are building law from the ground up, so shall we.* If the project of disappearance is scenographically arranged, the community can rearrange it.

Accompaniment

> You know you're doing the accompaniment wrong when you're
> talking. This whole meeting is about teaching you to keep
> quiet, teaching you to shut up.
>
> NEW SANCTUARY COALITION ACCOMPANIMENT TRAINING

Immediately, the accompaniment trainer's humorous injunction to "shut up" challenges participants' notions of what it means to advocate. The righteous fury of the assembled activists simmers down and becomes attentive. In other contexts, these people—students, social workers, retired teachers, community organizers, labor organizers, rabbis, priests—chant, denounce, cry out, speak truth, and occupy. Expectations gearing the body for such confrontations are instantly quelled as participants consider this injunction to keep silent. You must be silent because any well-intentioned but nonstrategic attempt to intervene, expose, or persuade could cause the officers to take their anger out on the one you accompany or on the organization at large. Thus, every move must be carefully measured to balance system-level advocacy with individual-level caution. Importantly, members of the organization who have experienced the deportation regime firsthand are predominantly responsible for designing strategies that maintain this balance. Safety considerations require that only members of the organization with secure immigration status accompany friends into the Removal Room and to other immigration appointments, but the accompaniers do so according to the strategies designed by undocumented people directly affected by the system. In this sense, the program strategically instrumentalizes the privilege of citizenship and, to a less explicit extent, whiteness to dismantle a racializing assemblage, an inherently vexed strategy that requires continuous reflexivity (Henderson 2009; Koopman 2008). Yet it does so in a way that reduces the role of documented accompaniers to the elemental fact of our capacity to safely signal presence in the room. In other words, although accompaniers tend to have more social capital and a less precarious position than those they accompany, this privilege is not falsely conflated with expertise. Moreover, the possibility of developing some sort of expertise is continually blocked through instructions such as "Now is not the time to satisfy our curiosity about the system" and "The guards and officers are not our friends." People with particular privileges such as citizenship, money, or whiteness are accustomed to receiving special treatment from legal institutions. Such people—and

I include myself here—tend to seek a sense of mastery by making friends with officers, requesting special attention, demanding clarity from the system, and otherwise interacting with the room in the same ways we are accustomed to interacting with other institutions in our lives. But such a tendency only widens the distance from those who will never acquire such mastery because the space is designed to place them in a condition of absolute uncertainty. Thus, much of the work of accompaniment involves recognizing and accepting how little we know and restraining our inclination to resort to our privilege to alleviate our own discomfort.

As an accompaniment volunteer, you are told that your accompaniment should support the person you accompany as well as bear witness and hold the system accountable. You are also told how *not* to accomplish those goals (e.g., don't confront the officers, make judgments, give legal advice, or antagonize). This training provides the essentials of what you should do, including the basic choreography of movement through the building and the universal instruction to follow the group leader. But if these instructions provide a rough outline of the day, they do not clarify the central activity of the work: how exactly do you offer support, bear witness, and hold a system accountable through stillness and silence? It would be challenging, and perhaps beside the point, to explicitly codify how an accompanier should pass the time in a manner that furthers these three ends. Such questions must be directed to your body to work out. In this sense, accompaniment is a movement practice, and its features emerge only by cultivating a state of readiness, attentiveness, and responsiveness that allows you to gradually acquire a better sense.

I remember sitting in the cafeteria with someone who had just done her first accompaniment. She had admitted beforehand that she did not know how to be helpful. She was not a lawyer, she did not speak any language besides English, and she had no experience with this type of advocacy. She said: "I was feeling so helpless and scared for my friend. I couldn't say anything because we don't speak the same language. So finally I decided just to put my hand on top of hers, and then she put her other hand on top of mine, and I put my other hand on top of hers. And then we just sat there like that." [She demonstrates, looking down at her own hands as if the other pair of hands were still present.] "We said nothing for about an hour until her name was called."

Silence, like stillness, draws our attention to different qualities of presence, to the possibilities of sensation within a constrained terrain of action. Susan Leigh Foster describes the power of self-restraint in her analysis of the lunch counter sit-ins during the civil rights movement: "Filled with kinetic potential while seated, their stillness, not a state of non-action but rather a kind of motion, consisted in monitoring and refraining from casually abundant kinetic impulses" (2003, 412). Stillness can be motion insofar as it interrupts particular forms of expected flow. Stillness catches our attention because the body is more disposed to be caught up in "casually abundant" movement. As visual culture scholar Tina Campt puts it, "stasis is neither an absence nor a cessation of motion; it is a continual balancing of multiple forces in equilibrium" (2017, 9). When we continue to balance these forces, we accumulate potential energy. We can imagine this in the accompanier's story of holding hands with her friend for an entire hour. At any time, one of them could have removed her hand. Every moment they did not was a new commitment to uphold each other. A lifetime of cultural training signals that it is not normal, outside of intimate relationships, to hold and be held for so long. To resist such social training, override the instinct to recoil, and persist in touching sends a message that is both internal (proprioceptive) and external (semiotic).[14] In the prolonged layering of hands, the gesture works internally to sensitize each person to anticipate the other's movement and to initiate pathways of movement that flow in common. Externally, the gesture communicates to others present that something unusual is happening. Within the context of the Removal Room, the image of a group maintaining silence and stillness communicates meditative focus, collective preparation, and the capacity to adapt and endure. In this room of surveillance, magic doors, and arbitrary authority, the visible expression of such movement-in-common suggests the glimmer of a competing, unauthorized order.

Part of the power of accompaniment is that those who accompany are not expected to be present. Only removable people and their advocates are anticipated to have any business on the ninth floor. The project of removal thus depends both on the ability to coerce (im)migrants to participate in possible confinement and on the circulation of others away from this scene. Each implies a distinct type of power: the former is the power to seize people and hold them captive, and the latter is the power to remove potential witnesses. The latter can be seen as a form of "choreopolicing," in dance theorist André Lepecki's (2013) terms: this type of power is equivalent to the moment when a police officer directs passersby away from a crime scene, telling them, "Move along, there's nothing to see here."[15] In the Removal Room, both types of control over movement are enmeshed. A scene of confinement is contained within confusing displays of circulation—glass doors implying openness and circulation lead to unlabeled doors of disappearance. Exiting from the elevators on the ninth floor, the unaware person circulating through the building would see only a waiting room and would have no visual clue that those waiting, once directed to the inner offices, might be seized and dispossessed of their freedom to move. A multipurpose, heavily trafficked building plainly hides a pathway to incarceration. We appear to be free to go anywhere, until we cannot. It is eerie to see how fluidly the traffic flows above, below, and around the ninth floor, while people on that floor sit in terrorized anticipation of confinement.

The accompaniment program can disrupt the fragile stability of that arrangement. Although our friends checking in on the ninth floor cannot flee without severe potential repercussions, the people circulating around the area can stop to bear witness. By doing so, they demonstrate that such circulation is not as free as it seems; instead, it is working to shepherd us away from the fact that there really is, referring back to the police officer's statement, "something to see." Most urgently, the accompaniment program disrupts the terrorizing design of the room itself, which relies on isolating individuals from their social world (or terrorizing them with the threat of doing so).

When we bring unanticipated bodies into the Removal Room, we introduce an element of freedom into the choreography of the check-in, *even if the choreography itself does not change.* Thinking like a dancer, we might imagine that we have to change the choreography—block the doors, face the wrong way, refuse to sit down, or otherwise disrupt the sanctioned pathways through the space. Yet we radically change those pathways simply by doing accompaniment as a group. We take a route through space that was imposed on people and transform it into an intentional practice or exercise.[16] Doing so has radical potential in this context precisely because the Removal Room aims to annihilate freedom. If (im)migrants are coerced to enter the Removal Room through the threat of immediate deportation, then all the steps involved in entering that room—approaching the building, passing through security, ascending in the elevator, passing through the glass doors—bear the signification of coercion. By treating these same steps as a noncoerced practice, the accompaniment program introduces freedom into that choreography, fundamentally altering it.

When friends and accompaniers sit together in the Removal Room, they are not sitting but very consciously sitting-with (see TallBear 2014 on "standing with"). An accompanier's sitting and waiting are meant to echo another's sitting and waiting. As an accompanier, you are in a state of kinesthetic empathy, that feeling of virtual movement inside your own body that is activated when you watch another person move (Foster 2010). In this case, the movement in question is the accompanied person's internal battle with the room. That person's stillness, I would speculate, is not the product of motionlessness but of competing urges of the body *revuelto*: the urge to escape, to confront, to break down, to give up, to speed up or slow down time, to stay grounded, to conjure memories of better scenes, to rehearse possible scenarios, and so on. As an accompanier, you are inside that room and feel its currents, but you are not its target. As you pick up on your friend's scrambling nerves, you feel something of that scrambling in yourself. You too may have competing urges, such as the urge to scream or to cry, but you must quell those urges. All parties, it seems, are not motionless; rather, they are continuously battling other impulses in the attempt to stay still.

By committing ourselves to hold the experience, we work against the terrorizing attempt to eliminate the factuality of disappearance. We signal that disappearance is a fact, that the state's attempt to manufacture fear of disappearance is also a fact, and that we are committed to standing in solidarity for the duration. Potentially, this commitment works to collectivize and objectify the terror, counteracting the state's drive to "fix" it, in Taussig's (1992) words, in the individual imagination. By accompanying, we signal that there is an objective project of terror in place. The practice of standing with terror, however, is a volatile project. As accompaniers, our own imaginations and bodies can become the substrate of terror's expansion; if we let this sensation consume us, we could amplify the panic in the room. As Saidiya Hartman argues, empathy has the power to "obliterat[e] otherness" by turning "feeling for you" into "feeling for myself" (1997, 19). If such a turn were to occur, we as accompaniers might transfer the burden onto the one we accompany to help relieve our own anxiety. Instead of providing comfort, we end up seeking it. Yet the other extreme—to try to show (as I am often tempted to do) that we know exactly what we are doing and that everything will be okay—is also a false posture. We cannot guarantee that our friends will be safe, and trying to do so is simply restating our distance from the terror they face. In my case, as a white half-Latina citizen whose relatives were disappeared decades ago under another regime, I am aware that my whiteness and my citizenship allow me to feel safe in that room. At the same time, the inbuilt groove by which I recognize the room's terror stems from intergenerational memories that are both connected to and distinct from the terror of the Removal Room. In other words, my positioning recognizes and misrecognizes the terror in the same instant. Such questions of positionality remind us that to accompany is not to fully understand another's experience, but it is a commitment to support what we do not understand. The accompanied and the accompanier can experience very different realities in the same room, and in spite of that gap, being there still matters.

The relay of kinesthetic empathy between accompanier and accompanied, then, has nothing to do with any alignment in their realities (to imagine otherwise would lead to dangerous fantasies of sameness). Being targeted by the room and feeling effectively caught up in that targeting are worlds apart. Nevertheless, there is a sensation of being twinned in a mutual condition of frustrated flight yet mutually committed to holding the moment.

Every time I accompany someone, I learn from others about the subtle potency of that commitment. I learned a great deal, for example, when I saw Pastor Juan Carlos Ruiz smile in the Removal Room. There was nothing naïve about that smile. He was deeply aware of the terror people were feeling. But his smile caught on and seemed to have a general calming effect. There was an "illegal surrealism" to the act of smiling in that room, to borrow Fred Moten's (2015) phrase; the pastor's smile distributed permission for everyone to momentarily feel joyful without cause. By producing joy in a space where it seemingly had no place, he challenged ICE's capacity to disseminate terror. His smile signaled to those of us present, *Our gods will quietly outlast you.*

The New Sanctuary Coalition is an interfaith organization—a designation that reflects the personal practices of the founders and some of the members, as well as the role of houses of worship in the sanctuary movement. As someone raised (fanatically) atheist, I did not immediately identify with the framework of faith. Yet, when one is confronting a deeply violent legal system, few forms of resistance are more powerful than entering a room surrounded by one's higher powers. *Bring your own gods* is the nonverbal invitation I feel circulating among the group's participants— radical priests in the tradition of liberation theology, an ordained undocumented female minister, practitioners of sweat lodge ceremonies and ayahuasca, ghost philosophers, radical choir participants, Garifuna spiritists, and others whose breadth of spiritual inquiry is impossible to delimit or describe. These faiths, together, add up to abundance. There are abundant ways of radiating energy to others.

After being accompanied to the Removal Room, one friend told Sara, "I felt like I was surrounded by a ring of angels." The group worked like a conductor of energetic resilience. It is a good reminder of the promiscuousness of spirit, which changes form based on who calls it. If you and I were to imagine this promiscuity right now, our prayer might go something like this:

> Whatever spiritual channel allows you to mirthfully, irreverently, illegally endure, open that channel now so that it can partake of a relay of resilience.

> Together we generate a spreading ring of what reverses the flow and intent of the room.

> Whether we experience warmth, humor, levity, groundedness, fugitivity, or faith, that diversity itself shows the nontotality of whatever is trying to spread fear in the room.

> It means that ICE cannot contain what it has assembled.

Because it seeks to isolate individuals, ICE is not prepared for those assembled to act and move as one. When an ICE officer calls an individual's "alien" number to begin the check-in process, the entire accompaniment team stands up together, as if to say, *We are them.* This kind of doubling is a common practice in theater and dance. In a choreographed dance piece, a dancer's seemingly spontaneous gesture might happen onstage simultaneously in another body or at another moment in time. That doubling renders singularity suspect; it suggests that this might not be a brand-new moment, that you might not be "in" a mathematically divisible segment of space and that the performer might not be a singular, self-possessing subject (Schneider 2008; Schneider 2011, 111–37). If such doubling can generate a profound disturbance onstage, its effects are much more profound in the Removal Room, where ICE counts on the capacity to isolate individuals from their communities. It uses architectural, choreographic, and linguistic methods to threaten that the eclipse of one person's world will cause no tremor in the wider world.

When we stand together, we signify that tremor. And if our friends often cannot present themselves to the room hand in hand with their kin, we come to bear witness to that attack on kinship while standing for the principle of kin being greater than biological relation. We stand for the primordial "we," which is simultaneously a warning: *You cannot calculate, predict, or discern who will care about whom, or how many will care, inside and outside of this room.* Every related effort to desegregate and decolonize our social world potentially comes to bear in such moments. Our solidarity makes it harder for them to imagine the enemy, and it certainly makes it harder for them to disappear people.

Returning to the Room

One day, the guards moved their desk a few feet deeper into the entrance and announced that accompaniment teams would be prohibited from entering the Removal Room. New Sanctuary Coalition called a series of meetings to brainstorm what to do. There was a deep sense of indignation and incredulousness. Some wanted to demand to see the memo authorizing this change, if one existed, to follow the paper trail and identify the person responsible. Others wanted to call elected officials and denounce the move publicly.

But what law had been violated? What right did we have to enter the room? There was no clearly codified right of entry that we could claim. The Removal Room is neither an open court nor public space. Yet many of us invoked the language of rights, where the notion of a right is typically understood as an institution's obligation to guarantee protection. Many of us wanted to appeal to a higher level of institutional power. We felt it was our right to be there and that if we denounced the new policy to a congressperson, mayor, judge, or city councillor, that right would be restored.

The leadership of the organization reminded us that what we thought of as a right was in fact just the cumulative effect of the accompaniment program. "Ten years ago," Ravi said, "they wouldn't even let lawyers into the ninth floor. And in New Jersey, where they have no accompaniment program, no one is allowed in." By insisting that its members be present, the New Sanctuary Coalition had gradually established a tacit right to the space. And if that were true, it remained in the people's hands to reestablish our right to enter. After all, the concept of sanctuary, which we consider semisacred, is sacred only insofar as we treat it as such. Just as there is no law preventing enforcement action in a sanctuary church, there is often no law guaranteeing the right of citizens to enter the peripheral, merely administrative spaces where immigration cases are adjudicated.[17] In claiming our "right" to occupy such spaces, then, we are speaking less of rights guaranteed by institutions and more of a contested idea of rights in formation, like the first right in Hannah Arendt's phrase the "right to have rights" (1973, 296). The first right, according to Judith Butler (2015), is not guaranteed by any institution but is generated through social mobilization. By occupying contested spaces, social movements operate in the contradictory zone where the right to have rights develops. Social movements may make demands on institutions, but in reality, they instantiate the right to occupy through occupation itself. In other words, social movements "take what [they ask] for" (Butler and Spivak 2007, 68). In occupying a particular space, that space is both the ground and the object of contestation. It is thus the occupation itself rather than the sanction of the institution that installs the right to have rights.

Many of us, especially those with citizenship and other forms of privilege, feel a kind of cognitive snag in accepting this state of affairs. Our privilege has trained us to believe that we can call on superordinate governmental forces to correct arbitrary state violence. To us, such violence appears to be some sort of anomaly, irregularity, or error, and the irregularity of the state's surface seems to be a screen for the regularity that lies intact somewhere in the depths. We continue to believe there is something virtuous at the state's core, no matter how much evidence accumulates about its surface. For others, lifelong experiences of marginalization reveal such violence to be structural and systematic. For those whose communities have been torn apart by the deportation regime, the privileged citizen's faith in the state's virtuous core cannot hold. If all we have is surface, we have to play with the depth of that surface. We have to use the very textures of the scene—its arrangement, its physical materials, its choreographies, and so forth—to intervene directly on the mechanisms of disappearance. The community "jurisgenerates" rights through its persistent presence (Moten 2015, following Cover 1985). If our right to the space had developed through a decade of accompaniment in the Removal Room, we were now tasked with relearning how such a process might unfold.

Thus, the group began to propose ways to directly intervene in the room. All the elements of the Removal Room that performance makers would call props, set design, and choreography were considered potential sources of creative intervention: papers, chairs, elevators, pens, verticality, sight lines, voice, volume, rhythm, repetition, and duration. The following list summarizes some ideas suggested by community members during a series of strategy meetings:

- Play with verticality: Place members on all other floors simultaneously while a team on the ground circles the building.

- Play with language: Be creative when talking to the guards. As one person explained, "One time when we were on the ninth a guard turned his back to us and then said, as if he were talking to someone else, 'If you don't have a reason to be here, leave.' Well, we figured we all did have a reason to be here, so we stayed. Eventually, he did come back and tell us directly to our faces, but in the hour it took him to come back and say that, we were doing what we came there to do."

- Play with bureaucracy: Ask for written legal justification from any security guard or officer who denies accompaniers access to the room. Alternatively, when denied access, leave a form letter stating that an accompanier was present but barred from the room, ask the guard to sign it, and have another accompanier sign as a witness. Include a space to enter the officer's name and stamp the form with an official seal. Leave copies of these forms with the guards so they will have to report their existence at the end of the day. Leave copies of the signed forms for the judges on the twelfth floor.

- Play with rhythm and voice: When accompanying friends to the ninth floor, bring an even larger group than normal. Loudly state, so that the guards, the friend, and the other people waiting can hear, "We will be on the sixth floor waiting for you. We will be here all day, and every twenty minutes one of us will come back and wave to you through the glass so you know you are not alone."

This last strategy was eventually adopted and ended up having a powerful effect in the Removal Room. Instead of sitting in the Removal Room all day with our friends, which we were no longer allowed to do, we spent the days elsewhere in the building and sent one person to the ninth floor at regular intervals. That person would approach the guards monitoring the room and call attention to the fact that an accompaniment team was present—on another floor—despite the prohibition. If ICE had intended to eliminate New Sanctuary's presence, the plan backfired: accompaniment teams actually amplified their presence by playing on the dynamic of anticipation that already existed. If the room's power was based on making people wait, accompaniers devised a way to redirect that sense of anticipation toward the accompaniment program itself (figure 1.3). In addition to ICE officers emerging unpredictably from the unmarked office doors, accompaniers now appeared predictably at the entrance every twenty minutes, thus introducing a competing play of entrances and exits. When you return to the room every twenty minutes, eyes start to look up every fifteen. Those waiting in the room began to anticipate our return.

After following this strategy for a while, some participants added another element. In addition to verbally stating that the accompaniment team would return, we held up a sign reading: "[Name of friend], we will

Figure 1.3: The accompaniment team rearranges the room.

be here as long as it takes." Because the walls of the Removal Room are made of glass, our signs were visible to everyone present. The people checking in, the ICE officers, and the guards were all aware that accompaniers were in the building, that their presence in the Removal Room had been prohibited, and that this prohibition had been creatively overcome. The sign made it clear that the Removal Room was both the object and the ground of active contestation. Rumor has it that, during one check-in, a security guard pointed to the accompanier holding the sign and told the friend checking in, "Hey, your people are here, pay attention." In other words, the guards had begun to habituate themselves to a powerful new scenographic dynamic.

Our rhythmic returns made a new sense of the room's spatial arrangement. As previously described, the chairs in the Removal Room face outward toward the glass doors, so the suffering of those checking in is on display for all to see. Once accompaniment teams began to visit every twenty minutes, the orientation of the seats took on a different significance. Whereas the arrangement had previously framed those checking

in as objects, they were now positioned as an audience watching the re-
curring show of accompaniment teams arriving at the glass wall. Despite
the Removal Room's attempts to stage disappearance, this new spectatorial
orientation powerfully shifted the sightlines of the room.

During one accompaniment in which I participated, this new orientation became particularly significant. Because the person checking in faced
a high risk of being detained, a number of faith leaders had been invited
to assist in the accompaniment, but only one was allowed into the waiting
room. Rather than leave the floor, however, the rest of the faith leaders
stood in a row behind the elevators on the other side of the glass wall,
facing the seats of those checking in. As they stood there, everyone going
in and out of the elevators and everyone inside the Removal Room could
see the line of adorned faith leaders forming a kind of mystical wall. When
you move people into a narrower space, you increase their relative visual
weight. The faith leaders' presence was amplified by the architecture: they
were static in a place of passage, arranged widthwise in a space designed
for lengthwise movement, arrayed before a prohibited space that, by standing still, they charged with potential energy and threatened to cross. By
denying the faith leaders access, the officers had actually increased their
presence, allowing the architecture of disappearance to momentarily turn
into a theatrical frame. And what it framed was the standoff between ICE's
racializing assemblage and the higher forms of authority the faith leaders
represented. For those inside, it is hoped, this wall of faith signaled, if only
for a moment, the transcendent power of love.

During another accompaniment, our team leader asked a guard if she
could enter the room and give our friend a hug. The guard paused for a
split second, but it was long enough to tell us that he was not completely
aware of the new policy prohibiting our presence. Sensing us sensing him,
he changed key, feigning self-assurance and said, "There are too many of
you here." So our leader responded, "If there are too many in our group,
only four of us will go in and stay just until our friend's name is called." Her
statement was meant to sound like a compromise, but in reality, she had
reinstated the terms of accompaniment in effect before the prohibition.
As the least assured actor in that encounter, the guard seemed to be bas-
ing his attitude on how we, as repeat players, behaved. He was waiting to
fit his action into the groove of our expectations. The team leader's ability
to take advantage of this small window demonstrated the myriad opportunities to change the dynamics of a space. At that moment, it was possible
to imagine how a persistent community practice deeply engaged with the

material environment of a contested space can gradually develop, as Ravi explained, into an institutionally sanctioned right to such spaces.

Then, a few weeks later, ICE ended the prohibition and accompaniers were allowed back in the Removal Room. At the community meeting held a few days later, accompaniers told stories of many other such windows, cracks in the system that seemed to lay the groundwork for this reversal. Sara told us about another immigration justice organization that had been refused access. According to her source, the guard had said, "Well, you can't bring everyone in, but how about you go downstairs to the sixth-floor cafeteria and every twenty minutes send someone up with a sign." Another accompaniment volunteer added, "Once I was up in the ninth ready to hold up the sign, and then the guard said, 'Hey, don't you want to give your friend a hug?'"

The guards' adoption of our terms (friend) and our gestures (hug) signaled that the accompaniment program's patterns of repetition had become sedimented into habit. Perhaps ICE's withdrawal of its prohibition indicated recognition of the futility of barring community members when they would just develop new ways to magnify their presence. Perhaps ICE found those dynamics nonthreatening because of their predictability, regularity, and rhythm. The choreography of accompaniment may have predictable features, but New Sanctuary's presence in these spaces led to unpredictable and ultimately uncontainable possibilities. Our presence allowed the organization to bear witness, launch campaigns, raise awareness, produce alternative discourses, fight disappearance, hold the system accountable, and take advantage of subtle openings. If the Removal Room was both object and ground of contestation, then the community's capacity to jurisgenerate the right to accompany was both a metaphor and a physical platform for its broader transformative potential. That which oppresses through its scenographic arrangement can be inverted by rearranging the room.

Postscript

The text of this chapter was written in 2017, after several months of participation in the accompaniment program. It was written at a time when I saw the transformative potential of collective action. There was a sense of openness not only to the methods but also to the organizational structure of the movement. It felt, for a moment, that everyone—the directly affected and the supposedly unaffected, noncitizens and citizens of all races and backgrounds—was moving together without predetermined roles, sensing that we were all needed and might all play a part.

After a while, I stopped participating in the accompaniment program and got involved in other dimensions of the movement. When I considered returning a few years later, things were different. Much of the diversity among the participants had been lost. The accompaniment program had become almost exclusively white. The New Sanctuary Coalition had lost much of its ethos of horizontality and turned into a more hierarchical organization following an NGO model. Then the COVID-19 pandemic hit. Many immigration court appointments became virtual events, making the role of accompaniment unclear. Finally, after a series of internal conflicts, the New Sanctuary Coalition itself was officially dissolved. Some of those involved continued to accompany one another to immigration court appointments on an informal basis. At the same time, many of the New York–based (im)migrant leaders who had focused on fighting deportation now turned to other urgent areas that emerged during the pandemic.

Over the course of these developments, I tried several times to write a postscript to this chapter to account for these changes. But then a few months would go by, and things would change again. In light of this, I have no retrospective conclusion to offer about what was or was not bound to occur; nor can I say what warnings about the present were embedded in the past. Clearly, however, the New Sanctuary Coalition experienced some of the same issues affecting other social movements in neoliberal times, where the need to bring in money drives "NGOification," and activist groups forgo broader coalition-building activities to build relationships with the donor class (INCITE! Women of Color against Violence Staff 2007). In the process, roles that were once fluid become fixed, and the climate of openness gives away to the exigencies of meeting preestablished goals.

Clearly, too, the accompaniment program was affected by the same racializing processes it was designed to counter. If accompaniment involves a chorus of bodies mobilizing to signal safety, it operates in a social context where not all bodies send and receive the same signals. US legal systems evolved through histories of conquest and slavery to protect white property, such that whiteness, as Cheryl Harris (1993) argues, has come to represent a property interest in and of itself. But that history does not need to be recounted explicitly for it to be felt. It was present in the accompaniment program as a palpable intuition about race, safety, and institutional space, about who the law is designed to protect and who the law is designed to protect itself from. It was the obviousness of this divide that made certain wealthier white citizens feel comfortably insulated from the violence of the Removal Room, while Black, Latinx, and Asian citizens participating in the movement, some of whom had experienced the intersecting violence of criminal and immigration law in their own families or neighborhoods, enjoyed no such protection. The latter sometimes expressed a basic uncertainty about whether their presence was actually desired by the accompaniment program or whether the kind of protection the program offered tacitly relied on the power of white bodies to project institutional safety. Given what transpired, it appears that the patently contradictory tactic of using white privilege against itself collapsed under its own weight.

I cannot speculate further about these developments because I did not have access to the spaces where decisions about the program were made; nor did I undertake the kind of research that would allow me to provide a fair account. That would be another kind of book. More relevant to this project is the larger question of how practices of accompaniment intervene against the project of disappearance. And this question is not confined to the parameters of any individual organization. Rather, accompaniment is a deeply held spiritual value that permeates the broader immigration justice movement. Networks of deported people in Mexico operate teams to accompany those who have been recently deported.[18] Young activists have infiltrated detention centers to accompany the detained.[19] And countless individuals accompany (im)migrants along hemispheric migration routes, providing mutual aid, healing practices, political empowerment, and shelter.[20] These efforts form a vast—if largely unacknowledged—transnational accompaniment network.[21]

While this chapter has been about the accompaniment practice that developed in the context of one particular organization, the rest of the book considers unaffiliated acts of accompaniment in other realms. In particular, it asks how we might practice accompaniment in spaces where the basic tenet of physical co-presence, of moving *with* another person, appears to be impossible. In the coda I consider the possibility of accompaniment when we do not know the physical whereabouts of the person we accompany. In chapter 2 I consider the question of accompaniment in the absurdist theater of family detention.

TWO

The Prison-Courtroom
No-Show Justice in Family Detention

I attended a political asylum hearing in a courtroom inside a for-profit prison built for Central American mothers and children in Dilley, Texas. The judge was a no-show (figure 2.1). He was actually in Miami, Florida, and participated in the hearing via video chat, his torso appearing on a large screen installed in the customary place of the judicial bench in the little trailer dressed up as a courtroom next to the trailers dressed up as houses next to the trailers dressed up as schools. Also present in this two-dimensional image of no-show justice: a shiny spot on a bald head of the government prosecutor; bushy hair and the back of a computer screen hiding the face of the law clerk; a blurry map that appears to depict Central America; and, in the top right corner of the screen, the images of us that these people in Miami can see. You know what that reverse gaze of a video conference looks like. That's me in the corner sitting silently, attempting to draw a picture. That's my friend Emma, a lawyer, who has been told not to speak. That's Yesenia, who says to the image on the screen, "I'm nervous." She is about to be ordered deported and, as of this writing, continues to suffer the consequences of what happened in that courtroom.

Figure 2.1: The trailer-courtroom.

Yesenia was incarcerated in a detention center built on the colonial logic of racial elimination. And from inside that space, she was expected to seek asylum. She was expected to request protection from the officials that had incarcerated her and her children. She was faced with the delirium of what happens when the politics of recognition and the politics of elimination coincide. But in order to get to that scene, to even contemplate the possibility of accompaniment, we first have to contend with the fact that the presence of this courtroom processing claims for asylum was introduced as a prison reform. When the US government started detaining (im)migrant families in the early 2000s, it faced a series of lawsuits and public protests that challenged the legality of this practice. The institution managed to survive these legal challenges by reconfiguring the internal architecture of family detention centers to make them more "humanitarian" and less "prison-like." Since the opening of the South Texas Family Residential Center (known as Dilley) in 2014, (im)migrant detainees, journalists, and advocates have consistently pointed to these reforms as cynical and failed attempts to mask what this space really is. After Dilley tried to get state accreditation as a licensed child-care facility, the advocacy community called it an "insult to the common sense of the people of Texas" and likened the move to "putting lipstick on a pig" (Phippen 2016). Nearby, an oil company proposed to construct a "hotel-like" family detention center that marketed itself as an answer to the poor conditions in other centers. A representative from an antidetention group responded, "If you are not free to leave, then it doesn't matter how nice it is. It's a prison" (Feltz 2016).

We could follow these commentators and say these reform efforts are failures and Dilley remains a prison. But perhaps it would be more accurate to say that it is *not not* a prison.[1] In other words, it is a particular type of prison whose long-term survival strategy has something to do with manufacturing the delirious impression that it might be, but potentially is not, but definitely is a prison. In order to enter this space, then, we have to be prepared to contemplate the fact of a strategic investment in incoherence, a type of incoherence that is not just linguistic but also scenographic. Michel Foucault might call it "heterotopia." For Foucault, the term *heterotopia* designates a "single real place" in which "several sites that are in themselves incompatible" are juxtaposed (1986, 25). When this juxtaposition happens, the incompatible sites that are cited like terms within quotation marks inside the real place do not remain the way they would under other circumstances. Instead, the coexisting sites "suspend, neutralize, or invert the set of relations that they happen to designate, mirror, or reflect" (Foucault 1986, 24). In other words, a "home" or a "courtroom" nested inside a prison is not a home or a courtroom. It might not even be a home-in-prison or a courtroom-in-prison. Sites that are heterotopically introduced into other sites relate like a hall of mirrors to the customary meanings associated with those sites. In Foucault's definition, it is not just the elements but the *relation of the elements* that is suspended, neutralized, or inverted. In other words, if the compound terms "prison-home" and "prison-court" designate a relationship between two elements, the nature of that relationship is not a simple summation. A courtroom inside a prison does not imply that there is a courtroom and there is a prison and the latter is simply a container for the former. Rather, prison heterotopia expresses the basic point that these sites are necessarily deformed by their physical entanglement. When they are lumped together in the same space, the discrete categories of "prison," "home," and "courtroom" may each individually be transformed beyond recognition. But none of this means that a prison is not a prison. It might mean, instead, that the feeling of living among absurdly derealized forms comes to define the experience of imprisonment itself.

When I first arrived at the South Texas Family Residential Center, I spoke with a newly detained woman. She asked me, "Am I in prison? When we arrived, they told us it was a family center, but it definitely seems like we're in prison." How was I supposed to answer that question? I could tell her it was a family center, thus becoming complicit in the euphemism of benevolence and social service propagated by the industry. Or I could say it was indeed a prison, and by doing so, I would effectively be sentencing her to prison in the instant of that utterance. My confusion and her confusion were two separate but related manifestations of the same fundamental problem: a generalized breakdown of function and form. By choosing to rebrand itself a "family residential center," the prison company that ran this place set in motion a search for meaning. It made people on the outside ask themselves, what is a family residential center, and what distinguishes it from a prison? For the people on the inside, this ambiguity is not merely an intellectual exercise but rather an urgent process of getting a grip on reality. If you have to ask, "Am I in prison?" you are in a very specific kind of prison, one that attacks not only your freedom but also your right to know the basic facts about what is happening to you, including the elemental question of whether you are confined. In either case, whether one is detained on the inside or concerned on the outside, the incoherence of prison heterotopia is an incitement to meaning: our senses are activated by the prison's crisis of form.

The problem I identify here is connected to a larger conversation in carceral studies about the conundrums involved in depicting detention centers and prisons. How do we represent prison life without becoming complicit in the logic of prison? What does it mean to see or "unsee" the prison? (Schept 2014b). Given that these spaces are hidden from view, critics expose what happens inside prisons in the hope that doing so spurs the public to close them down. To that end, much of the cultural production around prison and detention involves what Michelle Brown calls "the quintessential carceral image"—the suffering of a racialized person in a cage (2014, 185). Often, these images aim to humanize people in prison—demonstrating that they are complex, relatable individuals who do not fit criminal stereotypes (Story 2017). While these scenes can increase the public's empathy for particular people in prison, they do not necessarily lead us toward abolition. They do not show us a vision of a world that does not rely on prisons or how we might transform society to get there. Instead, these scenes expose the fact that the internal culture of a particular prison or detention center is racist, misogynist, dysfunctional, or abusive, but the accumulation of this evidence does not necessarily catalyze social transformation toward a noncarceral world. Rather, the exposure of carceral atrocities often leads to reform efforts aimed at reorganizing the prison under more benign, humane, or population-specific terms.[2] And these efforts, in turn, tend to entrench rather than abolish the institution.

In light of these patterns, filmmaker Brett Story asks, "What does it mean to make something 'visible,' and why do we think seeing has the power of dislodging?" (2017, 455). Here, she implies that, rather than dislodging the institution of prison, seeing images of prison might have the opposite effect—namely, lodging the prison more deeply in the sphere of common sense. Extending this question, we might ask, what if the problem of reform and the problem of "seeing" were connected? As prison abolitionist Judah Schept writes, "while we often use the word 'reform' to suggest progressive, if incremental, change, the word also can mean 're-structuring' or, more obviously, 're-formation'" (2014a). By taking apart the word *reform*, Schept suggests that the institution of prison endures through its capacity to evolve—to form again. This implies that the cycles of reform that have produced prison heterotopias might involve the activity of sense-making itself. Prisons make no sense. The more deeply we peer inside them, the less their internal realities correspond to the rationales that supposedly give them purpose.[3] The process of reform is an attempt to resolve these contradictions and restore a sense of alignment between function and form. We come up with a new type of prison that seems to make more sense. We fold new logics—such as the "home" or the "refugee center"—into the space of prison. Yet these reforms only lead to prison heterotopia, mixed-up spaces where incompatible notions generate a new crisis of sense. What if prisons and detention centers are spaces that are structurally incapable of making sense? And what if this breakdown of meaning stimulates the process of reform as a restoration of sense, as *re-formation*? In that case, the crises of form generated in prisons and detention centers might actually be productive, rather than counterproductive, for these institutions' long-term viability. As César Cuauhtémoc García Hernández argues, "prison's failings are actually part of what makes the prison as an institution so successful" (2017, 274). If the supposed failures of prisons are not failures but actually invitations for re-formation, then the goal is no longer to catch the prison in a lie. The prison, so to speak, wants to be caught. The goal instead is to catch ourselves believing that a prison or a detention center can be made compatible with truth. It is more important to pay attention to how prison stages the shows, no-shows, and antishows that accumulate in and around prison and how we are implicated in that process. If the prison industry makes us complicit in its own reinvention, is there a way to refuse this process? How do we enter the space of prison heterotopia without unwittingly repairing it, without offering the prison more coherence than it offers back?

The rest of this chapter theorizes about these scenographic dynamics in the institution of family detention. The first section traces the history of reform that led to the expansion of the institution. In the second section, I retrace my visit to Dilley, Texas, in the winter of 2016. Here, I consider how detainees navigated the physical structures of a heterotopic space and what those journeys reveal about the enmeshed politics of elimination and recognition. In the final section, I return to the central theme of chapter 1 and ask what it means to accompany others in the space of prison heterotopia.

Family Detention: A History of Reform

The US government first attempted to detain families and unaccompanied minors arriving at the US-Mexico border in the 1980s. But a 1990s judicial ruling known as the *Flores* settlement effectively curtailed child and family detention.[4] The ruling in *Flores* prohibited the detention of minors except in exceptional circumstances, in which case the children were to be held only in licensed child-care facilities. Immigration authorities tried to get around this ruling by separating families and detaining the adult parents, but Congress directed them to end that practice in the interest of family unity. Thus, by the late 1990s, both children and their parents were considered exempt from detention. After 9/11, the so-called war on terror provided the political will and funding to revive the discredited concept of family detention. The newly created Department of Homeland Security took specific aim at Central American (im)migrants arriving on the US-Mexico border when it directed its agents to prioritize "other than Mexicans" and to funnel them into both existing and newly constructed, primarily for-profit detention centers (Martin 2012a). It was in the context of a wartime mentality and a newly bloated enforcement budget that the Bush administration managed to defy the *Flores* settlement and renew the project of incarcerating families.

That project was, by then, a well-established pattern in the history of immigration detention. The rhetoric of war inflates existing racial animus toward (im)migrant populations and creates a sense of urgency to contain them. This results in a perceived shortage of detention space and unleashes a scramble to convert prisons, military bases, and other abandoned spaces into detention centers, generating a windfall for the private and public entities involved in the business of prison.[5] The first entity to address this apparent shortage was the Corrections Corporation of America (CCA; later renamed CoreCivic), one of the major US prison companies operating both prisons and detention centers around the world. The CCA transformed an adult prison that had become unprofitable into the T. Don Hutto Family Detention Center in 2006, thus saving the corporation's failing investment (Libal, Martin, and Porter 2012, 255). As family detention served an economic function for the private prison industry, the Department of Homeland Security supplied the legal mechanism to facilitate the mass incarceration of (im)migrant families. It applied the concept of "expedited removal," a procedure invented in the 1990s that allows low-level immigration officers to deport people without a court hearing and to detain them pending deportation.[6] In doing so, the DHS claimed it was "closing down a loophole that has been exploited by human smugglers" (Department of Homeland Security 2006). This "loophole" was the *Flores* safeguard that limited the detention of children. According to the government's narrative, smugglers took advantage of *Flores* by "renting" children to accompany them across the border. Having conjured this improbable scenario, the DHS managed to do the impossible: depict the arrival of children and families as a threat to national security. The family was no longer conceived as a natural entity but rather as an artificial arrangement designed to undercut the law. As it had in previous moments of racial panic, the US government invoked the logic of deterrence when it initiated the detention policy, claiming that incarceration was necessary to deter other Central American families from migrating.[7] The DHS further argued that it would be unwise to "release families into the community where, more likely than not, they're going to abscond" (Department of Homeland Security 2006). This logic, of course, is endlessly circular. Families must be detained because otherwise they would be free; in other words, families must be caged because otherwise they would not be caged. The DHS had recently introduced a "catch and remove" initiative aimed at detaining and deporting 100 percent of undocumented people arriving in the country. "Catch and remove" evoked centuries-old practices of racial hunting in the borderlands, thus supplying the framework for configuring the mere presence of Central American families in US territory as a territorial threat.[8]

As Kelly Hernández concludes in her careful study of US prisons and detention centers, "incarceration is elimination"; it operates "as a means of purging, removing, caging, containing, erasing, disappearing, and eliminating targeted populations from land, life, and society in the United States" (2017, 1). As the institution of family detention took shape following 9/11, the logic of elimination could not be more apparent. At any given moment, there are many (im)migrant families living in the United States who are not documented. Yet, the policy of family detention did not target the undocumented family per se; rather, it targeted the specific population of Central American families on the US-Mexico border. It could not be argued that this particular population was conspicuous for its violation of US immigration law. Quite the contrary—these families often followed the established procedure for seeking asylum by turning themselves in to the Border Patrol and expressing a fear of persecution in their home countries. The families detained in this period were not accused of any crime. Their individual behavior was not the issue. Instead, they were incarcerated because their mere presence in US territory was construed as a weakness in the fortress of an insecure ethno-nation. To perceive children as a loophole makes sense only when the enemy is configured in civilizational terms. The fear of (im)migrants' reproduction, grounded in a colonial logic of elimination, supplies the unstated but clear reason why the Central American family was seen as a threat. Within the settler-colonial logic of elimination, sexual reproduction is a target because reproduction is considered an engine of racial contamination.[9] Since the 1980s, white fear of Black and brown women's sexual reproduction had been a central factor in anti-immigrant policies.[10] The particular discourse of "anchor babies" oriented this panic toward Mexican, Central American, and other Latina women (Lugo-Lugo and Bloodsworth-Lugo 2014). That discourse also situated racial panic at the US-Mexico border, recalling the anxiety of unfinished conquest that has played out incessantly in the borderlands region. As María Josefina Saldaña-Portillo (2016) argues, the US-Mexico borderlands continues to be perceived through the eyes of the colonists who struggled to maintain control over the region. Even as existing Indigenous communities with ongoing claims to sovereignty are disappeared from the map, the psychic residue of Indigenous resistance continues to define the borderlands as a fundamentally lawless region that must be brought again and again under white control. The enduring fragility of the settler psyche helps explain the shocking asymmetry of family detention, the sense of vulnerability invoked by US officials even as they wielded advanced surveillance equipment and carceral facilities against children and families. Many commentators tried to highlight this asymmetry by depicting the Central American family as vulnerable and innocent. Repeating this claim is unlikely to be useful, given the way a politics of innocence can lend itself to paternalistic forms of rescue and control (Ticktin 2017). Instead, it might be more important to address the *targeting of innocence*, the specific manner in which the US government—in yet another echo of US-sponsored Central American "dirty wars"—has gone after those members of society considered sacred or immune.[11] Considering family detention alongside these recent transnational projects of elimination points to a tactic of terror by which the state directs its violence against those we cherish most. This tactic of terror resounds in the silence of these pages, where I have managed to write about family detention without ever directly referring to a detained child. Even in the attempt to provide a basic history of what is happening, I quickly approach the limit of what I am able to write about—and this is the psychological component of elimination and disappearance. Anyone who understands what it means to love a child comprehends this terror because the extent of the violation is exactly proportional to the extent of the love. And so, if I am unable to write directly about what detention means for a family or a child, and if the nausea I feel when writing about this is anything like the nausea you feel when reading it, this is only because the impact of colonial terror reverberates widely and we are all living within its extended range.

Historians demonstrate that prisons tend to emerge in political contexts marked by deep, intractable contradictions. As Ruth Wilson Gilmore and Craig Gilmore explain, the "connection between the rise of the nation-state and the rise of the prison is located in the contradiction between mobility and immobility: when the conditions attending on a global system that requires constant motion (e.g., capitalism) clash with challenges to maintain order, spatial fixes such as racialization and criminalization temporarily settle things" (2007, 144). What Gilmore and Gilmore describe is the political use of prison as a (particularly cruel and ineffective) solution to contradictions that are not easily solved. Prisons arise not out of political certainty but out of ambivalence, of dependency mixed with fear, of mobility crossed with immobility, of the nation-state as an ethnic and territorial concept rubbing up against the dynamism of capital. In the case of Central American (im)migrants, these ambivalent relations are exceptionally clear. Central American (im)migrants trigger the anxiety of unfinished conquest (and settler fears of reverse conquest), yet they are integral to the US economy as a source of disposable labor. Capital is able to exploit the labor of racialized undocumented people because of the value created through their illegalized presence—that is, the legal and social mechanisms that marginalize them politically, deprive them economically, and enforce their deportability. When the state declares particular populations illegal, it delivers a "very prized kind of highly vulnerable, precarious labor" that contributes to US industries as a dependable source of surplus value (De Genova 2016b, 276).[12] But this relationship requires that illegalized (im)migrants continue to reproduce themselves as a class. It requires that (im)migrants continue to cross borders without authorization and remain in the United States undocumented. In this sense, US capital is actually dependent on the *autonomy* of (im)migrants: the persistence of human mobility beyond the terms of law. Central American (im)migrants are thus located precisely at the point of tension between capital and nation, mobility and immobility, labor and race. The autonomous movement of Central American (im)migrants is both a source of surplus value and a source of fear, a contradiction to which the state responded in the post-9/11 period through the temporary "spatial fix" of family detention.

In 2007 a lawsuit led to the closure of the T. Don Hutto Family Detention Center. That lawsuit played a significant role in shaping subsequent phases of family detention, so I will recount the details here. In their case against the DHS, the American Civil Liberties Union and other advocacy groups mounted three arguments to support the immediate release of families. First, they argued that the incarcerated families had a right to re-lease under the terms of the *Flores* settlement. Second, the plaintiffs de-scribed the conditions at Hutto as a violation of the *Flores* settlement's mandate that children be detained in the least restrictive setting possible. They argued that the architecture and protocols at Hutto were penal rather than "home-like." They described children being forced to wear prison garb and participate in headcounts; live in cement cells with only one hour of recreation a day; and submit to the orders of correctional officers who prohibited familial affection, used family separation as a tool to control behavior, and disintegrated care relations. Third, the plaintiffs sought the immediate release of the families based on the "irreparable psychological harm" that detention posed to children.[13]

The Texas district judge presiding in the case dismissed the first and third arguments but upheld the second. He denied the children's right to imme-diate release by affirming ICE's absolute authority to detain unauthorized immigrants. During the hearing he said, "So it is [plaintiffs'] position that as long as an illegal is in this country with a child, the placing of that person in incarceration in jail, where they usually go before I sentence them or before they're deported, they cannot go to jail anymore, they are—they get a free pass with their child?" (quoted in Martin 2012b, 498). This judge thoroughly reproduced the perception of children as a loophole within the armor of national security. His reference to a "free pass" depicted the Central American child as an obstacle to profit, thereby making the logic of commodified captivity particularly explicit. On the third point, the judge rejected the plaintiffs' argument that Hutto's conditions caused ir-reparable harm to children by finding, essentially, that the children were *beyond harm*, already irrevocably damaged by the process of migration itself.

The only point the judge agreed with was the notion that, as a "prison-like" facility—in fact, a former prison—Hutto could not satisfy the *Flores* settlement's stipulation that children be detained in the "least restrictive facility possible." Judge Sparks thus conceded a mismatch between the image of a Central American family and the architecture and protocols of an adult prison. He agreed that families should be detained in facilities that resemble homes rather than those that resemble prisons.

What is notable about this early chapter of family detention is how the prison industry and the government managed to shift the debate from one about *captivity* and *liberation* to one about architectural *form*. Judge Sparks saw Central American families as a naturally prison-bound population, yet he agreed that the terms of their captivity should be re-formed. The distinction between prison-like and home-like detention centers stresses imprisonment as a state of scenography rather than a state of confinement. This framework normalizes incarceration and suggests that this condition becomes unacceptable only when it mixes up two racial figurations of the enemy. Family incarceration should not resemble forms of incarceration associated with prison because prisons are for criminals. In the US racial imagination, "criminal" is code for Black.[14] Thus, an underlying anti-Blackness renders the spectacle of prison architectures, prison protocols, and prison discourses shocking in a way that other "softened" forms of commodified captivity do not. Central American women and children occupy a different, but also profoundly maligned, place in the US racial imagination. The home-like detention center, therefore, has the effect of aligning the scenography of family detention with the construction of a civilizational enemy—those who must be eliminated because of their capacity to reproduce. As Andrea Gómez Cervantes and her colleagues observe, the notion of a home-like prison "associates Latina immigrant women with the stereotypical images—their fertility and motherhood— that the public has been alerted to fear" (Gómez Cervantes, Menjívar, and Staples 2017, 279). The home-like prison effectively states that depriving Central American women and children of liberty should match the settler-colonial parameters of how their enemy status was conceived.[15]

The scandal of Hutto and the mounting public pressure caused President Obama to announce a period of reflection. He hired a special investigator to report on conditions in detention centers and suggest a less penal, more "civil" approach (Schriro 2017). For several years, no new family detention centers were built. But then, despite an overall decline in the total number of apprehensions at the US-Mexico border, the number of families and unaccompanied minors arriving at the border increased in 2014. The federal government and the news media depicted the increase as a "surge," relying on a familiar metaphor of flooding water to produce the impression of a national crisis (Santa Ana 2002, 72–79). If anything surged in the summer of 2014, it was the amount of federal money filling the pockets of the Border Patrol and the prison industry as a result of this supposed crisis. The rhetoric of crisis led to the sudden, dramatic expansion of enforcement infrastructures. The Obama administration hired new Border Patrol officers, expanded a militarized immigration-containment partnership with Mexico (Programa Frontera Sur), and awarded private prison companies contracts to build three new high-capacity family detention centers: Artesia, Dilley, and Karnes.[16]

The Obama administration's attitude toward family detention had shifted 180 degrees—from dismantling the practice in 2009 to vastly expanding it in 2014. Prison reform is about staying power.[17] It is the propensity of the prison-industrial complex to withstand resistance by reemerging under new terms. In this case, the Obama administration faced ongoing resistance from (im)migrant justice and human rights sectors, and it also had to justify the reversal of its own stance. Just five years earlier, the DHS special investigator had condemned family detention as poorly managed, ineffective, and inhumane, so how could the administration justify the new push to build family detention centers (Schriro 2017)? All of these factors contributed to the need to present family detention not as a revival of prior forms but as a meaningfully changed institution. Thus, when the new centers were built, they did not repeat the conditions at Hutto. It seemed that the Hutto lawsuit had taught the prison industry and the government about the importance of euphemistic language and architectural reform.[18] The new centers at Dilley and Karnes were marketed as "campuses." Promotional materials emphasized children's playgrounds and the ability of "residents" to move freely through the centers.[19] The distinction between home-like and prison-like detention centers had been given form.

Once the new centers were operational, they spurred a new round of lawsuits, this time taking aim not only at the conditions of the detainees' confinement but also at the violation of their right to request asylum. Both the Bush and the Obama administrations had implemented family detention as a gateway to deportation. When the detention center in Artesia opened, there were no provisions for families to apply for asylum, and many commentators argued that one of the purposes of the new detention centers was to prevent families from doing so.[20] But that changed in 2015 when a Texas district court struck down the legal basis of family detention. The judge rejected the government's deterrence rationale as a violation of detained families' due process rights. He ridiculed the notion that Central American families represented a threat to national security, and he affirmed what legal advocacy organizations had roundly proved: that the vast majority of detained families had strong cases for asylum and were therefore owed protection under US law.[21]

Faced with this challenge, the Obama administration chose to transform the institution of family detention rather than abolish it. Bizarrely, the government decided to incorporate this new understanding of detainees as rights-bearing asylum seekers into the very meaning of detention itself. The secretary of the DHS announced that "substantial changes" were needed in family detention policy. He promised that the detention centers would "ensure access to counsel, attorney-client meeting rooms, social workers, educational services, [and] comprehensive medical care" and stated that "families will also receive education about their rights and responsibilities, including attendance at immigration court hearings" (Johnson 2015). The same centers that had been implemented to facilitate the deportation of Central American families were suddenly recast as processing centers maintained for the nonpunitive, bureaucratic purpose of helping detainees prepare their immigration cases. The legal advocacy organizations that had regularly been denied access to these facilities were now allowed to operate inside them on a permanent basis. And contrary to their original purpose of expediting removal—that is, blocking detainees' right to contest their deportation in court—the new family detention centers were outfitted with immigration courtrooms and asylum offices built into the physical infrastructure of the "campuses" themselves.

By incorporating these reforms, the Obama administration achieved several contradictory things: it (1) meaningfully reduced the number of families deported from these facilities and increased the number released to pursue asylum claims in the United States, (2) bolstered the permanence and perceived legitimacy of family detention, and (3) created a kind of prison heterotopia that folds humanitarian premises into the very space of elimination. Family detention centers became spaces of racial elimination that paradoxically justified their existence by allowing detainees to exercise their rights. Legal rights, social services, and humanitarian protections were turned into unlikely alibis for the settler-colonial project of borderlands incarceration. Notions that appear anathema to prison were blended into the prison environment.

And nobody knew what to make of it. How do we condemn something we cannot conceive? In a 2015 *New York Times* article about the family detention center at Dilley, journalist Julia Preston catalogs the center's features—some of which she might have observed herself, and some of which might have been reported to her by prison officials. She does not clarify which is which. In either case, the information is filtered out to the public, and readers feel as if we have become part of the filtration system. As Preston lists the features that supposedly coexist at Dilley, we get a sense of the disorientation produced by prison heterotopia. We get a sense of the cynical profusion of incompatible functions and forms. We get a sense of being baited into the work of re-formation. It is difficult to say whether the goal is to convince or to confuse.

> A staff pediatrician performs weekly wellness checks, officials said. On a recent day, a nurse took the temperature of everyone entering the dining hall for lunch, to control an outbreak of chickenpox.
>
> In a school classroom, 17 lively children raised their hands and tried to outdo one another saying the English words for the apples and peanuts that a bilingual teacher displayed on a Smart Board. They all knew what to say when she showed a chocolate cone. "I love ice cream!" they shouted.
>
> Recreation specialists lead Zumba classes. In the one-chair beauty parlor, detainees earn $1 a day styling hair.
>
> A formal courtroom has a video screen beaming immigration judges sitting in Miami. This year, official figures show, 88 percent of migrants in family centers passed the first hurdle for an asylum claim, an interview in which they described their fears of returning home.
>
> Some women detained here said they felt relief at first, after bringing their children on a journey from Central America almost as perilous as the mayhem they were escaping. . . .
>
> But as weeks drag on to months, mothers struggle. Children become restless and wonder what they did wrong. (Preston 2015)

What happens when this article feeds the world these images of Dilley? We receive a barrage of incommensurable data points and struggle to give them form. "Zumba" leads to the image of a consumerist space. Suddenly there is a storefront. Suddenly there is music. Suddenly there is a coffee shop next door. When the nurse takes the detainees' temperature, we might assume a whole medical system with a public health mandate. When the children learn from a "Smart Board," we might picture a school outfitted with the latest technology. The reference to a "formal courtroom" has us imagining a baroque edifice. When the author refers to dollar-a-day labor, she conjures images of prison slavery. Yet when she claims that detainees are relieved when they arrive, the facility morphs again into a space of refuge. The differentiation of all these image clusters creates the impression of variety, texture, and depth. In reality, all this purported differentiation takes place in trailers that are more or less identical and minimally retrofitted to serve their alleged purpose. It all takes place inside a secure detention center in the desert. By creating an impression of diversity internal to carceral space, we are encouraged to ignore the violence of captivity itself. We are encouraged to be on the lookout for carceral atrocities while ignoring the atrocity of incarceration. We are encouraged to see a detention center as a neutral container that can accommodate benign or legitimate functions—if only the relations between those functions are slightly re-formed. When the debate centers on forms and reforms inside prison, we run the risk, as abolitionist Rachel Herzing puts it, "of exceptionalizing or isolating negative elements of the [prison-industrial complex], while normalizing its overall operation and underwriting its future" (2015, 194). It means that we have become, in the words of Jared Sexton and Elizabeth Lee, "unprepared or uninterested to contest the process of *roundup* at its most basic level" (2006, 1007).

The Zumba classes Preston references may or may not have happened at Dilley, but they are *staged* in the public's mind. Imagined theater is never meant to be physically staged; instead, the scenes take place in the reader's mind (Sack 2017). When the prison industry invites Preston to write about Zumba classes, a Smart Board, and a formal courtroom, the reader produces imagined theater. By calling it imagined, I do not mean it is not real. Quite the contrary, these scenes clearly fulfill a purpose, insofar as they are part of the process of prison reform. If we try to point out the failure of reform—if it turned out, for instance, that the Zumba classes were not actually held in the manner advertised or if they were discontinued—the prison industry might go ahead and announce a new dance program. We are egged on by the assumption that the detention center is attached to its own reasons. We are egged on by the pursuit of reason, by the assumption that there must be a way to resolve the contradictions and make a coherent statement about what this space *really* is.

Although we may be easily recruited into this drive for coherence, the truth is that, as long as it remains a space of incarceration, it remains a space that shelters incoherence. Between the inside world and the outside world, there is a tangent line, a nonroad. On the outside, there is a show the public can imagine but cannot see. And on the inside, there is a show the detainees can see but potentially cannot imagine. Remember her words: *Am I in prison?*

Dilley, Winter 2016

Parking Lot

I fly down from New York with Emma, a lawyer. We are going to spend a week with a team of legal advocates who have set up a permanent base near the detention center. They are part of a network of organizations in the Southwest that participate in lawsuits against family detention and provide legal and social services inside detention centers.

After one night of training we will spend the rest of the week traveling back and forth between our motel and the detention center, meeting with detained women and helping them prepare for their so-called credible fear interviews (a precursor to asylum).[22] To get to the South Texas Family Residential Center, we have to pass another prison and an oilfield.[23] The arid, unpunctuated landscape seems to do to space what indefinite detention does to time. There is not a contour or a curve in sight. In the parking lot, Emma and I are prohibited from taking pictures, although we are tempted to take one of the series of flags at the entrance that unabashedly proclaims a neoliberal trinity: the CCA flag, the Texas flag, and the US flag.

From the parking lot, I cannot see the campus or get a sense of its scale. I can only see the secure visitors' entryway, which is surrounded by fences; soaring above them is an array of floodlights that survey us. I am immediately mindful of the visual asymmetry that is characteristic of prison: from the parking lot, I have a very shallow view of the facility, while its surveillance towers ensure that I can be seen from a distance (Schept 2014b). In the parking lot we notice a bus with tinted windows (figure 2.2). The bus driver casually informs us that he deports people to Guatemala. Here is an actual instrument of banishment, seen up close. Yet because of the tinted windows, even seeing it up close and in person is to continue not to see it. The bus communicates to the public that the bodies inside are undesirable and forsaken, that they are kept in the dark because our world is better without them. The tinted windows of the bus are paradoxically turned out, in that sense, toward the public, even though they hide the deportees. The scene publicly announces a project of removal, asking us to consent to disappearance by giving us something to see. The tinting lays the basis for deportation, doing the theatrical work of making the prisoners seem as if they have vanished before the bus drives them out of the nation (Taylor 1997, 132).

The bus says, *These people do not exist because we just covered them with an opaque screen.* As an openly illusionary mechanism, the bus invites us

Figure 2.2: The bus with tinted windows.

to suspend disbelief, to concede to the power of props. There is, of course, something fragile about this operation. It is clearly the scenography, the act of tinting, rather than the bodies themselves that generates the fear from which we purportedly require protection. State regimes of disappearance use a psychological substrate of infantile images of cavernous spaces and darkness to create the impression of an unstoppable, diabolical, or indeed magical force separating the public from the people targeted for disappearance (Taylor 1997, 131). The bus says the deportees are dangerous, but its underlying message is that the state is dangerous. To this extent, the windows act like a magic line separating us from the interior—a solidarity inhibitor—making it seem as if, even if we possessed the will, we could not open the doors.

To be inside this bus is to perceive with absolute clarity the violence of roundup itself. The act of seizing a body transforms the nature of space, turning space into prison space. Prison space is infused with the illusion that nothing exists outside of what you are shown. Prison space cuts off the body's capacity to move through the world and watch it unfold.[24] Prison space is a global threat staged in a truncated universe. Sexton and Lee call prison "the prerequisite of torture" because of the enduring and generalized nature of such a threat. Once the body has been seized, they argue, "the necessary conditions for any subsequent brutality have already been met" (2006, 1007). If you were inside that bus being deported from Texas to Guatemala, you would experience that atmosphere of potential impunity. The sensation that *anything could happen to me in here* is a durational and spatialized condition with at least as much weight as the event: *something happened to me here.* The tinted windows make the project of disappearance paradoxically transparent. You gaze out the window and see hundreds of people looking in your direction without registering your face. There might be fear or curiosity in their eyes, but it would not be directed at you—not really. Their faces would reflect the fantasy of a mobile dungeon conjured by the darkened windows. Transported in a mobile prison across apparent national boundaries, you would understand the collusion of at least three nations in manufacturing your disappearance. You would see the irony of the transnational cooperation that goes into punishing your transnational life.

Visitation Trailer

We walk through the parking lot into the security area, where we have to submit our belongings for inspection. Before arrival, we were admonished to bring bottled water because the local water is thought to be polluted from fracking. Past the security area we arrive at the large visitation trailer, where volunteers associated with the legal services NGO have arranged a set of tables and a play area for the children. Against the far end, detained women and children sit in rows waiting to discuss the details of their cases with us.

The visitation trailer seems like a relatively benign and open space. There is a guard in one corner quietly monitoring the room, but apart from that, there is little overt evidence that we are inside a prison. In fact, pasted to the wall, the phrase *endfamilydetention* is conspicuously displayed as the Internet password for volunteers. The fact that this antagonistic message seems to cause no alarm gives the impression of an autonomous zone—a space physically inside the detention center yet controlled by the advocacy organization. Inside the visitation trailer, the advocacy organization is free to impose its own values: provide legal services to all, treat people with respect, protect detainees' privacy by allowing them to engage in sensitive conversations free from the guards' intimidation, and even paste an abolitionist message on the wall. Yet, to the extent we are making the prison space *ours*, we are also contributing to the idea that anything—even our own abolitionist politics—can be incorporated into the physical structures of prison.

During my time in the visitation trailer I made coffee, I made friends with detainees, and I had interesting conversations with volunteers about neoliberal trade policies. The strange implication of this experience is that prison can accommodate all of these things. The dangerous implication is that prison space can be made humane, habitable, and functional if we—the well intentioned and well informed—are given a larger say in its operations or a larger share of its square footage. With prison heterotopia, space is not unitary. It is never just one thing. It is a double paradigm where the action of reclaiming space is not necessarily the opposite of ceding it, where making prison *ours* is also expanding prison's scope, and where making prison meaningful can sometimes result in making prison last.

My responsibility, like that of many volunteers who arrived at weekly intervals, was to spend all day in the visitation trailer with Emma, meeting with detained women individually to prepare them for their credible fear interviews—a precursor to potentially winning political asylum. At the time of my visit, women who passed these interviews were eligible for release from the detention center with bond payments of around $10,000 or with electronic ankle monitors. Once they settled somewhere in the United States, they would pursue their asylum claims in immigration court.[25] Most of the women we worked with were successful in their interviews and were scheduled for bond hearings. Part of our job was to provide legal orientation and explain the possible outcomes.

As a result of our training, I began to absorb and reproduce the scripts developed by the NGO for interviewing women about their asylum claims. We explained that asylum exists to protect people who fear persecution if they return to their countries, and we asked them why they decided to leave. We encouraged their recollections to take the form of a narrative arc: "What was the first moment the violence started, the worst moment, and the moment that made you decide to leave?" We practiced the rhetorical art of making the "intelligible spring from the accidental," in Paul Ricoeur's terms, the legal and literary art of linear chronology (1984, 41). If our interlocutors tended to narrate collective realities as such—framing their own experiences in terms of overall conditions in their countries—we steered their narratives away from such statements. We had been informed that the women's greatest hurdle was convincing asylum officers of the existence of what is called "nexus." Asylum officers tended to agree that the women's suffering "rose to the level of persecution" but faulted them for not demonstrating a causal nexus between such persecution and the women's individual characteristics or actions.[26] Nexus functions in asylum law like a narrative hinge or motive, a tight cause-and-effect relationship between the asylum seeker's identity and the persecution she suffered. Nexus requires, first and foremost, that in the act of storytelling the asylum seeker emerge as a distinct individual with distinct characteristics—distinct enough for her to become the target of an individualized act of motivated persecution. To this end, we were trained to ask the women "Why did they choose *you* and not others?" and "What is it about *you* that made them target you specifically?" Mimicking what I had heard more experienced volunteers say, I tried to inculcate an individualist mind-set: "This is *your* story. No one knows this story like you do."

Strangely, phrases like "this is *your* story" bear no obvious trace of the neocolonial history they carry. Quite the contrary, such phrases sound a lot like the ubiquitous discourse of individual empowerment that circulates in contemporary culture.[27] I could sense that some of my fellow volunteers took pride in transmitting this discourse. In a liberal worldview, individual recognition is the opposite of racism.[28] So telling incarcerated women that they "own their story" sounds like good news. These volunteers did not see that the compulsion to "own your story" can be just as oppressive as the invisibility of that story. They did not see that the valorization of "special" or "unique" trauma is just as oppressive as the structural violence that produces trauma, nor did they see that these two processes are two sides of the same coin. It is the enduring neocolonial dynamic between the United States and Central America, and the obfuscation of that dynamic within the fabric of asylum law,[29] that makes it difficult for Central Americans to receive asylum and thus intensifies the pressure for individual Central American asylum seekers to portray their cases as unique. As I sat in the visitation trailer and told women "this is *your* story," I watched the faux optimism of my words register on their faces. I had a sour, guilty taste in my mouth. The language of individual exceptionality is not the happy antidote to racism but actually a deep sign of its persistence within a hostile legal code.

One of the women I met in the visitation trailer, Ana, was visibly shaking when we approached her. When we asked what had happened, she explained that when she presented herself to the Border Patrol at the US-Mexico border, she was asked what right she had to enter the country. She told the officers she had no visa or documents but that she had come to the United States to reunite with her husband in Montana. Upon hearing her response, they shackled her and, with sadistic mocking, told her they would take her all the way to Montana to meet him. In reality, they took her to Dilley. On the van ride from the border, Ana believed that she and her children were being kidnapped. She pleaded with the officers to tell her where they were really headed, but they only laughed at her and repeated, "We're going to see your husband."

Once Ana had caught her breath, we tried to reassure her that she was safe, that she had not been kidnapped, and that she had legal rights. We then proceeded with the standard orientation. We explained that she could apply for political asylum, which exists to protect those whose governments cannot or will not protect them from persecution. Except that Ana had no particular fear of persecution in her home country. We asked her many times if she feared being deported to Honduras, and she repeatedly said she did not. Quite plainly, she was more afraid of the US government officials who had just kidnapped her—the same government that was now offering protection—than she was of her life in Honduras. But our training had not prepared us to deal with this unexpected situation. The rules of asylum recognize only stories in which the United States acts as savior, not as persecutor. From this perspective, Ana's story was not acceptable; it constituted a kind of legal nonsense, being completely illegible within the parameters of the law. So, in rote fashion, we continued to tell Ana about her right to asylum but offered no suggestions about how she could reconcile the narrative plotline of asylum with the very different plotline of her lived reality. We simply gave Ana our standard speech and let the giant gap between our words and her reality float in the air.

In heterotopia, it is not just the elements but also the *relation of the elements* that is suspended, neutralized, or inverted. That is, a school inside a prison is not the same thing as a school outside a prison, and the incorporation of a home or a courtroom into carceral space can distort those sites beyond recognition. At the same time, however, by folding one logic into another, prison heterotopia draws diverse elements into relation and potentially reveals their underlying commonalities. As I reflected on the sequence of events that Ana experienced, I saw how kidnapping, detention, and asylum were meshing—for Ana—into a singular process. Those events, taken in the abstract, are so different that they are almost incompatible. They each belong to entirely distinct semantic spheres. But for Ana, prison heterotopia had pushed them together into a single slice of space and time. Prison heterotopia produced the compound phenomenon *kidnapping-detention-asylum*. This compound phenomenon was a three-part expression of the fundamental ambivalence toward Central American (im)migrants in US society.

As discussed in the previous section of this chapter, the history of family detention exposes profound contradictions regarding the role of Central American (im)migrants in US society. The anxiety of unfinished conquest in the borderlands underlies the eliminatory impulses of border policies, but additional anxieties are introduced by the global nature of capitalism. In its perennial search for surplus value, Central American (im)migrants have been racialized as a source of cheap labor. Thus, US capital depends on Central Americans' autonomous mobility, even if that mobility also provokes racial panic. For Ana, every stage of prison heterotopia (or the compound experience kidnapping-detention-asylum) manifested this structural ambivalence. At every stage, her autonomy was treated as a problem. Every stage attempted to correct her autonomy but did so in different ways. The Border Patrol punished it. The detention center "spatial[ly] fixed" it, in Gilmore and Gilmore's (2007) terms. And the asylum process silenced it and transformed it into something else.

Ana presented herself at the border not as a dutiful supplicant but as a person who knew where she wanted to go; she wanted to go see her husband in Montana. The idea that a Central American woman might have the right to exercise such autonomy was entirely off-script. Indeed, the Border Patrol officers apparently interpreted her stance as a brazen affront to the entire system, their personal authority, or both. So they decided not only to transport her to prison but also to make a show of their power to do so. The point was to teach her that she was not the author of her own movement—a seemingly gratuitous act, until we remember that state theater is not gratuitous. Rather, it is the means by which the state "shows itself to itself," bringing inchoate, ambivalent, or unresolved issues to the fore. In this case, the Border Patrol officers dramatized the ambivalence about human mobility underlying the detention regime. They transported her to the detention center and, on the way, employed theatrical means to teach her that she was not free.

Once Ana was incarcerated, that lesson did not end; it continued in a different form. In the visitation trailer, we informed her that her autonomous act of going to Montana to see her husband was ineligible for recognition. Instead, she could only earn recognition by silencing her intentions and turning herself into a victimized object awaiting rescue. When Emma and I recited our standard script about the asylum process, we were not punishing Ana's autonomy as the Border Patrol had, nor physically inhibiting it in the manner of the detention center. Instead, we were silencing her autonomy by introducing her to the parameters of a humanitarian legal system in which it has no place. We informed her that detainees can earn their release from the center if they have experienced persecution in their home countries and are looking to the US government for protection. Ana's *real* story—that she migrated to pursue a transnational family life and that her most acute experience of unsafety was not in Honduras but at the hands of agents of the US government—had absolutely no chance of recognition. We did not tell her to lie. We did not tell her to be truthful. We offered no advice at all. We simply showed her, through the automated quality of our speech, through the disconnect between our words and her reality, that her truth was, from a legal standpoint, moot. Our impotence was not a personal failure but a reflection of the system in which we worked. We were mouthpieces for a humanitarian mechanism structured by the assumption that violence happens elsewhere and safety happens here.

And then we met Yesenia. To our standard questions, she responded quietly, sparingly. She politely declined the demand for coherence, chronology, and self-performance. Yesenia had failed her preliminary hearing with an asylum officer, so we were preparing her to appeal that decision to a higher official: the immigration judge. Emma and I were afraid for her. We wanted her to feel safe in the courtroom inside the prison because we knew she would be deported if she didn't divulge everything that had happened to her. So we emphasized that the immigration judge was there to listen and would not reveal anything to ICE or to those who had threatened her in Honduras. We asked her the standard questions about why she was afraid to go back to Honduras, and her answers did not rise to the level of persecution that qualifies individuals for asylum. From her fearful and quiet demeanor we sensed—and many months later she confirmed to a member of our team—that she had experienced horrific violence in Honduras and did not feel comfortable sharing that information in prison. She had been threatened with death if she spoke about the circumstances that caused her to flee, and here she was in a detention center being told that if she didn't tell the truth she would be deported. The mirroring of a single threat by two nations traced a regional zone of state terror: all parties demanded that she shut up and speak. Her silence pierced the hallucinatory quality of the space. The gaps in her story pointed to the gaps in ours. They brought the fact of her captivity to the fore. Her posture, her voice, and her disjointed story spoke of the ongoingness of terror. Yesenia laid bare the "as if" quality of the labor required of her: suspend consciousness of imprisonment, perform as a legal subject while imprisoned for no legal reason, appeal to the US government as protector from violence in your country of origin even though it has set up an institution specifically to extend and extract profit from that violence.

Thinking of this moment now, I wonder what it would have meant to respect her reality, what it would have meant to insist on her freedom of movement without any corresponding obligation. Yesenia, in Andrea Smith's (2013) terms, "refused to be known and refused to be infinitely knowable." How could we simultaneously respect her unknowability and her autonomy? What needed to change so that she could make decisions without having to expose herself to anyone?

But at the time, I was not thinking along these lines. I was simply becoming more and more afraid. Emma and I wanted Yesenia to feel safe in court because we knew she would be deported if she did not divulge everything that had happened to her. So we assured her that we would be right there with her, that she could take as much time as she needed, that we were sorry she had to go through all this stress, that we were rooting for her, that everything was going to go well. In other words, we lent our good intentions to the prison courtroom and began to imagine—for we had not actually seen it—the discreteness of the courtroom, visualizing it as something separate from the rest of the prison. As we did so, the idea of the courtroom took shape as a form endowed with the miraculous capacity to deviate from the scene, as if, by the mere fact of being a courtroom, it could be a place inside the prison that was not part of the prison.

This is the essential lie of prison heterotopia. Prison lies when it claims to be a neutral container capable of accommodating other sites within it and preserving those sites intact without damage or deformation. Prison can never be a neutral container because its materiality—or, as Foucault puts it, "the very body of the prison"—is a spatial and temporal "vector of power" (2012, 30). Yet it is not surprising that Emma and I were compelled by the idea of a courtroom as a special place with the power to transcend prison. Historically, the courtroom has been understood as a place with very particular spatial properties: a "centrally located, locally anchored, spatially discrete, and architecturally symbolic" site (Mulcahy 2008, 465). The sense that the courtroom is "locally anchored" flows from the spatial concept of *emplacement*. Unlike a modern notion of space as substitutable or neutral, the courtroom is typically associated with a medieval notion of space as emplaced—imbued with special or sacred meaning (Foucault 1986). Inside the courtroom, particular places such as the bench and the bar are simultaneously architectural features and names defining the powers of those who occupy them. The courtroom thus affixes ritualized roles to physical locations, such that "where you are is who you are" (Radul 2011, 119). The subject entering the courtroom encounters a series of thresholds; thresholds demarcate the courthouse building from the rest of the built environment, the entry door from the courtroom, the observation area from the trial area, the trial area from the bench, the bench from the judge, the judge's adornments from his body, and his body from his "inner chambers" (Evans 1999). In the medieval period, when judges were endowed with ecclesiastical authority, even their physical bodies were conceived as thresholds where the sacred source of law met the mundane world of legal dispute.[30] It is not surprising, then, that this mystical residue persists and that we continue to imagine the courtroom as a kind of secular cathedral.

Back at Dilley, Emma and I hoped that the courtroom would transcend its surroundings. We tried to convince Yesenia (and ourselves) that the courtroom was insulated from the rest of the prison environment; that it was institutionally separate from the prison, even though it was physically located inside it; that it was run by enlightened judges rather than guards. It was as if, sweeping our hands across that miserable campus, we said, *Here's a captivity trailer, another captivity trailer, a captivity trailer, and then the trailer of impartiality, confidentiality, and justice.* In producing this image, I felt co-opted into prison heterotopia, in some sense exacerbating the delirium in order to help people, one by one, escape it. When you have heard yourself reassuring incarcerated people that they are totally safe, you have learned something about prison heterotopia.

Courtroom

On the day of the hearing, Yesenia, Emma, and I are escorted separately by guards to the trailer that serves as a courtroom. Yesenia is told to wait in another area while Emma and I sit in the courtroom itself. As we wait, we have time to take stock of our surroundings. We observe the thin plastic walls of the trailer—a symbol of impermanence, seriality, and poverty. The traditional design of the courtroom, with its medieval concept of *emplacement,* is here cited/sited in a transient container, like mobile quotation marks. It is an architectural joke.

In spite of the ironic quality of the courtroom, some customs are preserved. The scene of justice in its most ob*scene* iteration still attends to the scenographic, putting the threshold in the expected place (figure 2.1).

There are rows of pews and a gate separating us from the giant screen that stands in the place of the judicial bench and connects us to Miami.[31] Both screen and bench represent a point in the room that is simultaneously beyond it. Both have the property of beckoning and forbidding our approach. We sense that, by comparison, we have been reduced to singularity, to a mere here and now. Yet that little room somewhere in Miami has a mystical quality only because it represents the freedom of movement the prisoners lack. It seems remote not because it houses the sacred source of law but because it is a place people can freely leave. The placement of unincarcerated space in the structural position of a metaphysical threshold turns life outside prison into an inaccessible remove. For the detainees, the screen's technological tether to the outside world invites an exit from prison only to reinforce its prohibition. The world is round. No part is remote. But with a windowless trailer and a locked door and a judge's torso floating on a screen, it is certainly possible to produce the feeling that we have arrived at the edge of the world, *and even justice is a no-show.*[32]

A private lawyer arrives in a huff and apologizes to the judge, citing her long ride from another town. The judge begins an elaborate display of sympathy for her, mentioning multiple times on the record how sorry he is about the long drive. He never gushes over the prisoners' burden of confinement like he does over the lawyer's burden of transportation. This brief moment of levity, meant to go over the prisoners' heads (or outside their linguistic earshot), telegraphs a preemptive white supremacist community among the unincarcerated. At some point, I realize that the prisoners' confinement might be only minimally salient for the judge, who sees this constructed little courtroom scene only as it appears on his screen, which crops out everything beyond the walls of the trailer (figure 2.3). The judge's view of the scene is limited to a video image that more or less corresponds to his customary view from the bench. The screen allows him to enter the courtroom space virtually, without having to move his body through the desert landscape, pack his bottled water, notice the bus with the tinted windows, talk to the security guards, observe the "Green Turtle Neighborhood," or experience any of the other incoherent notions that lead to the courtroom where he seemingly presides.[33] How large would the frame have to be to capture the fact that the women presented to him as defendants are actually in a state of confinement? Confinement itself does not catch attention; its world-delimiting and time-torturing properties are internal experiences that may not be visible in images. The most insidious effect of Dilley's heterotopia, then, is that it seems designed to

Figure 2.3: The trailer-courtroom as seen from the judge's perspective.

make the basic fact of confinement forgettable for all parties except the one confined.

Like a "real" court, the prison-courtroom has rows of pews and a gate separating the spectators from the participants in the proceedings. But— ha-ha—these seats exist to welcome an imaginary audience: the hypothetical public that would attend this trial and oversee the activities of justice in the grand tradition of open court. Of course, the public is absolutely prohibited from entering the premises because this is a prison. So the pews become a no-one-is-coming display, a reminder that no public is watching the judge. We are seated in the courtroom, looking up at the image of ourselves from what would be the judge's view from the bench and adopting the posture of respectful subjects relative to that projected view. But— ha-ha—there is no actual principle of elevation here. The image from "on high" is an effect of the technology; the judge is actually gazing at a computer screen that might very well be at his eye level. Nevertheless, we watch ourselves framed in that screen showing submission to a concocted elevation. The scene invites us to experience judicial rapture, stimulating, in Judith Butler's words, "a certain desire to be beheld by and perhaps also to behold the face of authority" (1997, 112). Yet—ha-ha—we are beheld by a face we could unplug. If we did so, the thin film of static would go flat, 3-D would turn 2-D, color would turn gray, and the room would seem even more remote. The flimsiness of the connection to justice is on display. In one corner of the screen, we watch our own fearful, respectful faces. The screen holds a mirror to our participation, as if mocking us. We watch ourselves, framed for the judge, injecting belief into a process in which we cannot believe.

This type of gesture is something performers do all the time: practice an action independent of its object, play to the audience before the audience arrives, pretend to hold a prop before the prop has been brought in. At the level of kinesthesia, there is no distinction between expressive and instrumental gestures—that is, pretending to look up at a judge and actually looking up at a judge both involve the same movement (Noland 2009, 15). When we take away the context that gives that gesture purpose, the scene starts to resemble the absurdist play *The Chairs* by Eugène Ionesco, in which the protagonist delivers a dull speech to an increasing number of empty chairs. The absurd as a genre lingers in the moment after the gesture is cut off from its instrumental context, when bits of form, formerly rigged to a rationale, persist anyway. The absurd is thus interested in the qualities that actions obtain when outliving their function: speech beyond reason, gesture beyond purpose, bureaucracy beyond government.

We might assume that legal institutions are embarrassed by their own absurdity. And yet, as theorists of colonial and postcolonial law have argued, some legal systems are less interested in persuading the public of their legitimacy than in broadcasting a state of impunity—an official culture of open secrets and inverted truth.[34] In these circumstances, the absurd is not so much an embarrassment to the law as it is a technique of power. Perhaps the most iconic examination of such a scenario is in Franz Kafka's novel *The Trial*. When the protagonist, K, arrives in court, he faces a confusing scene.[35] Even though the court system appears to be deprived of reason, K is compelled to address it as real because he is under investigation and his life is in the court's hands. K is neither permitted to adjust to the faulty logic of the system nor to conclude that the system has no logic. Instead, the threat of violence compels him to search for meaning. The legal absurd as imagined by Kafka thus combines a state of restlessness on the part of law's subjects with a kind of restful abandon on the part of legal officials. The legal system freely dispenses contradiction, while the subjects of law pick up the pieces and try to make sense of them. There is a sadistic quality to this situation because the subject's belief in the law is simultaneously solicited and ridiculed. Power becomes the power to void the law of sense and yet compel the law's subjects to participate anyway.

Back in the prison-courtroom at Dilley, I have the strange feeling of being an object in this type of scene. The judge may be a no-show in this courtroom, but his absence has turned the room into a show of another kind. It is a show of absurdity in which the detainees and their advocates have been turned into unwitting performers. We are going through the motions of demonstrating fearful respect. We are making our cases and requesting recognition. Yet our compliance is ironized by the ha-has of the scene. How much longer can we continue to go through the motions? How can we take seriously a premise of humanitarian rescue nested inside an environment of commodified captivity? How will we manage to manufacture belief?

When Yesenia arrives, the judge asks questions about the transcript of her earlier hearing. He says he does not see anything to support a well-founded fear of persecution. I look at the map of Central America posted behind him on the screen. The institution of family detention evolved through a series of deliberate decisions on the part of the US government to exacerbate and commodify the precariousness of Central American (im)migrants. Yet this judge is allowed to situate himself in a centered, neutral position and from this position contemplate a version of violence in Central America rendered anthropological and aloof. Relative to that gaze, Yesenia is just another supplicant. She is just another needy person appearing out of nowhere and requesting mercy. He asks whether she has anything to add, and she says "No," but her "no" comes out like a scream behind barbed wire. I glance at the security guard positioned on the right side of the room. He has been there the whole time, but I have just noticed him because of the twitch in his face, and he looks down in what I perceive to be shame. He speaks both English and Spanish. I imagine that, like me, he feels himself straddling an invisible fault line in the room. Emma, the lawyer, is still not allowed to speak, and I can see the taut muscles in her face as she holds her words in. Our half of the courtroom is in a state of frozen panic.

The judge asks another question, and Yesenia responds, "I am nervous." Claiming nervousness disrupts the expectation of her response, disturbs the regulated turn-taking of courtroom speech, and asserts that she cannot answer the questions without addressing the conditions within which they are asked—namely, the fact that this scene, described to her as a scene of recognition, excludes, ridicules, and disappears her. The judge immediately confirms these conditions, joking, "Well, I have a dentist appointment today, so no one is more nervous than I am." He might have said, "While this society has collectivized responsibility for the care of my body, it has collectivized responsibility for the disposal of yours. The fear I have about others helping me live is more profound than your fear of others letting you die."

The silent scream does not penetrate the screen. I am two feet away from Yesenia, but I feel like she is actively being dropped from the room. Yet her removal from our shared world is not making a hole in that world because she has already been perceptually cut out of its fabric. Or we, in that moment, are enacting that cut.

And then the judge momentarily loses his Internet connection. He peers more closely into the camera (I'm assuming this, because his face gets larger on the screen) and says, "We're beginning to lose our picture here . . . it looks like every color of the rainbow . . . oh never mind, it's coming back now . . . I've lost my train of thought." His train of thought—the tether to law's mystical source—snaps when the visual field blurs. The law releases its hold on the body with a sudden awareness of the fragility of the medium, a flickering that is a faulty cable rather than a fluttering robe. The judicial pores fill up with blackheads instead of time immemorial, pus instead of wisdom. His face gets larger, we have been reduced to pixels, and it has scrambled his mind.

Nervous Accompaniment

There is no way to finish this story that would bring emotional resolution, no way to continue it without dragging Yesenia further into the self-disclosure she refused. I do not want to disrespect that refusal by telling her story. But based on the scene I described, we can retroactively consider what accompaniment might have meant or what it could still mean.

We can start by considering some of the proposals made by participants in that courtroom scene: the judge's little laugh as he shared the pain of the lawyer's long commute, the concocted judicial elevation, and Yesenia's nervousness instead of narration, or "the way the body slows down what's going down" (Berlant 2011, 5). Yesenia slowed down what was going on. She was the only one in the room requesting salvation within a space of confinement built on a racial project of elimination. Her nervousness in combination with her refusal to narrate claimed that impasse, because squaring salvation and elimination is a puzzle nobody can solve. When the body is pinned between incommensurable notions, it develops an energy that does not correspond to movement in space: nervousness.

Yesenia's nervousness was the physical manifestation of a scenographic mode in which we find no clarity in the concrete. And that is a surprising thing. In the study of legal ritual, the lens of mise-en-scène has often been invoked to describe how legal ritual clarifies meaning.[36] Most of the law's fundamental principles—authority, normativity, transparency, and so forth—are abstract. The concept of justice, for instance, is meaningless without some kind of embodied elaboration: as the popular saying goes, "Not only must justice be done; it must also *be seen to be done*." Law is thus fundamentally dependent on staging to make its core processes concrete, where *concrete* means: "Combined with, or embodied in matter, actual practice, or a particular example; existing in a material form or as an actual reality, or pertaining to that which so exists. Opposed to *abstract*" (*Oxford English Dictionary*). Thus, when legal theorists argue that mise-en-scène makes law concrete, they mean that abstract values such as authority and justice are embodied in "material form" (a bench, a robe, the closed door to the judge's chambers) and in "actual practice" (the reading of rights, the format of cross-examination, the ritualized act of swearing to tell the truth). All of these things give visible and tangible form to abstract processes. And so the concretizing function of mise-en-scène supposedly helps the law make more sense.

But what if we take the comparison further and consider that, for theater producers and filmmakers, concrete form is not necessarily associated with perceptual clarity. In fact, theater and film tend to treat concrete form as the staging ground for experiments in multiplicity, disjuncture, and even derealization. Some approaches to theater mise-en-scène, for instance, explore how settings with "too much furniture, or walls that [a]re too tight" turn concrete form into an active force enacted on the characters, while other experiments in mise-en-scène reverse that relationship and treat concrete form as "the visible extension of [a character's] ravaged state of mind" (States 1985, 90, 84).[37] Filmic mise-en-scène likewise shows that it is not necessary to venture into abstraction to lose one's mind. Director Sergei Eisenstein, for example, explored concrete arrangements in which our minds are incapable of synthesizing what they perceive. He realized that he could show viewers successive angles of the same space, and even if the angles were not continuous, the viewer would string them together based on an assumption of continuous movement.[38] Through these experiments, Eisenstein created the effect of irreconcilable spatial properties: interiors that are larger than the spaces containing them, staircases that can be climbed but neither ascend nor descend, the eye lured to a point of implied depth that never appears. Without ever departing from concrete form—in some cases, without ever leaving the room—film achieved a sense of the surreal by exploiting the multiplicity inherent to concrete reality.[39]

Like the surrealistic experiments of theater and film, concrete reality at Dilley induced a state of derealization. Every bit of form baited us to synthesize what we could not. A detained woman looked around the visitation room and asked, "Am I in prison?" The concrete reality of that room offered no clear answer. In the courtroom at Dilley, an elevated screen dissolved into a blur of pixels. People who had been kidnapped were told they were safe. The re-formed form of the detention center made things concrete (visible and tangible) without making anything clear. And in the process, all parties were robbed of reason and of rest. The heterotopic nature of this detention center delivered incoherence and invited us to participate in a futile struggle to restore sense.

And at a certain point, Yesenia refused. She refused to repair the fundamental incoherence of prison heterotopia. She refused to believe. She refused to feel safe. She refused to compartmentalize the detention center into zones of commodified captivity and zones of refuge. Her body refused by producing a nervous signal that her mind refused to dismiss. She refused to treat her nervousness as an aberrant, internal experience and instead offered it to the room as a fact about the room, submitting her nervousness like one submits evidence to the court. To accompany Yesenia is to carry her nervousness as something that needs an echo instead of an answer. By carrying her nervousness, we double it. Doubling Yesenia's nervousness does not resolve anything, but it adds energetic evidence to the fact that the attempt to erase Yesenia from that room is not the only thing happening there.

Yesenia is nervous, and she voices it ("I am nervous"), amping up the signal on an impasse. Those of us in the room with her experienced "the contagion, the contact of being with one another in this turmoil," as Jean-Luc Nancy puts it (2000, xii). And this is a contagion the judge cannot catch. When he says he is nervous about his dentist appointment, he is inviting some of us—the unincarcerated—to forget that Yesenia is held captive. He is also in that moment announcing his exclusion from contagion. He announces an impenetrability that is not only technological but that the technology of the computer screen certainly supports. Thus, to let Yesenia's nervousness spread, to double it, is to add intensity to the capacity to be nervous in common. And the spreading ring of what the judge cannot catch unplugs him, for a moment.

Yesenia's nervousness is a refusal to participate in the work of re-forming prison. As I have argued, prison re-formation is not limited to the history of lawsuits recounted in the first section of this chapter. On a more basic level, prison re-formation might be conceived as a property intrinsic to prison space—a space whose colonizing partitions and heterotopic inversions produce a crisis of form that calls out for repair. Like the absurdist and surrealist modes of theater and film, concrete reality in prison is not clarified reality but rather the staging grounds of derealization. The ambient threat of violence—which the physical elements of prison enable, symbolize, and also occlude—is the necessary condition for re-formation. If we were not compelled by the threat of violence, we could abandon the search for sense. Like the protagonist in Kafka's novel, it is the threat of violence that compels our participation.

During my visit to Dilley in the winter of 2016, the person most directly subject to imminent violence was the one who managed to refuse. Yesenia came to the United States to escape the people who had brutalized her, and in the detention center she was told that she could win asylum by speaking about that experience and requesting protection. But she did not feel safe and did not comply. As a result, she was deported and faced a series of hardships that, in order not to break her trust, I will describe only with the legal term *persecution*.

Those of us who are not facing these circumstances might be moved to criticize or, alternatively, idealize her act. Some of the lawyers and volunteers present at the hearing were angry at Yesenia for not disclosing the truth and angry at themselves for failing to convince her to trust the process. But instead of submitting her refusal to judgment, we might acknowledge that her refusal defies judgment. Yesenia was coerced to assert her social value or face social death. And in such circumstances, writes Grace Kyungwon Hong, "the refusal of social value is an impossible, unthinkable option, one that exists, in truth, outside of any available notion of the political" (quoted in Cacho 2012, 31). The courtroom is not prepared to deal with a person who refuses to accept its premises, even when their survival is at stake. Yesenia's refusal, in this sense, cannot be judged from within the scene because it breaks the coercive bonds that hold the scene together. Her refusal implies that impossible, unthinkable acts occur.

At that moment in the courtroom, I fell into a well. I did not know how to accompany Yesenia. But if I had it to do over again, I would hold her hand and offer her my nerves. I would help conduct the current. I would accompany her refusal to give the prison form.

THREE

Bring Me the Room

Tragic Recognition and the Right Not to Tell Your Story

In a class I taught at Brown University called Performance and the Law, I decided to show the film *A Well-Founded Fear* (Camerini and Robertson 2000). This documentary offers a glimpse into the world of asylum officers as they attempt to determine which asylum seekers qualify for asylum. As an occasional Spanish-English interpreter at asylum hearings, I had been in the asylum office depicted in the film and others like it. I appreciated that the film offered viewers a rare insight into legal processes that are otherwise hidden from public view. My intention was to use the film to demonstrate the role of gestures, scripts, and stereotyped characters in legal determinations. In other words, I wanted my students to think about the ways the law expects asylum seekers to *perform*. I wanted them to realize that "asylum seeker" is not a self-evident identity but rather a product of historical constructions, generic conventions, and the continuous negotiation of these elements through embodied performance.

I asked my students, "What do you think of how these asylum decisions are made? Does it seem fair to you?" One student, Siena Rafter, undercut my question and responded, "No one should have that much power." Her statement concluded the activity before it began. Rather than taking for granted the exercise of identifying with the position of an asylum officer, Siena critiqued that very act of identification. Her critique suggested that there is something fundamentally unacceptable about the distribution of power in the asylum hearing and that by undertaking the classroom exercise of evaluating the fairness of these procedures, we would be uncritically participating in the asymmetry of the scenario. By identifying the people we deemed deserving of recognition, we would bolster the criteria that make other people undeserving. And by correcting the blind spots we perceived in the asylum officers' perspective, we would become invested in the bordering activities of immigration law. It is difficult to conceive that a system that could be made fairer is also fundamentally colonial, and perhaps it is even more difficult to conceive that a system *I* made fairer, that *I* filtered through the felt wisdom of my own empathy, remains a structure of domination. Siena's statement implied that she would not feel comfortable making a decision about who deserves to migrate, nor would she feel comfortable living in a world where such decisions are made.

In this chapter, I ask what it would mean to commit to Siena's stance—to refuse to be compelled by individual processes of legal recognition because of a deeper respect for the freedom of movement. Scholars have defined the freedom of movement as "the freedom to move and . . . the concomitant freedom to not be moved (i.e., to stay)" (B. Anderson, Sharma, and Wright 2009, 11). Some (im)migrant groups in the United States define it as the right "to live, love and work anywhere you please" (Fernandez and Olson 2011). Siena's statement made me wonder whether there is another form of freedom embedded in these definitions: freedom *from* individualized, asymmetrical processes of legal recognition. We might call this *the right not to tell your story*. To suggest such a right might seem appalling, given that individualized, asymmetrical processes of legal recognition are often at the center of immigration advocacy. Legal mechanisms like asylum grant rights to (im)migrants based on individual recognition, and a great deal of cultural production aims to support legal recognition by circulating (im)migrant stories in the public sphere. These activities are bolstered by the widely held belief that institutional recognition satisfies a universal human need. Yet, if there is a universal human need to be recognized, why do we believe that need can be met by a legal system that kidnaps, terrorizes, and banishes people? In other words, why do we continue to believe in the ethics of recognition when it is administered in an environment of terror?

In chapter 2 I demonstrated some of the ways that terror envelops the asylum process, throwing the potential moral value of recognition into crisis. There, I told the story of Yesenia, a detained asylum seeker, who refused to participate in the ritual of seeking recognition. This chapter continues that discussion by imagining a complementary form of refusal from the other side of the room. When Siena stated that "no one should have that much power" and put an end to our classroom exercise, she enacted a distinct but related kind of refusal. Whereas Yesenia refused to seek recognition, Siena refused to adopt the sovereign position from which recognition is granted or denied. Yesenia's refusal interrupts the scene from within the thick contradiction of its awful duration. Siena's refusal stops the scene before it starts, as if the immigration judge, rather than taking his seat, chose to pause, linger, and then throw the chair out the window. Siena's refusal is not the same as Yesenia's—certainly, the low stakes of refusing a classroom exercise have absolutely nothing in common with the perilously high stakes of Yesenia's refusal. Nevertheless, we can see the affinity between them. We can see that each echoes and enables the other. We can see that if the two refusals were combined, their effect would be multiplied. Siena's refusal is an act of accompaniment from an unlikely corner of the room. It is a refusal to be captivated by sovereign generosity when sovereign generosity presupposes too much power. It is a refusal to feel good in the environment of sovereignty because the universal, horizontal, and enduring commitment to freedom feels better. This chapter is dedicated to rehearsing that act.

Why is this rehearsal important? Although Siena's refusal may appear inconsequential, her act resonates far beyond the context of the classroom. Indeed, it resonates across many settings in which US residents are literally or figuratively invited to sit in the judge's chair. Many instances of citizen "allyship" reproduce the basic asymmetry—if not the actual interrogatory format and content—of the asylum hearing, where citizens make decisions about whether to award recognition to (im)migrants. I became familiar with such scenes when I participated in the new sanctuary movement between 2013 and 2019. That movement embraced a universal stance against deportation, yet participants worked in an environment where the most effective way to combat any individual deportation was by operating within established legal channels. Practically speaking, members of sanctuary organizations spent a lot of time filling out immigration forms, learning the criteria for different types of legal status, soliciting help from lawyers, and launching public campaigns that asked supporters to make phone calls and send letters to deportation officers, immigration judges, and directors of various immigration agencies. In the process, movement participants with citizenship or relatively secure immigration status sometimes ended up performing a gatekeeping function. For instance, some organizations that offered physical sanctuary conducted an informal screening process to exclude people who were considered unsympathetic according to the good/bad binary enshrined in immigration law.[1] Similarly, lawyers who were otherwise critical of that binary chose "winnable" cases in order to maximize the impact of their labor.

In these instances, movement participants were more or less compelled to reproduce the basic asymmetry of the immigration courtroom because they were embedded in, and dependent on, that system. In other instances, however, US citizens sympathetic to (im)migrants—sometimes called allies—reproduced the basic format of the immigration courtroom not out of necessity but out of goodwill and sincere belief. Such scenes are so ubiquitous across activist, academic, and arts contexts that performance theorist Ana Elena Puga (2012) has coined a term: *migrant melodrama*. As Puga elucidates, the courtroom format of an asylum hearing reproduces fundamental tenets of melodrama—namely, that the suffering person is virtuous, that this virtue must be recognized, and that by recognizing virtuous suffering we reaffirm the moral clarity of the world.[2] Migrant melodramas are those spheres of cultural production that operate outside the immigration courtroom and yet reinforce these basic melodramatic features. Puga focuses on a series of films and novels that address US citizens and "depict undeserved suffering by innocent victims as the implicit price of inclusion, or even fair treatment, in a new nation-state" (2016, 75). During my time in the new sanctuary movement, I saw migrant melodrama play out in many contexts. There were rallies and fundraisers where (im)migrants were asked to share their stories of suffering before an audience composed mostly of citizens who were then encouraged to lobby for policy change or to donate money. And in the field of documentary theater, in a series of works sometimes termed "refugee theater," actors reanimate courtroom testimony drawn from the transcripts of real asylum hearings.[3] In some of these plays, the theater is staged to resemble a courtroom, and the audience is encouraged to see itself as a "court of public opinion" that decides whether to grant asylum to a particular individual (Puga 2013, 161). Often, the creators of such works are critical of xenophobic policies and see themselves as trying to rehabilitate immigration law by staging opportunities for members of the public to symbolically award recognition.

The scenes I just described encompass a wide range of cultural forms, and the scenographic details, participation formats, and intentions of their creators clearly vary. I draw them together not to suggest that they are the same but to focus on the one aspect they have in common: the basic asymmetry that Siena recognized as too much power. This asymmetry is so assumed, so unquestioned that it is barely noticeable. In the immigration courtroom, there is no welcome without judgment, no freedom without evidence, no compassion without scrutiny. As a citizen occupying the judge's chair, you cannot assert that an (im)migrant is right with you without asserting that she is right with the law—or, more strangely, you assert that she is right with the law *because* she is right with you, an argument that turns the citizen-judge into the very personification of sovereignty.[4] Either way, you end up speaking in the name of the law, as if your friendly feelings and the law's parameters of inclusion were organically aligned. As if you— by virtue of your citizenship, by virtue of possessing a microscopic share in sovereignty—can exercise recognition on the sovereign's behalf, extending the stately (and churchly) hand that awards recognition as an act of grace.[5] In these scenes, we identify with the privileged gaze of sovereignty in order to recuperate its potential for goodness. We set up a distance between (im)migrants and citizens so that in the highly charged moment of recognition, we can feel that distance dissolve. When you occupy this position in the room, you take for granted that the noncitizen's transnational status is a problem that must be rectified through a judgment of law. You assume that the (im)migrant's freedom of movement must be justified, while your freedom of movement goes without saying. You expect privacy in the encounter but assume the person before you has no right to the same. And whatever your final decision might be (exclusion or recognition), your feelings about that person—either compassion or disdain—are deputized. That is, they have a direct impact on the other party's livelihood.

We generally think that recognition, including institutional recognition, generates good feelings. This chapter disrupts that commonsense notion by rehearsing how the room looks and feels from the perspective of an immigration judge. When we participate in scenes that ask us to identify with the judge and sit in the judge's chair, we quickly realize that the sovereign act of recognition is not what we think it is—or, rather, that it does not feel how it is supposed to feel. From a sovereign position, the room becomes saturated with a sense that the truth is elusive and the evidence inadequate. This sensation of inadequacy, which I explore theoretically and then invite the reader to rehearse, might be a sign of wielding too much power.

This chapter takes us to several rooms of asylum adjudication: first, the asylum office featured in *A Well-Founded Fear*, and then a similar asylum office I visited while serving as a Spanish-English interpreter during a young woman's asylum hearing. By taking the reader through this rehearsal process, I hope to demonstrate what it feels like to have too much power and what it might feel like to let that power go.

The Politics of Asylum Recognition

Given the problematic nature of this scenario, why would we want to practice identifying with sovereignty as opposed to simply declaring, as Siena did, that no one should have that much power? It strikes me as important to do so because the sensation of having too much power is not immediately obvious. The recognition of the (im)migrant by the state or the citizen is deeply asymmetrical under current conditions, yet that recognition does not *feel* asymmetrical. When we recognize another person as a "real" asylum seeker or refugee, we tend to lose track of the asymmetry presupposed by that determination. Alternatively, if we are aware of that asymmetry, we tend to assume that, with recognition, the asymmetry will be overcome. To offer an alternative to recognition, then, we first have to consider its enormous pull.

According to philosopher Georg Hegel, recognition is a fundamental stage in human development: the individual achieves self-consciousness only insofar as others see him for who he is. For Hegel, recognition is meaningless when conceived as a one-sided action; true recognition must involve the double action of two parties recognizing each other. Each is the other party's "middle term," the vehicle through which he sees himself and actualizes his identity. Both parties thus "recognize themselves as mutually recognizing one another" (1977, 112). Hegel's theory posits a social universe in which we materially assist others by recognizing them and in which all of us require and offer such social validation in turn. This equalizing tendency is thought to be so powerful, in fact, that the drive for mutual recognition leads to the dissolution of social hierarchy. In Hegel's well-known example of the lord and his bondsman (more commonly known as the master-slave dialectic), both parties' desire to be recognized by the other leads them to become equals.

Many scholars of postcolonial and settler-colonial settings take issue with Hegel's transformational optimism on this point. For decolonial theorist Frantz Fanon, recognition represents one side of the twin structure of colonial society. On the one hand, colonialism is perpetuated through objective, structural features such as settlement, enslavement, and the suppression of Indigenous knowledge and forms of life. On the other hand, colonialism also involves the "capacity to transform the colonized population into *subjects* of imperial rule" (Coulthard 2014, 31). Colonial states encourage colonized subjects to see themselves through the eyes of the colonizer and thus to seek the colonizer's recognition and validation and inclusion in its systems.[6] The drive toward recognition assists the colonial project by binding the colonized at the level of a psychological attachment. Recognition of the colonized by colonial authorities might mean gaining a degree of social status, political inclusion, or legal rights, so this attachment is not just psychological, but also material. Because recognition is imagined to fulfill a universal need, the benevolent nature of state recognition typically goes unquestioned, and this impression masks the continued violence of colonialism. As Mohawk scholar Audra Simpson writes, regimes of recognition are "seen as invariably virtuous," and this perception makes them difficult to overcome (2014, 20). Following Fanon, Déné scholar Glen Coulthard concludes that the "interplay between the structural/objective and recognitive/subjective features of colonialism" ensures the capacity of colonial systems to endure over time (2014, 32). While the structural/objective features enable the colonizing class to consolidate economic and political power, scenes of recognition disguise this structure of domination by staging encounters that carry the potential—but lack the actual effect—of transcending coloniality. In other words, recognition puts social equality *on the horizon*, or potentially *on stage*. But in colonial contexts, that horizon is never reached.

I received an email sent by a sanctuary organization to its supporters after one of its members received asylum. I quote it not to criticize the author but as a sample of how the transformative power of recognition is misconstrued within immigration justice organizing. It read: "Every victory, every chance to stand in solidarity with each other brings us a step closer to a world where everyone has the right to live in dignity." On a personal level, it is clearly true that every act of legal recognition counts. There is no way to underestimate the victory when someone gains asylum because there is no way to underestimate a person's life. On historical and conceptual levels, however, it is not necessarily true that recognition for one asylum seeker brings us closer to a world where everyone can live in dignity. For many decades, the scope of the asylum process has expanded concurrently with the punitive aspects of the system. Beginning in 1980, the United States passed landmark legislation to make asylum a universal right available to individuals from any part of the world. In subsequent decades, many battles have been fought (and some won) to expand courts' interpretation of the definition of *asylum* and reduce barriers to particular groups. For instance, legal advocacy has had a profound effect on asylum claims based on sexual orientation.[7] Across these decades, the field of asylum advocacy—both the sophistication of its legal arguments and the extent of its reach—has grown. Yet in the same period, there has been a steady intensification of the punitive, violent activities that go by the name of immigration *enforcement*. These include spectacles of racial terror conducted by state and nonstate actors, border militarization, crimmigration (the integration of criminal and immigration law), deportation, and detention.

The historical coevolution of these enforcement activities with the humanitarian apparatus of asylum might seem like an anomaly or an error. It might seem that the humanitarian apparatus supporting recognition for asylum seekers must grow stronger to counteract the forces of state violence associated with enforcement. Within a liberal political system, the interpersonal act of recognition is interpreted as benevolent, while the violence associated with enforcement activities is interpreted as a psychological error, an expression of irrational prejudice and xenophobia.[8] The opposition between state violence and recognition thus appears to be as clear and straightforward as the opposition between hatred and love. And once the issue is conceived in these terms, it is natural to assume that recognition for asylum seekers automatically advances a larger cause of justice. It is natural to assume that if we scaled up the humanitarian apparatus, we would automatically scale down the carceral system. It is natural to assume that improving the social image of racialized (im)migrants leads to a reduction in harsh, racist policies.

And this is where immigration law appears to share something fundamental with the settler-colonial paradigms analyzed by Simpson, Coulthard, and Fanon. Similar to those contexts, asylum law is embroiled in a twin structure where hatred and love, recognition and racism, are more functionally integrated than we might suspect. There is an interplay between apparent opposites. Recognition for asylum seekers tends to simultaneously mitigate and perpetuate the larger global inequities engendered by imperial and colonial histories. And this interplay marks a conceptual limit that contributes to the durability of the current system. It is very difficult to envision a different system when the current system seems to contain its own remedy. It is very difficult to perceive the urgency of a decolonial vision when the humanitarian regime administered by international bodies and individual nation-states appears to have a pure ethic at its core. Yet, contrary to this impression, there is no original moment of pure inclusion that we can extract from the history of asylum law. Instead, asylum law has functioned as an ambivalent and partial mechanism since the inception of the international humanitarian regime.

In the wake of the Holocaust, there was an unprecedented impetus to create an international system of human rights. The establishment of international norms around human rights represented a major transformation in world politics, for it implied that "states could no longer be regarded as the sole arbiters of the needs and entitlements of their citizens" (Bhabha 1996, 5). Universalist principles of human rights were thus perceived as a challenge to the nation-state system of territorial sovereignty (6). The nations that negotiated the foundational human rights agreements on which contemporary asylum law is based wanted to ensure that provisions for asylum seekers did not infringe on their power to control migration into their territories and establish procedures for citizenship. Policymaking in that period and throughout the subsequent decades manifested a profound "fear of the floodgates," an ongoing fear that, by recognizing asylum seekers, nation-states would open themselves to an uncontrolled influx of poor, racialized people (Gorman 2019).

The legal procedure of asylum that emerged from these political negotiations thus reflects a compromise. Asylum law establishes universal eligibility for a particular type of protection while simultaneously reinforcing the territorial system of sovereign nation-states. Even though it recognizes a class of mobile people on an individual basis, the legal imagination of asylum remains firmly rooted in a worldview in which the autonomous mobility of poor and racialized people is seen as a legal anomaly and an existential threat. The asylum system does not aim, even in its most generous interpretation, to rectify the global inequities engendered by imperial and colonial histories. It does not cover people who migrate for economic reasons or those who participate in circular migration or remittance economies. It does not cover people who migrate because of a general lack of safety in their home countries if the violence does not target them specifically. It does not cover people who live transnational lives or who are part of transnational families if they do not have an individualized fear of persecution.

Instead, the asylum system accomplishes a much narrower task. It establishes a legal mechanism known as *non-refoulement*, which prohibits nation-states from deporting arriving (im)migrants who meet the internationally established definition of *refugee* (those who have a "well-founded fear of persecution" in their countries of origin based on race, religion, and other protected grounds).[9] In order to apply for asylum, (im)migrants must first make their way to a country where they are not citizens. Through their own initiative and means, they must arrive at that "host" nation's port of entry or in the territorial interior of the country.[10] The asylum process therefore always begins with some kind of unsanctioned, unanticipated, unregulated mobility. But even if the host state recognizes that person as a legitimate asylee according to the refugee definition, it does not recognize the person's autonomous mobility per se. In fact, the legal construction of asylum effectively erases (im)migrant autonomy by positing that no unauthorized migration ever took place. According to the international standard, a refugee becomes a refugee the minute events occur that fulfill the refugee definition—for instance, the minute an individual's country of origin fails to protect her from certain types of persecution. When she arrives in a host country and is granted asylum, that official act does not make her a refugee; it only "declares" her to be what she already was.[11] In this way, the legal construction of asylum generates a fictional idea that "there is no gap" between the moment an asylum seeker loses membership in her country of origin and the moment she gains membership in another country (Noll 2005, 206). As immigration law scholar Gregor Noll argues, this legal construction is a manifestation of the fear—or, as he theorizes, the *taboo*—of poor and racialized people's autonomous mobility.[12] To say "there is no gap" between membership in one nation and membership in another is to say there is no life outside the nation-state system, and this drive to erase undocumented and transnational life reverberates throughout the asylum process. When the host country recognizes someone as an asylee and agrees not to deport that person, any legal status conferred in that moment is typically contingent on the asylee remaining in the host nation and not returning to the country of persecution. The original country is therefore renounced on a permanent basis, reaffirming the idea that each person is exclusively under the authority of one nation. And if an individual is denied asylum, she is typically not allowed to simply continue her journey or seek asylum in another country; she is deported to her country of origin. Here, the assumption is that if the individual is not eligible for inclusion in the new nation-state, it is because her bond to the country of origin was never broken and she must immediately be returned to that country's authority. In either case, both recognition and denial aim to rectify transnational and undocumented existence and reaffirm the territorial nation-state system. Because asylum is triggered by unsanctioned and unpredictable acts of mobility, the legal process is always subject to accusations that it legitimizes the autonomy of poor and racialized people. Asylum recognition is thus tied up in a kind of reaction-formation with the larger terrain of autonomous mobility that initiates and engulfs it (De Genova 2016b, 273).

And this dialectical tension between asylum and autonomy is not confined to the internal contradictions of legal constructs. Rather, it extends to the work of asylum seekers and asylum advocates, who are often at pains to distinguish asylum from unauthorized migration. At the start of this chapter, I mentioned some of the ways citizens in the new sanctuary movement and other immigration justice groups end up reproducing the power dynamic of the asylum hearing—either explicitly assuming a gatekeeping function or implicitly identifying with sovereign generosity through scenes of migrant melodrama. Many of the organizations I worked with implemented norms and mechanisms to avoid these patterns and set up more horizontal, less paternalistic dynamics between (im)migrant and citizen participants. Yet in practice, it is often difficult to maintain such horizontality because the power asymmetry is not simply an outgrowth of social hierarchies between citizens and (im)migrants; it is intrinsic to the asylum process and its condemnation of undocumented transnational life. It is very difficult to advocate for asylum seekers without becoming embroiled in the dialectic between the supposedly legitimate (authorized, morally sanctified) mobility that is asylum and the supposedly illegitimate (legally impermissible and morally dubious) mobility that exceeds the asylum definition.

We can see this difficulty most clearly in the original sanctuary movement of the 1980s, which inspired the new sanctuary movement of the 2000s. At the time, the US government was systematically discriminating against Salvadoran and Guatemalan asylum seekers and denying their claims. The Central American (im)migrants and US citizens who participated in the movement condemned this legal discrimination, provided physical sanctuary for those at risk of deportation, launched a powerful critique against neocolonial interventions in Central America, and worked to promote asylum's moral and quasi-theological meaning (Cunningham 1995). As a result of the movement's legal advocacy, the US government was forced to acknowledge its discriminatory stance against certain Central American asylum seekers and to award them temporary legal status.[13] Yet, even as the sanctuary movement was effective in shifting attitudes toward Central American immigration and instigating policy change, it also participated in—and arguably strengthened—the moral distinction between asylum and the larger terrain of (im)migrant autonomy. Movement workers, who were often US citizens, conducted their own screening processes to determine which Central American (im)migrants fit the legal definition of asylum—and therefore who would be included in sanctuary activities—and which (im)migrants were classified as "economic migrants" and excluded on that basis. These citizens became so accustomed to playing the role of immigration judge that they felt capable of making asylum determinations "as accurately as could government officials" (Coutin 1993, 109). Such screening processes were not incidental to sanctuary activities; they were fundamental to the movement's political agenda and legal viability. By limiting sanctuary support to those who fulfilled the legal definition of asylum, the movement was able to consolidate its critique of US interventions in Central America, promote the spiritual value of sanctuary, and defend the legality of its actions when the government brought criminal charges.[14] Thus, just as governing bodies tend to downplay the acts of autonomous mobility that initiate the asylum process (declaring there is no gap between membership in one state and membership in another), the sanctuary movement could promote the moral and legal sanctity of asylum only by excluding those whose mobility raised the specter of unsanctioned transnational life. And in the process, these citizens, who were certainly sympathetic to the plight of Central American (im)migrants, nevertheless reproduced the interrogatory format of the asylum hearing in their movement spaces, with all the colonial paternalism such a scene implies.[15]

The history of asylum law in the United States thus tends to manifest the twin structure of colonial recognition. The legal recognition of individual asylum seekers appears poised to transcend the colonial legacies of global human mobility, yet it consistently works to consolidate them. The scene of asylum may represent the triumph of individual freedom yet subtly reinforce the precepts of (im)migrant illegality that allow the criminalization and systematic exploitation of poor and racialized (im)migrants. The rest of this chapter is dedicated to asking how this elusive twin structure plays out at the level of mise-en-scène. How, by rehearsing the theatrical parameters of these scenes, might we better understand the counterintuitive role that recognition plays in (im)migrant criminalization? Puga's notion of migrant melodrama goes a long way toward theorizing the underlying theatrical structure of asylum law. Her analysis of the melodramatic imagination helps explain the moral dichotomies that abound in immigration politics and why suffering is so central to asylum scenes. Although I draw from Puga's work, I also propose to see the theatricality of asylum in a different way. The asylum process is triggered by the unsanctioned mobility of poor and racialized people, and yet the territorial system of national sovereignty depends on disavowing this fact. In scenographic terms, then, we might say that the specter of (im)migrant autonomy is *always already in the room*. It is both the cause and the enemy of the event. A scenographic analysis might then focus on how this disavowed reality takes up space in the room. After all, the term *mise-en-scène* captures the idea that absent events nevertheless *take up space*. Images in the background put pressure on the foreground, events that happen offstage reverberate onstage, and what might have taken place coexists alongside what does, in fact, take place. Absent and present realities rub together, producing a sense of dynamism. We might analyze the asylum hearing in similar terms: as a scene whose dynamism arises from the co-presence of contradictory forces—namely, the tension between the moral sanctity of the refugee definition and the moral condemnation of autonomous mobility and transnational life. Asylum narratives that tend to be recognized by the law and upheld by civil society as emblematic of the refugee condition are those that seem to resolve this tension *of their own accord*. In other words, a "good" asylum story (1) distinguishes an individual from others who are similar, (2) puts forward a narrative of mobility that can be seen as virtuous or innocent, (3) reaffirms the sovereign control and territorial system of nation-states, and (4) downplays the (im)migrant's freedom of movement. In other words, there are certain stories whose singularity, cohesion, and affective pull make it seem possible to reconcile the moral imperative of human rights with the sovereign imperative to exclude. The "good" asylum story makes us feel that there is no contradiction between the two. But how is it that stories that just so happen to fulfill a sovereign imperative are also the ones that particularly move us?

Here, it is useful to remember that the term *recognition* describes not only a legal determination and principle of interpersonal ethics but also a particular climactic moment within a tragic plot. Asylum law is invested in singularity, and it is the function of tragedy to depict the singular importance of a particular tragic tale. The basic principle of tragedy is that not all suffering is tragic. Tragic suffering is elevated above suffering in general: "significant suffering" versus "mere suffering," in Hegel's terms (quoted in R. Williams 2006, 54). For much of the history of tragedy, this distinction was accomplished in part through socioeconomic criteria: only the suffering of the demigods, the aristocracy, or the nobility aroused the pity and fear necessary for a compelling tragic plot.[16] As cultural theorist Raymond Williams argues in *Modern Tragedy*, the meaning of tragedy has evolved over time. Within our contemporary liberal—and neoliberal—era, "ordinary people" can be tragic protagonists, yet tragedy maintains a preoccupation with individual distinction. In modern times, the tragic hero has become the "liberal tragic hero," who strives to surpass her social context in pursuit of her own individual truth (or, in neoliberal times, her individual brand). Greek tragedies featured individual characters, of course, but they were understood to function as representatives of general themes. Whereas Greek tragedy presents "general action specified," liberal tragedy—and perhaps liberal common sense, more broadly—presents "individual action generalized" (R. Williams 2006, 114). The individual is special because she is different from the rest of us, and yet the act of recognizing her specialness somehow elevates us all.

Sociologist Olga Jubany spent four years investigating the internal culture of immigration officers in Spain and the United Kingdom who process asylum claims. As part of her research, she accessed the officers' handbooks, participated in their training courses, and interviewed the officers. Her principal finding was that above and beyond any strict technical criteria, the immigration officers based their asylum decisions on what they considered a professional intuition—that is, an ability to distinguish authentic from inauthentic stories on the basis of a feeling. As one officer put it, "I would not know how to tell you but you do feel it, you just know it" (quoted in Jubany 2011, 86). I saw something similar when I attended a conference at a New York law school, where several asylum officers appeared as panelists. I approached one of the officers and told her that I was engaged in a project that compared immigration law to theater. I asked what she thought of the idea that there is an embodied, performative dimension to her work. Her eyes lit up as she told me the story of a man who had petitioned for asylum on account of his sexual orientation. Her initial impulse had been to deny asylum because she did not find his story of persecution credible. But then she asked, "How is it that people in your country know you are gay?" This question presumably implied that if his homosexuality were socially "invisible," he would have no reason to fear persecution. The man responded, "Because of how I am with my boyfriend." She asked him to explain. The asylum officer then looked at me and delicately, tenderly swept her hair away from her own forehead, imitating the gesture the man had made to demonstrate: "He touches me like this." At that moment, she knew the man was telling the truth and decided to grant him asylum.

What did she feel when she witnessed this gesture? What did I feel when I witnessed it replayed secondhand? A kind of synthesis. A kind of pull. A kind of sadness. A kind of beauty. In his *Poetics*, Aristotle defines recognition as the moment in the tragic plot that produces "a change from ignorance to knowledge, producing love or hate between the persons destined . . . for good or bad fortune" (section I, part XI). In the moment of recognition, we feel that we have perceived something significant. In a flash, we realize the power of the forces conspiring against our protagonist. We make a leap in understanding and a leap in compassion at the same moment. We are simultaneously wrought with pity and moved with beauty. Tragedy is art, after all, and it is an art form tasked with answering the question: "how can the suffering in tragedy give pleasure?" (R. Williams 2006, 65). Although it is uncomfortable to speak of pleasure in the context of asylum law, it is relevant to note that the pursuit of a singular feeling of cohesion is common to the dramaturgical craft of tragedy and the legal construction of asylum. In liberal tragedy, recognition of a special individual is imagined somehow to be a victory for us all. And perhaps this is why we assume that we can counter the punitive side of the immigration system just by scaling asylum up ("every victory, every chance to stand in solidarity with each other brings us a step closer to a world where everyone has the right to live in dignity"). When we recognize someone as special and encourage the law to do the same, liberal tragedy would have us believe that a more beautiful and just world is on the horizon, even though, structurally, nothing has changed. Liberal tragedy blinds us to the twin structure of colonial violence because it teaches us that the individual is the most meaningful unit of society; thus, recognition for one socially condemned person is more real than the machinery of state violence that brings the scene into being.

During the time I was involved with asylum cases, there were often victories. These victories were the result of a tremendous amount of unpaid labor and community mobilization that resulted in a particular person being upheld as a singularly valued individual. In the jubilation of these moments, activists who were new to the field would invariably comment that the immigration judge or asylum officer had been surprisingly nice. Such activists had likely joined the movement because they thought the system was cruel and heartless, and in these moments of victory, it appeared that we had "humanized" the law. The impulse, then, was to believe that if we could just reproduce that scene on a larger scale, the system would tilt toward justice. But as they spent more time involved in the work, these activists realized that the system is both humanized and dehumanized, both compassionate and heartless—dualities that are just another way of expressing the twin structure of colonial rule. The quasi-beautiful cohesion offered by asylum recognition is the moment when our capacity for compassion seems most awake, when we are most sensitized to the pain of the refugee condition. Yet, the terms by which we recognize the singular are not the terms by which we recognize the general. The singular asylum seeker is recognized for her unique traits, her plausible story, and her coherent narrative and for the way all these elements come together in a flash of recognition. But these same criteria make it impossible to recognize the general cause of asylum seekers because their pain is the pain of criminalized mobility, which is the pain of border imperialism.[17] The general cause is the decriminalization of transnational and undocumented life, and this implies unpredictable, unsurveilled, and unknowable mobility. How can we support such mobility when we have made the singular coherent narrative a condition of our compassion? The tragic frame of asylum installs a problem of perception: the general pain is perceptible only when it is crystallized in the singular, which raises the question of whether the general pain is perceptible at all.

Asylum is not numerically limited in the United States, but perhaps it is dramaturgically limited. Perhaps it is limited by recognition itself and by all the theatrical and literary conventions that condition our preference for the types of stories that come together. How is it that recognition covertly performs a policing function, even though—and this is the strangest part—it catches us at what appears to be our best moment, filled with fellow feeling and opening our arms? Like the asylum officer whose mind was changed by the reenactment of a boyfriend's caress, we are touched by the beauty of the singular—so touched, in fact, that we might easily forget the officer's readiness to deny the claim before being presented with that bit of embodied evidence. Before that evidence emerged, the asylum seeker was just another threatening manifestation of (im)migrant autonomy, part of the murky, unknowable phenomenon that is both the cause and the enemy of the event.

Well-Founded Fear

Siena refused to be touched by the beauty of the singular "good" story. She declared that it entailed too much power. She suspected that recognizing it might work against a wider cause of freedom. To consider this possibility, it might be necessary not only to analyze but also to rehearse the asylum hearing—that is, to experience what happens to the scene of individual recognition when it plays out over and over again. We need to see the scene's cumulative weight—the room of law when it begins to look like a theater, a space of ongoing labor where the same magic comes to life night after night (figure 3.1). From the spectator's position in a theater, one is privy to both the achievement of a theatrical world and the labor that sustains it. But if one stays past the show, there is even more to see: the cleanup, the set shifts, the daily re-creation of the carte blanche. The room of asylum recognition is a physical room where the labor of many people—clerks, security guards, officers, translators, judges, lawyers, and asylum seekers themselves—makes the figure of the successful asylum seeker and the figure of the failed asylum seeker appear. From the judge's chair, the show cannot be the same the first time and the thousandth time, because between an elusive ideal and its laborious reenactment, we cannot help but experience a certain decay.

A Well-Founded Fear premiered on PBS in 2000. The documentary depicts a typical asylum office and features scenes of recognition and compassion, happy outcomes, extraordinary tales of survival, insightful and compassionate asylum officers, applications denied, truth and lies, linguistic and cultural misunderstandings, botched language interpretations, officers grown jaded and callous, and evidentiary voids that no one knows how to overcome. The film, in other words, reveals the asylum hearing as "engrossing," "dramatic," and a "mix of emotions," in the words of one reviewer (Genzlinger 2000). Directors Shari Robertson and Michael Camerini acquired permission from the Immigration and Naturalization Service (INS)—since replaced by the Department of Homeland Security—to film individual asylum hearings and interview asylum seekers and the asylum officers who act as judges in these cases, giving US viewers a glimpse into a process they have likely never seen before. The film continues to be used as an educational tool in law schools as well as an internal training tool for asylum officers.

We see people in a waiting room, fidgeting, nervous. Over the camera's searching close-ups, we hear the voiceover of the asylum officers' standard questions: "How did they find out about you?" and "Tell me again, sir, what you're afraid of?" and "You say you were tortured, what do you mean by that?" The scene then jumps to a traveling shot over the open ocean, as if from the perspective of a low-riding boat, which fades into a shot of the red chairs in the asylum office waiting room. We then ride up the

Figure 3.1: The room of law when you are a repeat actor and it has begun to look like a theater—a space of ongoing labor to make the same magic come to life night after night.

contours of an American flag, close enough to see the individual stitches of the stars and stripes. Then the scene reverts to a static shot of those empty red chairs, and a layer of text is superimposed over them. It is the standard application for asylum (Form I-589). The effect of this montage suggests, *I crossed the ocean to access the American dream and now I have to scale the cold, dry room of bureaucracy.* Framed as a perilous bid for freedom, the montage traces a direct sequential relation between the decision to cross the ocean and the bureaucratic scene of recognition. We meet an asylum officer who says, "My supervisor came up to me after I had discussed a case with him. I told him what my decision was and he said, 'How are you going to feel if this guy goes back and someone puts a bullet in his head,' and I said, 'I'm going to feel terrible about it, obviously, but I have to make a decision and I have to live with it.' That's what this job is about. You make a decision about people's futures." Now we understand the importance of our participation. We must learn as much as we can about asylum seekers if we hope to get this process right. The stakes of not doing so could be death.

The pan across the ocean, up the American flag, and into the asylum office implies a direct movement from foreign lands to US rooms of bureaucracy, as if one gets off the boat and immediately knocks at the door of an asylum office. Central to the asylum scenario is the construction of a figure motivated solely by a desire to see the United States as savior, one who *seeks* the state's promise of inclusion and relief from a nation that has become unlivable. The horizontal crossing of the ocean leads directly to the vertical ascent up the flag. Yet many of the asylum applicants we meet in the film live and work in the United States. In the vignettes about individual asylum seekers we see scenes from their everyday lives: their families, their jobs, their homes, and their places of worship. One couple explains that they have lived and worked in the United States for seven years and built their lives here. Given this contradiction, a *New York Times* film review asks, "What finally lands applicants in the hearing office, when some have been living comfortably in this country for years?" (Genzlinger 2000). Indeed, why do undocumented people seek the bureaucratic recognition of asylum at a particular moment in their lives? And why, in spite of the heterogeneous mobility projects depicted in the film, do the directors choose to frame asylum seekers' stories in the simpler, paradigmatic terms of the ocean and flag montage?

The direct trajectory across the ocean into an asylum office is, in many cases, a myth produced during the asylum hearing itself. The purity of asylum seekers' trajectories is a reflection of the generalized disavowal of autonomous and transnational life. Applicants for asylum must establish that they applied for asylum within one year of arrival or, if not, demonstrate exactly why the application was delayed. In other words, they must demonstrate that their migration was and remains unilaterally motivated by fear of persecution in the country of origin and a desire for refuge in the United States. Every moment one remains in the United States without seeking recognition from the US bureaucracy raises the specter that one's presence and activities go beyond that purpose. Additional reasons for entering the country, such as to reunite with family, to find work, or to temporarily escape a difficult situation with plans to return, are all seen as evidence of a complexity and heterogeneity anathema to the proper construction of the asylum seeker. (Im)migrant advocates are afraid to question the purity of asylum because any indication of its complexity, in the words of one legal advocate, "plays into the anti-immigrant narrative that people (who claim the need for asylum in the US) are just coming to fix their papers" (quoted in J. Williams 2014). This narrative traps (im)migrants into a Manichean innocent/evil binary in which "fixing papers" is morally wrong. This binary, of course, is fictitious. It is entirely possible for a person to simultaneously have a well-founded fear of persecution and an urgent need to fix their papers. It is entirely possible for someone to require refuge from persecution in their country of origin and relief from the pains of undocumented life in the United States.

In the past few years, I have occasionally volunteered as a translator for asylum hearings, and I have been present when people were deciding whether to apply for asylum. Those who applied affirmatively did so for a variety of reasons. They had all experienced some form of persecution in their countries of origin that clearly or at least arguably fell within the type of persecution protected under US and international definitions of the refugee. In other words, nothing in my experience confirmed the anti-immigrant narrative of "bogus refugees" because all the asylum seekers I knew had indeed experienced some kind of political violence. Yet their decision to apply for asylum at that particular moment did not spring automatically from their eligibility to do so but rather from personal calculations that weighed the potential recriminations of an encounter with the immigration bureaucracy against the necessity of regularizing their status. There are certainly many people who fully identify and qualify as asylum seekers, and I do not intend to discredit or devalue that. In my limited experience, however, many of the people who applied for asylum had very little attachment to the symbolic or affective reasons for seeking protection from the US nation-state. Instead, they saw asylum as a way to *arreglar papeles*—that is, to attain relief from criminalization not for abstract reasons of national belonging but as a way to ameliorate the pain of illegal status and its interference with their lives (Coutin 2003, 58).

Living undocumented or precariously documented in the United States entails myriad stressors. For adults, it can mean employment only in industries where the threat of deportation is used either explicitly or implicitly to justify subminimum wages, wage theft, and substandard working conditions.[18] Students may be excluded from universities or allowed to matriculate but denied federal grants. Being undocumented is not just a juridical status but rather a "practical, materially consequential, and deeply interiorized mode of being—and of being put in place" (Peutz and De Genova 2010, 14). Those who apply affirmatively for asylum seek relief from the state-induced and socially enforced condition of illegality, and they integrate that decision into their own plans and projects, which might include attaining housing or employment that requires papers, obtaining a different type of visa, accessing affordable legal services to help legalize their status, falling in or out of love, and planning for long-term mobility within a family network. All of the asylum seekers I knew already considered themselves, to various extents, members of and participants in their local worlds: a New Yorker, a resident of a particular neighborhood, a coworker at a certain work space, a member of a place of worship or community group, part of a transnational family, and so on. That is, their sense of membership in the United States was based on the worlds they had built around themselves. Some people were motivated to apply for asylum because immigration agencies target undocumented activists (see Ludwig 2019; Mukpo 2018). Paradoxical from the standpoint of asylum's rescue narrative, these activists required legal recognition so they could more safely express dissent. Another great paradox is that, for certain precariously documented (im)migrants, legalizing their status in the United States allows them to leave the country (Coutin 2010). Many (im)migrants have family networks spanning multiple nations, and their projects, fantasies, and opportunities for employment are similarly transnational in scope. For such people, political asylum may represent a pathway not toward the exclusive embrace of the United States but rather toward eventual citizenship, which means decriminalized travel to their countries of origin. In other words, some seek asylum not to rectify their transnational existence but to remove the obstacle of border violence so that they can live that existence more fully.

None of the people I have in mind are "bogus" refugees. They are people whose life experiences fulfill the refugee definition but who also have qualities, ambitions, and identities that surpass the asylum plot and thus call its purity into question. The population of asylum seekers is more complex than the idealized narrative of asylum on which we construct the humanity of humanitarian recognition. The room of asylum adjudication is perpetually confronted with forms of life that exceed its terms.

After the ocean and flag montage, *A Well-Founded Fear* shows us clips of asylum hearings and interviews with asylum officers. The officers discuss the evidentiary dilemmas and emotional struggles involved in their work. In one such interview, the officer responds with her own rhetorical question: "How do you decide whether someone's telling the truth or not? It's not simple. You're never sure. And that's the problem. If you're pretty sure it's not the truth that's at least a comfortable position to be in, in that you know you're making a decision based on something that's real. But in a case like this where it's just plain fuzzy, I have to talk to somebody else about it to get another perspective." The interviewer then asks, "Some of them stay fuzzy, right?" and the asylum officer responds: "Yes. That's life. I mean it's real life. We're dealing with real situations and some of these stay fuzzy forever. And we still have to make a decision . . . based on fuzziness."

Clear lies are comfortable. Clear truth is comfortable. What is uncomfortable is entering a fuzzy room with a knife and being instructed to make the cut. The fuzziness is nothing other than the structural tension between asylum and autonomy, between the crystallization of the singular and the opacity of the general. The fuzziness is the continuous encroachment of unrecognizable life. And yet the asylum officers must find a way to make sense of their jobs. The same officer says, "This is not a moral situation. If somebody's lying because they want to stay here, that's perfectly understandable to me." She compares the violation of immigration law to a traffic ticket. Her perspective is uniquely pragmatic. She seems to understand that (im)migrants may choose to seek asylum under false terms because it is in their interest to legalize their status. And although she must make a judgment on their cases, she does not morally condemn them for their actions.

That perspective, however, does not seem to be widespread. Several other officers express a moral attachment to the idea of the asylum seeker and feel personally offended when (im)migrants lie. One explains, "I believe in this. I believe in this kind of work. And maybe at first, I was more gullible. I was more naïve. I believed everybody." He explains the other officers used to call him the "grant king." Subsequently, this officer learned that in some cases he had granted asylum based on false statements, and this revelation led him to change his approach. He says, "Geez man, I'm pretty gullible," with a look of reckoning. Another officer says, "I think you certainly become extremely cynical. And I think at some point you don't want to take crap from people. That you certainly don't want to do. If you gain anything from this job it's that. I mean in the beginning, you're more reasonable, you're more naïve, and your grant rate is probably a lot higher." The officers' moral attachment to the act of recognition continually exposes them to evidence that such attachment has been undervalued and abused. This same officer asks another, "Don't you think they privately laugh at us?"

As Sara Ahmed writes: "The construction of the bogus asylum seeker as a figure of hate also involves a narrative of uncertainty and crisis, but an uncertainty and crisis that *makes that figure do more work.* How can we tell the difference between a bogus and a genuine asylum seeker? It is always possible that we may not be able to tell, and that the bogus may pass their way into our community. Such a possibility commands us (our right, our will) to keep looking, and justifies our intrusion into the bodies of others" (2014, 47). It is the assumption that every racialized (im)migrant *could be the enemy* that requires (im)migrants to perpetually work to prove that they are not. Ahmed's reference to "more work" marks the unsustainability of a system that racializes and criminalizes migrants collectively yet asks them to individually redeem themselves through performances of innocence and exceptionality. The scene Ahmed depicts here reveals why such performances are perpetually insufficient. From the sovereign perspective, the migration of racialized peoples is framed as a potential threat to the self-preservation of the state. The figure of the (im)migrant who might attack, corrupt, or otherwise destroy the nation exists as an "enemy that must always be fought but can never be conquered," and every scene of immigration law is potentially the one in which this spectral figure takes bodily form (Gilmore and Loyd 2012, 45). The courtroom appearance "fleshes out" these figures of alterity—the "bogus," who is a liar through and through—but also the "genuine refugee," who is equally one-dimensional because that person's mobility falls squarely within the terms of suffering and rescue delineated by the asylum plot (Ahmed 2014, 3). In either case, the (im)migrant, from the judge's chair, is invested with potential life before taking bodily form, and the process of the "reveal" drives the drama of the asylum scenario. It also means that (im)migrants' performances can never be adequate because both the enemy and the innocent are idealized categories—simpler than any existing person. Perpetually failing to discover the purity we seek, we are compelled to keep looking, to peer deeper into the lifeworld of the (im)migrant to reveal either a diabolical intention or a previously undisclosed "humanity" and merit. Either it all comes together in the singular terms of tragic recognition or it all falls apart.

One asylum officer asks, "Don't you think they privately laugh at us?" Indeed, many scholars who have studied the transcripts of asylum interviews—and many appellate judges who review the same transcripts—have documented patterns of interaction in which the asylum officer treats the asylum seeker as an actor in the pejorative sense: a "subject of trickery, one who uses deceit and guile to get what she wants" (McKinnon 2009, 217). (Im)migrant autonomy is both the cause and the enemy of the event. (Im)migrants land in these rooms through their own decision-making processes and for their own reasons, and the officers, sensing the unknown and knowing that the unknown is the enemy of the verdict, locate a cause: the asylum seeker is a deliberate imposter playing a role. As a semiscripted plot with well-defined features, the asylum hearing, of course, is a kind of theater, one that blends the melodramatic exposition of virtuous suffering with the tragic recognition of singularity. The extent to which asylum applicants deliver what they are supposed to is also the extent to which they introduce doubt. The asylum officer, in Diana Taylor's terms, perennially "suspect[s] that the devil hides in the performances taking place before his very eyes" (2003, 64). In the very act of succeeding, the asylum seeker demonstrates familiarity with the terms of the encounter. The asylum seeker becomes, as Judith Butler (2014) theorizes, "more knowing about the law and less known by the law": "knowing" because the asylum seeker understands what the law wants, and "less known" because, in assimilating the "good" identity, the asylum seeker "safeguards" those subjective aspects of identity that exceed the law's terms. Successful asylum seekers may have suffered persecution exactly as required by law but may also have dimensions of their lives that they know enough not to disclose. Successful asylum seekers may fear persecution in their countries of origin and also be willing to do whatever it takes to prevent deportation. The fact that these two things can simultaneously be true undergirds the ubiquitous fear of the fake, the intolerance of fuzziness, the hatred toward those who tell the law what it wants to hear. In this "wanting to hear," there is anxiety not only about virtuosic imposters who might elude detection but also about the "wanting" as such, the structures of desire within the scene of recognition, the desire to see the "real refugee" unambiguously revealed.

To adopt the position of the asylum officer who called himself the "grant king"—that is, to believe in the good mission of granting inclusion to "real" refugees—is to expose oneself to serial disappointment. As Sara Ahmed argues, hatred is a form of intimacy that "cannot be opposed to love" (2014, 50). Insofar as the officer's "belief in the work" constructs an attachment to an ideality, it establishes the conditions for attachment to turn to hatred when those terms are not met. Belief and disbelief, in this sense, are not so far apart because they both emerge through attachment to the idea that the real refugee—uncoerced, unmotivated, and grateful—exists and requires rescue. Asylum officers grow cynical and start to wonder whether asylum seekers are laughing at them. In this fantasy, the asylum officers imagine that asylum seekers are laughing because they have caught the officers *believing*. What some of these officers have grown to hate, then, is not the deceit of asylum seekers but rather their *disinterest*. If an undocumented person submitting an affirmative case for asylum makes her own decision to apply for asylum and does so by weighing her own life projects against the potential violence of detention and deportation, then her application for asylum does not necessarily imply a desire for recognition in its moral or affective dimensions. In other words, she might need papers and protection from deportability, but she might not need the compassionate arbiter of the state to show his bureaucratic love.

As a psychologist and decolonial theorist, Frantz Fanon was particularly concerned about how colonial scenes of recognition encourage colonized people to form a subjective attachment to colonial power. For Fanon, the colonial encounter is deeply asymmetrical because while the colonized are encouraged to desire recognition from their oppressors, the colonist does not similarly require recognition from the colonized. Instead, what the colonist wants "is not recognition but work" (2008, 95). Thus, for Fanon, as for Coulthard (2014), the colonial situation marks a breakdown in Hegelian reciprocity because the colonist has no need for recognition from the colonized. Yet in the asylum office depicted in *A Well-Founded Fear*, we can see that state officials (and sympathetic citizens) do seek recognition from asylum seekers. They want to be recognized as rescuers. They want to see themselves playing a necessary role in (im)migrants' lives. They want asylum seekers to affirm the necessity of their compassion. And these desires are threatened by the autonomy of mobility, by the fact that (im)migrants exercised their own initiative and judgment in the process of arriving in the room. Against this, the asylum officer wants to say, *You need my love* and *Your need for my love has nothing to do with my power.*

What the officers need to overcome, then, is both what is unknowable—namely, the full scope of asylum seekers' subjectivity—and what is entirely knowable but fiercely disavowed—namely, the legal framework that criminalizes racialized mobility and thus encourages people to squeeze themselves into narrow categories of individual redemption. Both these factors call into question the purity of the asylum seeker as a figure with a distinct nature; they interrupt the idea that the asylum seeker exists outside the terms of its legal construction. They call into question asylum as a neutral space in which US imperialism can be bracketed and cross-cultural encounters of recognition and compassion staged (Fassin 2011). They call into question the moral clarity of asylum as a politically innocent commitment to the alleviation of suffering—an activity, or even a mission, in which the officers can *believe*. When the officer asks, "Are they laughing at us?" and vows not to "take crap" from anyone, he shows how the asylum office is waging "war against its own condition" (Harney and Moten 2015, 83). The officer revolts against the fuzziness of the room.

In one scene of *A Well-Founded Fear*, two officers discuss the problem of repetitive testimonies. The film has, at this point, introduced the audience to the notion of asylum "preparers," coaches who help (im)migrants submit canned asylum scripts.

OFFICER 1: How about this, though? When you hear a story over and over again, does that affect your decision?

OFFICER 2: No, I still listen. This may be the one who's telling the truth. I mean, how many hundreds of thousands of times in Rwanda did somebody see their family slaughtered right before their eyes?

OFFICER 1: Right, but I think that then the demand for details is increased because you've heard the story ten times.

OFFICER 2: You know, you get a Mauritanian. They all say the same thing. In such and such a month of such and such a year they came to my home, they said I wasn't Mauritanian, they took my documents, they put me in a truck, they took me to a camp, yada yada yada. The same thing over and over again. Does that mean it didn't happen? No, because it could have happened the same way to thousands of people.

OFFICER 1: Right, but what happens? Is it just hearing it over and over again?

OFFICER 2: No, you hear one thing that doesn't ring true, and something clicks, like they say, "I'm a farmer." Well, what do you farm? "Well, I raise rice." Well, how do you plant rice? "Well, you know, I throw the seeds in the water." Uh oh!

Do the stories repeat because the same thing happened to many people or because many people were trained to recite the same story? The officers do not know what repetition signifies. But they have to make the cut somewhere and determine which of the repetitive stories is sincere. Asylum officers are instructed to credit testimony if "it is believable, consistent, and sufficiently detailed to provide a plausible and coherent account" (Paskey 2016, 474). They try to discover a world beyond the agency and design of the person testifying, searching for the verisimilar, for the ring of truth. An implausible account is thin, implying that reality has thickness, vividness. A true account, therefore, can produce details with a little probing. Scratch the surface, and you will either hit a wall or open up a world. Ask about the techniques of farming rice, and if the person is telling the truth, the grains should take shape. "If you lived it," one of the officers states earlier in the film, "you should be able to give me detail." As Roland Barthes (1986) theorizes in what he calls the "reality effect," it is the absence of signification that gives the superfluous detail the quality of verisimilitude. It is this very superfluity—the fact that the detail is irrelevant to the author's point—that signifies, by convention, that the text in question refers to the real world because the real world is presumably a place where things happen outside our representations of them. Similarly, a good asylum story produces a world beyond the design of the author, a world of detail. The officer asks the farmer about rice and wants the farmer to provide something that indicates his story is based on more than his desire to win his claim.

The demand for detail is yet another kind of cry against the fuzziness of the room. It is yet another way in which (im)migrants' autonomy, though disavowed, continues to exert pressure in the room, reverberating through its mise-en-scène. Sitting in the asylum officer's chair, we watch the asylum seeker tell a story about what happened in that individual's personal corner of the world. The asylum seeker brings us the story and also the world in which it fits. When we sit in the asylum officer's chair, the only thing we can do is execute a kind of geometric proof to make sure the world is larger than the story, that the world is populated with details that exceed the story and its author. We want to know that the asylum seeker is just an inhabitant of that world, rather than its creator, yet it is the asylum seeker who brings us both the story and the world. When we ask for details, we reveal our dependence on the asylum seeker to bring that world to life through story. The world is the story and the story is the world.

Aristotle, whose writings greatly influenced the histories of law and theater, recognized this problem as common to both fields. Lawyers and playwrights both rely on the craft of storytelling, but when their craft is visible it ceases to persuade (in law) or entertain (in theater). As theater historian Kathy Eden argues, Aristotle's solution was the same in both contexts: rely on plausibility to establish the appearance of truth. He argued that a plausible arrangement of chronological events leads to artistic satisfaction (in tragedy) and persuasive argumentation (in law) (1986, 10). A tragic plot, like a good legal argument, should unfold according to "necessary or probable" relations—common understandings of cause and effect—rather than through the obvious intervention of the writer (*Poetics*, section II, part XV). If done well, the tragic plot makes it appear that the laws of the universe, rather than the writer's creativity, are responsible for the protagonist's fate. Of course, the shared Aristotelian lineage of law and theater implies that our aesthetic tastes and legal intuitions are not disconnected: they both derive from a kind of craft that aims to reduce the visibility of craft itself. In both cases, we rely on the notion of plausibility to make a claim that we know how the world generally works. In both cases, the best story is the one that makes the storyteller invisible. But the storyteller is not invisible; she is right here in the room, saying, "in such and such a month of such and such a year they came to my home, they said I wasn't Mauritanian, they took my documents, they put me in a truck, they took me to a camp, yada yada yada." How are we to know if this story is plausible? If it follows the general tendencies of the world? We have nothing but the storyteller's word. As the officer, we supposedly have all the power, yet we feel engulfed, toyed with, and suspicious that the power actually resides on the other side of the room.

We long for relief. It comes in the form of tragic recognition, in the story whose singularity, cohesion, and affective pull make it seem possible to reconcile the moral imperative of human rights with the sovereign imperative to exclude. In one part of the film we meet a Chinese man, a poet. His case file is thicker than the others, thanks to the human rights organization that compiled stacks of documents to support his case. To the asylum officer, this pile of evidence makes his job easier. It will be easier to recognize this man because he has already been recognized by others. The asylum applicant recites his poetry during the hearing, breaking into tears as he recounts being tortured and explains that he would not have survived his time as a political prisoner had he not concentrated on his love for his wife. He says to the officer, "I hope that my sad life can be taken by the American government to give the protection of freedom." He represents the paradigmatic image of the asylum seeker, persecuted because he refused to give up his identity, disassociated from his culture not only because of his dissent but also because of his sensitivity. He appeals to the grace of the US government, reaffirming sovereign control and the territorial system of nation-states. And even though, at some point, his mobility must have temporarily transgressed that system, it does not incite the same anxiety as other stories do, perhaps because his story is comprehensible and seems to follow a straight line: individual difference, persecution, flight, and recognition. Every time I watch this film, my tears well up when this man is told that asylum has been granted. Although the film includes several scenes of asylum seekers receiving positive decisions, his is the only one accompanied by music: a swelling major chord progression. My guess is that the film's creators chose to insert an unambiguous affective cue at this moment because this is the one case for which we all come together in unanimous feeling.

I do not mean to diminish this man's suffering, which is, by all accounts, incalculable and fills me with compassion and tenderness for him. My intention is not to ridicule that feeling, which I clearly share with the asylum officer who approved his application, the human rights organizations that supported him, and the filmmakers who enhanced the emotional response with a musical cue. To the contrary, I hope that by rehearsing compassion in this scene of recognition, we gain an appreciation for how easy it is to participate in bordering activities without realizing it. This man's story is terribly sad and unique, and the poignancy of that combination moves us. It moves us to open the gate. No one else is exactly like this person; no one else is this special. When we recognize his specialness, we do not fear "opening the floodgate" to all (im)migrants because the same criteria that opened the gate for him close it for others. The gate opened for him because of a mysterious synthesis of individuality and universal resonance that produces recognition in the tragic frame.

In the depth of that moment, in the poignancy of my own tears, it is difficult for me to perceive my affiliation with sovereignty. It is difficult to see that, as Siena recognized, we still have too much power because recognition offers the feeling that boundaries are dissolving and that the system possesses an ethical core. As sociologist Didier Fassin notes, "If there is domination in the upsurge of compassion, it is objective before it is subjective (and it may not even become subjective). The asymmetry is political rather than psychological: a critique of compassion is necessary not because of the attitude of superiority it implies but because it always presupposes a relation of inequality" (2011, 4). In drawing a distinction between the "political" and the "psychological," Fassin implies that dominance and compassion function on separate planes. While we experience compassion as an affective upsurge, dominance may not even rise to the level of consciousness. Dominance, instead, is an objective feature of the arrangement. Dominance is expressed by the fact that this man's freedom from incarceration and deportation is contingent on eliciting certain feelings in government officials. Dominance is the naturalized distribution of economic and political power through which nation-states selectively open borders to capital while criminalizing transnational and undocumented life. Dominance is conferred by this man's dependence on people with cultural capital and their ability to see him as special and expend resources on him—such as the human rights organization that took his case—resources denied to others not because of a lack of commitment but because there is not enough to go around. And there is not enough to go around because the population of those who need relief from criminalization is larger than the idealized narrative of asylum. Dominance is the reason the room exists, and yet dominance is fervently displaced by feeling.

In the film, we meet a pregnant Algerian woman from a politically active family. In the asylum office, she explains that she was threatened for refusing to wear a hijab. She testifies that her father and his friend were kidnapped and tortured. The officer seems sympathetic. We see the woman in the park with her children and her partner. Then she returns to the office to learn the decision. The clerk tells her that the officer "was unable to come to a decision," so her case has been "referred" to an immigration judge, where she will have another "opportunity to tell her story." Then the camera follows her and her partner out of the office and into the hallway, where they look at the document they have been given. They attempt to make sense of it, speculating that maybe the facts of the case went over the officer's head or perhaps some documents were missing. They discuss whether the date of the immigration court appointment will conflict with the due date of their child. Finally the woman's partner, reading to the end of the document, says, "But practically speaking, it was denied." In a voiceover, the narrator informs us that although cases denied by the asylum office are retried in immigration court, only one in five negative decisions are reversed. Thus, the narrator explains, "In practical terms, the decision is made here." The symbolic divide between the space of pure recognition and the space of deportation is managed scenographically by allocating those functions to different rooms. Even though the negative asylum decision leads directly to the possibility of deportation, the woman will have to enter another building on another date to fully understand that fact.

As the very pregnant Algerian woman and her partner walk down the hall, the viewer feels the dramatic irony. She is still planning her life on her own terms, even though she has just been handed a decision that will, in all likelihood, criminalize her existence and lead to her deportation. She and her partner are still talking about her due date and the missing documents as if they have not yet realized that their world is about to be eclipsed.

The asylum officer looks into the camera in the next scene and explains that he "feels like shit" about his decision. But he has to follow the criteria; he has to hear an individualized narrative of persecution. And in this case, he "just [doesn't] see what she's got to be afraid of above and beyond what every poor soul who lives in Algeria has to be afraid of, which is a lot of civil strife and violence and wickedness." He is sympathetic, but he has a job to do, and this woman has failed to differentiate herself from his generic image of Algeria, which entails a generalized atmosphere of dysfunction. Nevertheless, he acknowledges that she has "had a hard time and she's got little kids and about to have more little kids and all she's trying to do is be safe." One's instinct might be to criticize this asylum officer's lack of compassion, but he is actually quite compassionate. He is moved by the woman's situation. He just does not have enough evidence to demonstrate that she rises above and beyond the fuzziness of abstract third-world misery. And it is entirely understandable that he sees Algeria in this light, because in case after case he has heard asylum seekers and their lawyers describe that country (and other countries) in such terms. As former immigration attorney Jawziya Zaman (2017) observes, "Over time, the names of our clients' countries become sounds that call forth a series of images unanchored from political context and history—images of gang violence, hungry children, and oppressed women. We think we know the most important thing there is to know about these places: people leave."

Indeed, the asylum office is structured to filter in certain kinds of information and filter out others. It filters in a daily barrage of portraits of foreign nations replete with peril; it filters out the reasons people stay in those countries, consider them superior, or long to return. This latter class of sentiments does not enter the room because it would contradict the asylum narrative. And if we were sitting in the officer's chair, hearing story after story, we too would probably imagine a classically colonial map of the world—where the United States is the center of safety and civilization, and the other side of the world represents an amorphous scariness. The Algerian woman's asylum officer regrets the burden of rendering this decision—that is, deciding whether the woman can officially exist in the room and reconcile her position vis-à-vis the nation. From his perspective, her body hovers in the room, awaiting his word. Yet it is also clear that she inhabits another plane of reality where the attempt to engulf her future simply fails. The room fails to close in around her because her life was never truly suspended, and her body was never truly hovering. She wonders about the date of the court hearing and her due date, implying, perhaps, that if the two dates conflict, the law might have to wait. More profound than this question of scheduling, I sense, is the fact that she is engaged in the process of making physical and spiritual room for the emergence of new life. This process involves a type of world making that might take up more room, for her, than the room of sovereignty. Sometimes what you carry inside you is larger than the container they put you in (figure 3.2).

Figure 3.2: Sometimes what you carry inside is larger than the container they put you in.

What we can see is that this woman is already engaged in an array of activities to make her body and her space sustainable for the life she is sustaining. The film shows her with her partner in the playground, and into that fundamental work of sustaining life this woman has subsumed the law as one of the various things she must resolve in order to get back to what matters. Obtaining the right papers to live in the United State without fear might represent for her yet another obstacle she has to clear.

On one plane of reality, the Algerian woman is building a world for her family, and legal recognition is just one nuisance among many that she has to resolve before inaugurating new life. In this plane of reality, the law is subsumed, which means that it is "include[d] or place[d] within something larger or more comprehensive" (Merriam-Webster). Her world-making activities are larger than the law. On another plane of reality, the law aims to subsume her by placing the details of her life within a general framework of eligibility. In legal terms, to subsume is "to bring a specific occurrence within a broad rule" (Cornell Legal Information Institute n.d.). Both recognizing her claim and rejecting it, both fervently believing and disbelieving her, require that we turn a blind eye to the existence of the first plane of reality in which her life is larger. These two planes of reality reverberate in the asylum room, coexisting without the possibility of synthesis.

We might remember here Foucault's caution, following Nietzsche, that "there is nothing in knowledge that enables it, by any right whatever, to know this world" (2001, 9). From the asylum officer's chair, the room is perpetually fuzzy because it depends on an abstracted position of total knowledge that is impossible to achieve. From the judge's chair comes the argument that we need to climb above the lived abundance of human mobility in order to understand its true cause. The fuzziness is a function of the perspective of having too much power.

The other option is to step down from the judge's chair and step into other ways of being in the room. The discussions of accompaniment throughout this book suggest some of these ways. Another way is modeled by the birth process itself, inspired by the pregnant asylum seeker who both subsumes and is subsumed by the law. As Adrienne Brown writes about her work as a doula, supporting the birth process involves "staying focused on the possibility and wisdom of the body. Standing or sitting with someone as they realize, remember their own wholeness" (2017, 25). The type of accompaniment performed by doulas is the opposite of subsumption. It is about realizing that the individual being accompanied has everything she needs, or would have everything she needs were it not for that which is in her way. This is a humble act of clearing the way, and it is born out of respect for what we hope to enable yet do not presume to understand.

Like the birth process, migration is another context in which "there is no eventual elimination of mystery" and "chaos is an essential process" (A. Brown 2017, 65, 20). Having too much power, in Siena's words, is the pain of believing that your job is to eliminate the mystery and chaos intrinsic to human mobility. When you step down from the judge's chair, however, you make a little more room for that which you do not understand to grow.

The Right Not to Tell Your Story

> For if I am right about the problematic of pain installed at
> the heart of many contemporary contradictory demands for
> political recognition, all that such pain may long for—more
> than revenge—is the chance to be heard into a certain release,
> recognized into self-overcoming, incited into possibilities for
> triumphing over, and hence losing, itself.
>
> WENDY BROWN, *STATES OF INJURY* (1995)

A Well-Founded Fear shows that recognition is unsustainable. By definition, it cannot work for everyone because it is structured as a dialectic between the "one" and the "everyone"—the individual who is worthy because she is special, and the many who are not worthy because they are unclear. Over time, this theater produces more and more fuzziness. It produces more and more frustration, turning belief into disbelief. The room fills up with an impression of third-world misery so ponderous that it feels like a flood. Over time, some officers rail against the idea that their compassion is being abused. Others are frustrated with the format that prevents them from expanding the terms of their compassion. Repetition, in other words, wears the room down.

Perhaps this accumulation of recognition could be "recognized into self-overcoming," in the words of Wendy Brown. Instead of hearing the message of the individual, which is the premise of recognition, we could hear the message of the collective, which is that recognition is not sustainable and we need a new orientation toward immigration. As Miriam Ticktin argues, the goal is to ensure that we can all live in a world that does not criminalize mobility and does not depend on any assertion of purity for undocumented people, a world that accepts that undocumented people, like everyone else, inhabit a "contaminated reality" (2017, 588). Such a political vision conceptually decouples the singularity of tragic recognition from the freedom of movement.

Recognition in the immigration context means being seen and heard as one is, and also being granted redemption from criminalization. This coupling means that whatever interpersonal reciprocity there might be in recognition cannot express itself. Our hearts are continually recruited into scenarios of domination. An alternative vision would be the right to "live, love and work anywhere you please" (Fernandez and Olson 2011). Here, freedom of movement implies mobility in terms of locomotion but also mobility of feelings and desires; it is the freedom to want what you are not supposed to want and perhaps also the freedom not to tell your story—or not to tell it when doing so is the "implicit price" for achieving rights (Puga 2016, 75). This implies not only the freedom to move but also the freedom to have your movement count as movement—in other words, respect for your autonomy. The room of recognition insists that the (im)migrant has not yet arrived in the room until an official decision is made about her status. Yet here she is. Why does she owe us her story?

In these final pages, I share my experience as the interpreter for a young woman at her asylum hearing. My hope is that this memory provides a space in which to consider alternative endings, endings that can overcome the scenario of recognition. In relating this memory, I have omitted certain things. I do not want to subsume this young woman within legal categories, yet I need to present sufficient details to set the stage.

Karen, a pro bono lawyer, has asked me to translate at the asylum hearing of a young woman. Karen tells me to brace myself for this case, which involves some brutal material. Dania was kidnapped from her home at a young age, locked in a room inside a brothel for several years, and then managed to escape and migrate to the United States to live with her aunt. Even writing about Dania now makes me feel as sick as I did when participating in her hearing. My feelings are based on a combination of what Dania survived and the forensic gaze to which her memories were subjected. Karen tells me this might be a difficult interview because Dania often exhibits an unexpected affect, laughing or looking bored when talking about the trauma she endured.

The asylum office is located in an industrial office park. We walk in, show our IDs to the security guard at the desk, and sit in the waiting room until Dania's number is called. Dania, her aunt Karen, and I sit together for a few hours, exchanging small talk. Then a female officer emerges and takes us back to one of several small offices for the asylum interview. After she asks Dania some basic questions about her history and fear of persecution, the officer begins a line of questioning about the physical appearance of the room where Dania was confined for all those years. Although asking for details about the sexual slavery Dania endured would have been unbearable and gratuitous, the officer is required to establish that Dania is a credible witness and that the facts she relates are plausible. The asylum officer needs to develop the world in which Dania's story fits. So, in the scenographic poverty of this asylum office, the officer asks to see the room of sexual enslavement brought to life. She does not need Dania to describe the *act*, but she does need Dania to describe the *room*. She asks, "What material was the floor made out of?" She asks, "What color were the walls?" She asks, "Was there a bed or just a mattress, and did anyone come to change the sheets?" We do not need to rehearse her responses or peer further into that room. But suffice it to say that the asylum officer is not satisfied with the fullness of Dania's description. Perhaps it is too simple or too repetitive; perhaps there is not enough detail. Perhaps the officer believes every word Dania said, but for that very reason she feels obligated to develop the record comprehensively so that her supervisor will not question or undermine her decision. At a certain point, this officer asks, "The men that came, were they short or tall?"

At this point, I am having trouble translating the officer's words without transmitting her frustration, which is conveyed by the repetition of the questions. Every question feels like an attack, and as the translator, I have to embody this interrogatory rhythm. Probably some part of my body manifests my resistance and conveys to Dania how I feel about these questions.

When the officer asks whether the men were short or tall, I am sure I make some kind of face as I translate the question to Dania in Spanish. Dania responds, "Some were short and some were tall," and then she raises her eyebrows as if to say, "What a fucking idiot." At this moment, I understand the utter impossibility of reconciling the two planes of reality in the room. The officer is trying to help Dania by subsuming her story, by making it credible and plausible, which means making it fit preexisting assumptions about the ways of the world. The basic pretentiousness of the law begins from the dubious notion that it has the transcendent capacity to judge the veracity of whatever new situations and new forms of life it encounters. The officer needs to find in Dania the hidden domain of superfluous detail behind the surface of her testimony that can definitively deliver the appearance of truth. As one asylum officer states in *A Well-Founded Fear*, "If you lived it you should be able to give me detail." When Dania says, "Some were short and some were tall," her smirking gestures to the idiocy of this exercise. Maybe they were giants. Maybe they wore masks. Maybe they had fangs. I am mocking the moment, but the moment needs mocking because Dania's response held a mirror up to the plausible monstrousness we all expected her to deliver. Dania did not conjure a plausible monster. She answered with a statistical average: some were short and some were tall.

Dania has in fact survived both rooms. She has seen them from an angle that Karen, the asylum officer, and I cannot understand. She has experienced what is unimaginable to the rest of us. We imagine the room of sexual slavery as worlds away from the room of the asylum hearing. The former is supposed to be the room of persecution, and the latter is supposed to be the room of recognition; the former is the room of damage, and the latter is its rectification. But who knows how continuous or discontinuous those rooms are for Dania? We do not know what continuities and discontinuities she perceives. Many have critiqued the asylum hearing as a form of retraumatization, where the repetition of interrogation reproduces the abusive experiences of persecution or torture.[19] What was shocking about the officer's question and Dania's response was that the judicial gaze appeared not only abusive, in the sense of retraumatization, but also, and perhaps more surprisingly, infantile. Dania had to help the officer understand what the officer could not possibly know. She had to indulge the epistemological pretensions of empire and help its representatives feel capable of imagining that which exceeds their experience. Dania had to help the officer feel larger than the evidence.

Despite answering the questions posed to her, Dania fails to bring the room of her confinement to life. Perhaps the room lacks life because of all the terror it supposedly held. It was, after all, just a room, in the sense that nothing about its architecture, materials, or dimensions makes the occurrence of unimaginable horror seem more or less likely. Per Dania's account, the room contained a certain type of floor and certain dimensions and certain objects—nothing exceeding the known world. We are flickering between the institutional need for Dania to say something lifelike that will allow the asylum office to sign off on the image and the absolute estrangement of the officer, the lawyer, and myself from the reality of that room. At a certain point the frustrated officer asks, "Is there some reason you are having trouble answering these questions? Is it because of your trauma?"

Karen decides to speak up. She is not supposed to interrupt the proceedings, but she does. She questions the effectiveness of the officer's line of questioning. She explains that Dania has had almost no formal education, that she was placed in an environment of sensory deprivation during her formative years, and that she was denied normal opportunities for language development and family and peer interactions. She argues that the lack of complexity in Dania's speech patterns is commensurate with those circumstances. This is Karen being a good lawyer. If she can explain the failures of the encounter in psychological terms, Dania will become more legible to the institution. Karen is providing a scientific line of reasoning the officer can use to fill the gaps in the record and the gaps in the room. But then

Karen changes course. As if fed up by recognition itself, she says something like—and I am paraphrasing: "Actually, I think she remembers that room about as well as I remember the places I've lived in. I don't think I would have been able to describe it better." In this moment, Karen switches from pathologizing Dania to pathologizing the process. She mocks the sovereign need to peer further into the room.

What I am suggesting is that this need is scenographic; it is a function of the perspective of having too much power. The officer was not a villain. In fact, she granted asylum to Dania, and my impression is that she believed her all along. My point is that, in the room of recognition, the only way to affirm Dania's credibility was to identify something about Dania—her trauma, her body, her voice, her story, her country, her history, or her culture—that has the ring of virtue or the ring of truth. When we take our place in the officer's chair, Dania's suffering comes into view as a fuzzy reality that must be overcome. In Dania's case, ironically, her story was fuzzy because it was too concrete. It was too concrete to make terror plausible. From the judge's chair, the truth was elusive and the evidence inadequate. When the evidence is inadequate, imagination is piqued and deputized, but perhaps it is hard to feel that. It is hard to recognize the feeling of having too much power.

Another option is to hear the low pulse that is typically crowded out by the theater of recognition. That low pulse is the freedom the (im)migrant represents and exercises: the "spatial disobedience" of migration itself, the fact of having an unknown relationship to the asylum narrative, the fact of having, in Dania's case, a sense of humor (Tazzioli, Garelli, and De Genova 2018, 245). This unknowability is what we annihilate when we convince ourselves that Dania requires our recognition. What she might require, instead, is the removal of all the obstacles placed in her path, including the obstacle of our border-patrolling compassion.

To accompany someone is to go somewhere
with him or her, to break bread together, to be
present on a journey.
PAUL FARMER, "ACCOMPANIMENT AS POLICY" (2011)

To walk with the wrong persons in the wrong
places.
ROBERTO GOIZUETA, *CAMINEMOS CON JESUS* (2003)

Wherever you are is where I want to be.
MIA MINGUS, "WHEREVER YOU ARE IS WHERE I WANT
TO BE" (2010)

Coda

Theorists of accompaniment take the politics of place seriously. They argue
that if we want to accompany another person, it is not enough to advocate
for them from a safe distance. Instead, accompaniment means inhabiting
the spaces they inhabit, which are generally spaces of struggle, danger,
or isolation. For illegalized (im)migrants, acts of accompaniment take
place within a segregated and policed land. The experiences of the asylum
seeker, the deported, and the undocumented are the experiences of people
perpetually considered out of place, people whose oppression resides in
a generalized but not always disclosed spatial order. Such people are *put
in their place* at the spectacular site of the geographic border, in everyday
spaces of public and private life, and in the sites this book calls *disappearing
rooms*—the hidden theaters of immigration law, where the legal system's
fundamental contradictions reverberate as mise-en-scène. In these contexts,
the physical presence of the *acompañante* matters. Our physical presence
is the difference between what Paulo Freire calls "false generosity" and
"true solidarity" (2014, 44, 50). The former implies an act of generosity
that maintains the presiding spatial order, while the latter transgresses that
spatial order in order to dismantle it.

So what do we do when we are faced with a system of oppression that
disables the possibility of physical presence? What if we cannot walk
with another person down a road because we cannot find that person on
any map? What if we cannot move with another person because we do
not know whether that person is in motion? What if we know neither

the coordinates of the journey nor whether, in fact, that journey has come to an end?

I cannot say her name because her name, for reasons I will soon explain, has itself become implicated in the process of disappearance. But I cannot refrain from naming her either, because her name is the closest thing we have to her location. She might be here or there. She might be dead or alive. But wherever she is, her name clings to her body. The syllables of her name evolved through the interaction of multiple languages. If we traced their etymological pathways and arrayed their meanings together in English, it would produce something like *Honeyed Herb and Stone*. So that is what I will call her.

Honeyed Herb and Stone crossed the border with a group and fainted in the desert. We found this out from someone who traveled with her. Her fellow travelers said they left her there because they could not afford to stop. We found a news report stating that a woman in the same location on the same day had been sent to a hospital in a helicopter. We identified all the hospitals in the area with helicopter landing pads. We called them. We asked whether they had a patient named Honeyed Herb and Stone, but they would not give us any information unless we had a signed consent form from the patient. How can we obtain a signed consent form from someone we cannot contact? *We need written consent.* How can we obtain consent when we cannot reach her? *Ma'am, if you want information about a patient, you need to obtain consent.*

We called a local organization that searches for disappeared people in that part of the desert. They looked in the area where she supposedly fainted and found nothing. They spoke to the local Border Patrol agents, who said nothing. We looked her up on the Online Detainee Locator, in case she had been picked up by immigration authorities and detained. We tried every variation and misspelling of her name. We called every detention center in the area, and they all asked us, "What is her alien registration number?" We did not have that information. If we knew that number, it would mean we knew she had been detained. And again, we explained, we do not know if she has been detained. We do not know if she is alive. That is what we are trying to find out. *We can't give you information without the alien registration number.*

Her family published her name and photograph on the Internet, hoping to reach someone who knew something. Instead, the information attracted scam artists. Scam artists called the family every few months, claiming to be government officials. They demanded that the family send thousands of dollars in bond to secure her release. Or they claimed to be (im)migrants who had met Honeyed Herb and Stone in a detention center; sometimes they even offered details about her life. Each time, the stories were just plausible enough to make us believe they could be real. Each time, we warned one another about the laws of probability. If she were really detained, she would have called. If the callers really knew her, they could put her on the phone. If she were using a fake name, they could give us that name and it would appear in the database. There was always ample reason to dismiss the story but an even more profound reason to maintain hope. So we would call the detention center and ask for information. We would contact immigrant advocacy groups that worked in a particular geographic area and send them a picture of Honeyed Herb and Stone. Over time, the family got more discerning and learned to recognize the signs of a scam. They started recording all the conversations with scam artists and submitted a police report. But the police chose not to investigate.

Who manufactured the disappearance of Honeyed Herb and Stone? There were the policies in place since the 1990s that deliberately funneled (im)migrants into physically hostile terrains and exacerbated the rate of deaths attributable to heat, drowning, and other environmental causes. There were the hospitals with their protocols. The detention centers with their cages. The police with their apathy. The Border Patrol with their silence. The scam artists with their scams. None of these entities contrived her disappearance single-handedly. Instead, her disappearance was the result of gaps within and between these entities. It has been three years since Honeyed Herb and Stone went missing, and her family has not given up the search. They want facts. They want answers, including negative ones. Even if they do not know where she is, it would be helpful to know where she is *not*. It would be helpful to be able to cross places off the list. Yet in most cases, we have not been able to do so. We never received proof of her presence, nor did we receive proof of her absence. So the list of possible places grows. The map of the United States is dotted with potential locations—places she might have been but probably never was, places she probably never was but might still be.

A person is in either one place or another. A person can be here or there but not both. Except if they are disappeared. Except if they are Honeyed Herb and Stone. None of our investigations has determined where she is. But none of our investigations has determined where she is not, either. She is not somewhere, but she is *not not* everywhere. She is not dead, but she is not alive. She cannot be nowhere, yet she cannot be found.

How do we accompany Honeyed Herb and Stone?

....

In his performance, "Evidence," in Japan in 1963, Thelonious Monk is playing piano and accompanying Charlie Rouse on the saxophone. At a certain moment, Monk stands up and stops making any musical sound.[1] He is still accompanying, though, by allowing his body to collect vibrations. It seems as if he needs to stand up to expose more of his surface area to the music. His accompaniment is not producing sound. Instead, his silence and his standing draw attention to the fact that he is paying attention. In this hiatus, he allows himself to support impulses without responding to them. At a certain point, this process leads him to sit back down and play the piano again. But the music he now plays seems to accompany what he heard before. His accompaniment paves a road post facto for a previous moment in another's journey. It is in synchrony but out of phase.

Ethnomusicologist Steven Feld uses that phrase—in synchrony but out of phase—to describe the music of the Kaluli people in the Bosavi rainforests. Their music is composed in dialogue with the sounds of the rainforest. According to Feld, the Kaluli people see the process of musical composition as a state of ecological receptivity. Writing a song is like "getting a waterfall in your head," like bubbling over with the memory of a previous flow. When Feld listens to music—the people singing, the song of birds, the flow of waterfalls—he perceives a kind of wholeness. But it is not the wholeness of unison, of sounds coming together at the same pitch, rhythm, and moment in time. Instead, the sounds of the rainforest and the voices of the people never line up exactly. They are out of phase. They seem to be "at different points of displacement from a hypothetical unison" (Feld 1994, 12). They are not simultaneous, yet they are perpetually linked because they inspire one another to continue. They are committed to the mutuality of this inspiration. And in this commitment, some kind of accompaniment happens, even if it is displaced in space and time. The sounds never touch, but they mean to. They never line up, but they would like to. Each sound expresses the memory and the hope of touching another source of sound. If "in synchrony but out of phase" were a theory of accompaniment, it might be the sense of wholeness produced through the mutual commitment of an intention to touch.

How many times has her family imagined getting a call from Honeyed Herb and Stone? How many times have they grabbed the phone and hallucinated hearing her voice? How many times has Honeyed Herb and Stone imagined calling them? Call without a response. Response without a call. Calls placed on a family line. Calls within a family plan. Accompaniment out of time and space. In synchrony but out of phase. Out of unison yet in touch. Together at a remove.

We cannot accompany her in space. We cannot commit to a physical presence. We cannot map out the geography of her disappearance and, by retracing it, dismantle it.[2] We cannot sit with her in the spirit of healing, holding hands while contemplating the enormity of what has happened. We cannot do that powerful thing of standing together at the side of unthinkable experience, closing the physical gap between us while maintaining the existential one. We don't have access to the spatial or temporal dimensions of accompaniment. We are not in the same room.

Nevertheless, we share a desire. I wish I could hear the voice of Honeyed Herb and Stone. You wish you could hear the voice of Honeyed Herb and Stone. The chorus of that wish is an echo. That echo is a response. Her name is a call—a call we cannot trace. The sound is *not not* everywhere.

NOTES

Introduction

1. In employing the term *(im)migrant*, I follow a group of scholars who aim to disrupt assumptions about human mobility built into terms like "immigrant" and "migrant" (Escobar 2016, 21). In this book, I use "(im)migrant" as an inclusive term encompassing those who might choose to seek permanent residency in the United States and those whose mobility is more transitory, circular, or not yet defined.

2. See Faudree (2012) and Taylor (2003, chap. 2) for intricate theorizations of the Requerimiento as a legal performance.

3. The dynamics of imported colonialism have also been described as a revolving door. At various points in US history, the government has facilitated the recruitment of particular groups of (im)migrants to serve as a transient and disposable workforce, only to criminalize and expel them once political conditions have changed. As migration scholar Nicholas De Genova (2013) theorizes, the illegalization of (im)migrant labor is highly productive from the standpoint of capital. Although the spectacle of border policing projects the image of absolute exclusion, the state is typically less invested in excluding racialized (im)migrants than in including them *as illegal*—in other words, available for purposes of labor, yet disciplined and subordinated by the threat of deportation.

4. It has been difficult for (im)migrants and their supporters to communicate the complex violence of immigration law because doing so requires deconstructing the popular assumption that recognition and racism are opposed processes. Some migration scholars have tried to break through this conceptual impasse by documenting the deep historical entanglement between colonial legacies and humanitarian immigration policies (see, e.g., Fernando 2016; Loyd and Mountz 2018; Razack 1998). By pointing to the ongoing colonial patterns that shape global human mobility, these scholars denaturalize the idea of (im)migrant vulnerability that allows the humanitarian state to stage itself as a benevolent protector. Shannon Speed's *Incarcerated Stories: Indigenous Women Migrants and Violence in the Settler-Capitalist State* (2019)

argues that Indigenous Central American (im)migrants to the United States are not naturally vulnerable but rather *vulneradas* (i.e., rendered vulnerable through long enduring settler-colonial dynamics exacerbated by immigration policy). See chapter 3 of this book for a discussion of the powerful critique of recognition mounted by a decolonial lineage of thinkers that includes Frantz Fanon, Audra Simpson, and Glen Coulthard.

5. Almost all of the Central American (im)migrants whose courtroom experiences are analyzed in this book would likely identify as Latinx or Hispanic, but many would also identify as Indigenous, Afro-Latinx, or both. In particular, some of the people I worked with or accompanied were Garifuna Hondurans and Guatemalans whose language and cultural identity reflect a history of encounter between Carib, Arawak, and African communities. If I refer to the "colonial project" writ large, it is because the colonial systems that shape Central American (im)migrants' courtroom experiences are multiple and overlapping. While centuries-old processes of settler colonialism in Central America continue to influence contemporary patterns of displacement, racism, and gendered violence, the neocolonial flows of transnational capital intensify the theft of ancestral lands and maintain the asymmetrical economic relations that drive transnational migration (on Central American (im)migrants' experiences in the United States, see Cárdenas 2018; for an introduction to the historical forces shaping contemporary migration, see Chomsky 2021). Meanwhile, when Central Americans arrive in the United States, many find their racial identities reconfigured within a US racial matrix—a process Devon Carbado (2005) calls "racial naturalization." Thus, while Garifunas may find themselves newly racialized as Black and subject to overpolicing and other forms of criminalization on that basis, Central Americans of all backgrounds may find their racial identities reconfigured as they enter highly racialized industries or segregated neighborhoods in which they are seen generically as Latino or even—not uncommonly—as Mexican (Arias 2003). Truly, then, there is an irreducible complexity to the historical processes of overlapping racialization faced by the people whose courtroom experiences are described in this book. Thus, I use terms such as "racialized (im)migrants" to refer to this complexity, and I draw from Latinx studies, Black studies, and Native studies to elucidate issues of criminalization, coloniality, and abolition. My use of the term *racialized (im)migrant* differs from its use in other works on US immigration politics, in that *Disappearing Rooms* does not focus on racial identity as such. Instead, it focuses on the scenographic arrangements that racialize people by subjecting them to colonial displays of criminalization, paternalistic rescue, or disappearance. Rather than the racialization of identity, the term designates a physical position within a scene. It designates the racialization of the room.

6. A report by the American Immigration Council (2021) provides data on the increased spending for immigration enforcement operations over the past thirty years during both Republican and Democratic administrations. The annual budget of the US Border Patrol increased from $263 million in 1990 to nearly $4.9 billion in

2021 (2). Since the establishment of ICE in 2001, the budget for that agency also grew steadily, from $3.3 billion that year to $8.3 billion in 2021 (3).

7. Since the 1990s, the US government has intentionally funneled (im)migrants crossing the border into physically hostile terrains (De León 2015; Nevins 2010; Rosas 2006). As Karma Chávez explains, "The rationale for what the University of Arizona Binational Migration institute describes as the 'funnel effect' was that both the deaths that would undoubtedly occur as well as the danger posed by the desert would be enough to prevent people from making the clandestine journey" (2012, 53).

8. The good/bad immigrant binary arguably dates back to the inception of immigration law, but the contemporary variation was consolidated through a series of policies in the 1990s and 2000s. As immigration scholar Alfonso Gonzales shows, the legislative history of this period was discursively dominated by what he terms the "anti-migrant bloc," a coalition of antimigrant forces that drew on criminal stereotypes and war-on-drugs imagery to construct the image of a "bad immigrant" who deserved detention and deportation (2013, 6). The powerful criminalizing discourses of this period led (im)migrants and their allies into a corner, where they needed to present particular (im)migrants as exceptionally vulnerable, innocent, or upwardly mobile (thus playing into the idea that others were undeserving criminals). From the 1980s to the time of this writing in 2020, no pro-immigrant policy proposal at the federal level has been considered politically viable unless it limits benefits to those populations considered exceptionally innocent or deserving and unless it promises to ramp up enforcement activities against those defined as "bad"—generally by increasing spending for border policing and detention. Even the Development, Relief, and Education for Alien Minors (DREAM) Act—which would have legalized the status of undocumented youth—was initially introduced as a border security initiative (Fernandes 2017, 107). While writing this book, as I watched the 2020 debates among the candidates for the Democratic presidential nomination, it was clear that the good/bad immigrant binary was alive and well. When asked about immigration policy, every candidate passionately denounced the detention and separation of families. Yet, when pressed by the moderator to state whether this stance indicated support for open borders, every candidate rushed to reaffirm the importance of border security and deportation. Joseph Biden made the good/bad immigrant binary particularly explicit when he spoke of "cherry pick[ing] from the best of every culture" while characterizing undocumented (im)migrants as criminals who should be deported. The transcript of this debate is available at https://www.nbcnews.com /politics/2020-election/democratic-debate-transcript-july-31-2019-n1038016.

9. Undocumented youth in the early 2000s pushed for the DREAM Act, national legislation that would have granted temporary residency and a pathway to permanent residency for undocumented youth who had migrated to the United States as children. Young activists undertook this legislative campaign in collaboration with politicians and Democratic Party strategists, who steered the movement toward narratives of exceptionality, innocence, and assimilation—that is, the "good immigrant" story (Fernandes

2017; Gonzales 2013). Over the course of several years, the DREAM Act was replaced by Deferred Action for Childhood Arrivals (DACA), a more limited measure that lacks a pathway to citizenship. At the same time that legislative solutions were weakened, undocumented activists saw their political demand for legalization on the basis of exceptionality, innocence, and assimilation was co-opted to legitimize the criminalization of their parents and others who fell outside the "good immigrant" narrative (Nicholls 2013). Some of those who received the benefits of DACA spoke of adverse consequences, including increased surveillance (Mena Robles and Gomberg-Muñoz 2016). These developments spurred a period of intense reflection about the inadequacy of measures based on individual status to address the deep criminalization of (im)migrant communities, and various sectors of the youth movement reorganized under more inclusive, coalitional terms (see Movimiento Cosecha, https://www.lahuelga.com/#header-eng).

10. To get a deeper sense of the widespread frustration over recognition politics among (im)migrant activists, see "Call for (a Different Type of) Solidarity," produced by the No Name Collective (reprinted in Chávez 2013, 109). At first glance, the document looks like a traditional call for solidarity produced by immigration justice organizations in support of individuals facing detention or deportation. The reader's attention is drawn to the bold letters that say, "Sign Jose's Petition" and the hand-drawn, cartoonish sketch of an individual labeled "Jose." However, upon closer inspection, the document contains a powerful critique of the individualizing format of such activism. A section called "Biography of Worthiness" states: "Here is where we would typically tell you all the ways in which Jose is good and worthy unlike the 'unworthy' immigrants. . . . And here, while advocating for one of the 'worthy ones,' you would implicitly accept the system that condemns the rest." The document calls on Jose's supporters not to tacitly accept a system that divides people against one another but to remain committed to a vision of liberation that includes everyone.

11. For more on the recent evolution of the (im)migrant justice movement, see Martínez et al. (2020). The authors, all of whom are longtime activists, reflect on the limits of state-based recognition and legislative campaigns and describe their reorientation toward a broader abolitionist struggle.

12. See the website of the organization Otros Dreams en Acción (http://www .odamexico.org/) and Fernandez and Olson (2011).

13. See Tamez (2012) for a historical account and theoretical discussion connecting genocidal acts against Ndé people to the contemporary militarization of the border. On resistance by members of the Tohono O'odham nation, see the nation's official website: http://www.tonation-nsn.gov/nowall/.

14. Performance theory holds that institutional arrangements of bodies in space concretize otherwise abstract social processes, making those processes visible and available to common perception and social transmission. These institutional scenes

are thus "scenographic models of sociometric process," in Richard Schechner's words (2003, 184). For instance, the staging of social hierarchies in a court of law is reflexive: we are both the subjects and spectators of those arrangements. In this vein, Barbara Myerhoff offers the phrase *showing ourselves to ourselves* to describe the political function of mise-en-scène (1982, 105). Scene study contemplates the theatrical means by which societies hold their own value systems up for observation.

15. See Schechner (2003) on the distinction between "doing" and "showing doing."

16. In his analysis of the macabre ritual of the death penalty, performance ethnographer Dwight Conquergood observes that the "regular rehearsals, precise stage directions, and obsessive planning" of these rituals actually reveal their "fragile and volatile nature" (2002, 362). The primary "performance challenge" of these events, as Conquergood puts it, is for participants to act *as if* the death penalty were a medical event rather than an act of judicial murder. Thus, the state's meticulous attention to staging these rituals indicates neither certainty nor self-assurance. Rather, it represents a fragile attempt to fabricate a reality other than what is taking place. Drawing from Conquergood, *Disappearing Rooms* treats the minute staging decisions that take place in immigration courtrooms not as unthought hand-me-downs of tradition but as indicators of the ongoing attempt, by state officials, to resolve the contradictions embedded in their mission.

17. Wendy Brown might argue that both the Requerimiento and the hidden theaters of immigration law operate beyond the pale. The "pale" was originally a fence used by British colonists to demarcate the boundaries of their colonial territories in Ireland (as well as a term for the entire territory itself). The phrase *beyond the pale* captures two enduring facets of the colonial worldview: on the one hand, the space beyond the pale is conceived as external to the protected sphere of civilization; on the other hand, it is a "threshold beyond which the law does not hold." The space beyond the pale is therefore a space of hypocrisy. It is "where civilization ends" and "where the brutishness of the civilized is therefore permitted" (W. Brown 1995, 45). My reference to *nobodies* and *somebodies* draws from Denise Ferreira da Silva's (2009) discussion of legal racialization. Her term *no-bodies* expresses the fact that "that which should happen to nobody, to 'no human being,' has consistently delineated the existence of so many human beings" (234). Per Silva, legal racialization produces a class of people whose killing does not generate an ethical crisis because their death is already legally defined as necessary for the self-preservation of the nation-state.

18. Indeed, one of the primary ways US immigration law has justified its deportation and detention policies is through an array of legal fictions by which (im)migrants who are physically present in US territory are legally treated as if they never arrived. See Fong Yue Ting v. United States (149 US 698, 1893) for an early example of this reasoning and Volpp (2013) on the enduring use of spatial fictions in immigration law.

19. See, for instance, immigration activist Marco Saveedra's reflections about his experience of being detained in Martínez et al. (2020, 38).

20. I am grateful to Rebecca Schneider, from whom I lifted the phrase *in our hands*. Her extensive work on the topic inspired my thinking regarding the transmission of gesture.

21. Such observations about the temporal life and social transmission of performance have been subject to extensive theorization and debate in the field of performance studies. For more on the political implications of theatrical casting processes, see Joseph Roach (1996), theorizing on the manner in which individuals inhabit social roles. For more on the scene as a lens for understanding historical process, see Diana Taylor (2003), who proposes the "scenario" as a vehicle of both repetition and change.

22. Here, I draw from the constellation of perspectives that combined to create the "autonomy of migration" approach. This approach follows in the wake of the Sans-Papiers movement in France, which spurred new interest in theorizing on the freedom of movement. To some extent, autonomy of migration draws on autonomous Marxism, a branch of Marxist thought centered in Italian workerist communism. Just as that branch of Marxism foregrounds the self-activity of the working class, the autonomy of migration approach posits the constitutive power of precarious migrant laborers within the transnational labor-capital relation. Although focused on the economic aspect of migration, the autonomy of migration approach is more broadly an attempt to decenter statist perspectives on human mobility. Dominant approaches foreground institutionally recognized citizenship as the ultimate object of noncitizens' mobility. In contrast, the autonomy of migration approach treats migration as a primordial element of human experience that conceptually precedes the nation-state. In order to change the way we conceive migration, scholars following this approach have worked to deconstruct the statist vocabulary that naturalizes an insider-outsider relation. As De Genova notes, "even to designate this mobility as 'migration' is already to collude in the naturalization of [borders]" because if "there were no borders there would be no migration—only mobility" (2017, 6).

23. Some modes of theater are particularly interested in highlighting the gap between what happens onstage and what might have happened. The Brechtian theater tradition, to name a prime example, attempts to show that whatever action is ultimately undertaken by the characters is not inevitable and that all possibilities coexist in the same scene (Brecht 1964). This type of theater may offer the plot of an individual protagonist as the seductive center of meaning, yet it continuously employs devices of mise-en-scène to point at the limits of representation itself. The dialectic between onstage and offstage space (as well as onscreen and offscreen space) has also been a persistent site of scenographic exploration in film. For instance, Nöel Burch describes how glances directed offscreen and narrative events elided by the camera turn the experience of film into a dialectic between onscreen space and the "espace-hors-champ [out-of-field space]" (1969, 36).

1. Removal Room

This chapter is narrated in the present tense, but it was written in 2017, six years prior to the publication of this book. At that time, I observed how a place called the Removal Room turned disappearance into an architectural and theatrical theme. Since then, the exact spatial configuration and the nature of removal operations in Manhattan have changed. The theatrical framework of disappearance, however, remains relevant to removal proceedings and their varied and evolving spatial designs.

1. When filmmakers and theater producers create a scene, they manipulate objective design elements such as furniture, color, spatial proportions, and trajectories of light. Yet such elements relate directly to the subjective experience of the characters. In the realist theater tradition, for instance, the characters are "soaked" in the domestic spaces that comprise that genre's typical mise-en-scène (Chaudhuri 1997, 6). Scenography, in this instance, is not considered a passive backdrop but rather an active force constraining and expressing the psychology of the characters.

2. It is possible that check-in times are standardized in some fashion. According to a report by the American Friends Service Committee, there may have been some central standardization at some point (Rutgers School of Law 2012, 6). However, this is not apparent to those checking in and thus does not alleviate the profound uncertainty produced by the process.

3. I am inspired here by Judith Butler (2016) in thinking of a frame both as a delimitation of the field of vision and as a ruse that "frames" a person for a crime. See Allan Sekula (1986) on how the invention of photography spurred attempts to identify the criminal as a phenotypic type. The idea that criminalization involves visual framing has also been explored in television and film. Feminist studies scholar Gina Dent has examined representations of prison across the history of film, noting that "the prison is wedded to our experience of visuality, creating also a sense of its permanence as an institution" (quoted in Davis 2003, 17). Following Dent, Angela Davis argues that "our sense of familiarity with the prison comes in part from representations of prisons in film and other visual media," and this televisual "comfort" informs the historic lack of public outcry over mass incarceration (2003, 17).

4. When I say that removal is founded on white supremacy, I do not mean this in an abstract sense. Rather, I mean that the legal and physical infrastructures of deportation were built through successive attempts to control the racial composition of the country by physically removing groups of people seen as undesirable. See, for instance, the work of historian Daniel Kanstroom (2007), who shows that immigrant removal has roots in what he calls the "forgotten century" of immigration law, with Indian removal programs, the capture of fugitive slaves, and the local custom of removing poor people from the colonies.

5. As Lisa Cacho argues, the enhanced criminalization of (im)migrants means that "the punishments for committing an 'aggravated felony' by a noncitizen are almost

always far worse than the punishment for the same crime committed by a citizen under criminal law. . . . Because freedom is understood as a 'gift,' freedom is easily revoked. Any transgression—large or small—is an inexcusable act of ingratitude deserving of detention or deportation" (2012, 95).

6. In those histories, the very definition of what counts as a crime (and what does not), as well as the geographic distribution of police forces and their activities, is based on the assumption that those who require policing are poor people of color and those who need to be protected from crime are wealthy white people and property owners. See Alexander (2012), Reiman (2007), and Simon (2007), showing that the classification of particular activities as criminal is not directly related to the social harm they cause. See Muhammad (2010) on the history through which crime and criminality were defined as Black. See also Moreton-Robinson (2015) on the decriminalization of whiteness through the legal protection of white property.

7. For instance, the Bush administration took advantage of the relative laxity of immigration law when it launched surveillance programs in Muslim and Arab communities following the attacks of 9/11. Policy makers favored the use of immigration law because it presented fewer procedural hurdles than the criminal legal system (Stumpf 2006). The Bush administration also employed immigration law in its legal justification for the indefinite detention of individuals at Guantánamo Bay. In these and other instances, immigration law has been utilized for purposes other than to regulate immigration.

8. It is not possible to make a blanket statement about the constitutional protections legally owed to noncitizens. Instead, the status of noncitizens continues to evolve in response to ongoing legal challenges and competing interpretations. See Carrie Rosenbaum's discussion of the constitutionality of immigrant detention (2018) for an introduction to this complex and contested topic, and Markowitz (2011) on the standard notion that deportation is not punishment and the consequences for (im)migrants.

9. Nicholas De Genova (2016a, 3) shows how immigration law takes processes with deep cultural meanings and philosophical histories (such as "trial," "verdict," or "imprisonment") and replaces them with "nondescript," "understated," and "unexamined" terms that have no cultural resonance and no indication of the stakes of the processes they name.

10. Kelly Hernández (2010) uses the term *Mexican Browns* to differentiate the customary targets of deportation policies from light-skinned Mexicans, who possessed a greater degree of political power in the borderlands region.

11. On the entanglement of antiterrorism and immigration enforcement in the wake of 9/11, see Chacón (2013), Chávez (2012), and Lugo-Lugo and Bloodsworth-Lugo (2014).

12. Racialization is defined by Michael Omi and Howard Winant as a process that "[extends] racial meaning to a previously racially unclassified relationship, social practice or group" (1986, 111).

13. I take the idea of the "removed" as a race from abolitionist geographer Ruth Wilson Gilmore. In an interview regarding the prison-industrial complex, Gilmore writes about a former white supremacist who organized a prison uprising with Black and brown inmates. When Gilmore asked the prisoner about this seeming contradiction, he responded: "Well, maybe what we are is the prison race." For Gilmore, this statement captures the idea that imprisonment constitutes its own process of racialization (Gilmore and Loyd 2012, 50).

14. Gestures operate simultaneously on these two planes, inwardly retraining the learned pathways of our tissues while outwardly projecting meaning to others (Noland 2009).

15. Per Michel Foucault, the institutional confinement of prisoners and the mentally ill combined permanent surveillance with the social scientific production of knowledge about non-normative subjects to produce a deeply internalized form of power that he called "discipline" (2012). The hegemony of this mode has arguably been replaced by what Gilles Deleuze (1992) calls "control societies": new, decentralized forms of policing that produce the sensation of free movement through urban space. Yet such movement, often unbeknownst to us, is heavily directed and surveilled. As a paradigmatic instance of what he calls "choreopolicing," André Lepecki (2013) draws on Jacques Ranciere's parable of a police officer who tells the curious passerby, "Move along, there's nothing to see here." In this instance, the police officer controls not through confinement but through choreographed compulsory motion. Such choreopolicing implies that it is no longer the enclosure but rather the entire range delimiting one's perception of free options that is subject to control.

16. In Judith Butler's analysis of the politics of public assemblies, she discusses the difference between having a certain identity and publicly claiming it. "When one freely exercises the right to be who one already is, and one asserts a social category for the purpose of describing that mode of being, then one is, in fact, making freedom part of that very social category, discursively changing the very ontology in question" (2015, 61). Following this logic, we could argue that when we move through the Removal Room as an intentional practice, we make freedom part of that choreography.

17. In a published memorandum, ICE limits immigration enforcement action in churches and other "sensitive locations," but this is ultimately an internal guideline rather than a binding law. Those (im)migrant activists who take physical sanctuary in houses of worship thus draw on a quasi-legal and quasi-symbolic form of protection.

18. The group Otros Dreams en Acción provides accompaniment and organizes political action with people who grew up in the United States and find themselves in Mexico due to deportation policy. For more on its work, see www.odamexico.org; https://www.youtube.com/watch?v=OE4kCdTHiEY; and J. Anderson and Solis (2014), a community-published anthology profiling the individual stories of members.

19. The infiltration of detention centers was undertaken by members of the National Immigration Youth Alliance (NIYA), who risked their own immigration status in

order to free undocumented people from detention. For a summary of these actions, see May (2013). Democracy Now conducted an interview with NIYA infiltrator Viridiana Martinez, who was detained at Broward Detention Center; see https://www .democracynow.org/2012/7/31/dream_activist_speaks_from_broward_detention _center_listen_to_exclusive_audio. The infiltration project also inspired a film, *The Infiltrators* (2019), directed by Cristina Ibarra and Alex Rivera.

20. These examples focus on accompaniment practices within Latinx (im)migrant communities. Certainly, accompaniment is practiced by other (im)migrant and citizen communities and goes by many names. Their omission here merely reflects the limited scope of my research process.

21. For a sense of the scale of these efforts, see the Ecologies of Migrant Care project, an initiative of the Hemispheric Institute of Performance and Politics at New York University (https://ecologiesofmigrantcare.org/). This website contains almost one hundred interviews with "churches and religious organizations, secular NGOs, religious leaders, political movements, think tanks, specialized media outlets, international forensic anthropology teams, as well as state bureaucracies and human rights commissions, and private contractors." This interconnected network engages the work of accompaniment as well as many other forms of support and political action to protect and advocate for (im)migrants across the region.

2. The Prison-Courtroom

1. I have borrowed the phrase *not not* from performance theorist Richard Schechner, who introduced it when writing about the liminal zones created through performance practice (1985, 127). In referring to Dilley as a prison in this chapter, I do not mean to ignore the distinction between detention centers and prisons. They are managed by different government agencies under different terms. However, by referring to detention centers as prisons, I hope to emphasize that detention centers are part of the larger prison-industrial complex and connect the issue of family detention to the prison abolitionist movement.

2. The term *prison-industrial complex* captures how prison scandals have consistently been turned into new pathways for industrial development. Industrial development includes not only the most obvious "bad actors"—the private prison corporations— but also, and more disturbingly, the entire class of NGOs, health workers, transportation companies, consultants, and even educators who have, in the words of abolitionist geographer Ruth Wilson Gilmore, "[swept] off from the top, as it were, the value that is circulating in the form of expenditures in policing, courts, and prisons" (Gilmore and Loyd 2012, 48). In particular, prison reforms have given rise to a class of NGOs that focus on the long-term provision of social services within prisons while enforcing a "staunchly anti-abolitionist political limit" (D. Rodríguez 2017, 22). This

is particularly true of women's prisons, where attempts to reform prisons on feminist or women-centric terms often lead to expansion of the prison system (Schenwar and Law 2020). For instance, in its policy toolkit *Meeting the Needs of Women in California's County Justice Systems*, one such NGO makes the expansionist logic of reform particularly explicit. Its stated aims are to (1) "ensure that local justice systems are more gender-responsive and that women and their specific needs are not over-looked . . . in a changing criminal justice landscape," and (2) "enable county justice systems to take full advantage of significant new state and federal funding streams available to implement rehabilitative alternatives to jail incarceration" (Bloom 2015, 4). Fusing pro-woman discourse and economic interest, both the immigration system and the criminal legal system have expanded incarceration in the name of what Rose Braz (2006) sarcastically refers to as "kinder, gentler, gender responsive cages."

3. As an empirical matter, prisons and detention centers generally fail to achieve the purposes that justify their existence (e.g., deterrence of crime, rehabilitation of prisoners, deterrence of illegal immigration). Studies show that prisons tend to amplify harm rather than diminish it and to expand criminal networks rather than eliminate them. See Stemen (2017) for an empirical study of how prisons amplify harm, and Dixon and Piepzna-Samarasinha (2020) on transformative justice, an approach that seeks to break cycles of harm by addressing root causes.

4. See *Flores v Meese Settlement*, case no. CV 85-4544-RJK(Px), filed January 17, 1997, http://www.aclu.org/pdfs/immigrants/flores_v_meese_agreement.pdf.

5. See Loyd and Mountz (2018) for a geographic analysis of detention facilities since the 1980s.

6. Expedited removal was established in 1996 and has become a major force in the expansion of immigration detention. Before the introduction of this mechanism, (im)migrants had more opportunities to appeal deportation decisions before immigration judges (Gebisa 2007).

7. US policies toward Haitian asylum seekers in the 1980s and 1990s set an important historical precedent for the detention of Central American families in the 2000s. The rationale of deterrence was invoked in the 1980s to justify policies of detention, deportation, and the denial of asylum (Loyd and Mountz 2018). The details of this history reveal that the seemingly neutral language of deterrence masks biopolitical calculations about racial undesirability, calculations that continue to drive detention policies.

8. The history of racial terror in the US-Mexico borderlands is an immense topic that encompasses everything from massacres of Native peoples and the vigilante practices of Anglo settler communities to the policing of *Mexicanos* following the US annexation of Mexican territories, the nineteenth-century capture of runaway slaves under the Fugitive Slave Act, and the lynching of Blacks, *Mexicanos*, Native people, and others in the border states of Texas, New Mexico, Arizona, and California in the twentieth century. In the long history of US settlement, the western frontier (both

as a geographic area and as a fixture of the national imagination) has functioned as a paradigm of perpetual war. As historian Clyde A. Milner writes, "With the exception of the Civil War and the military occupation of the South during Reconstruction, the U.S. Army throughout the nineteenth century was largely a western army, manning posts and pursuing native peoples" (1994, 183).

9. In this sense, the detention of (im)migrant families can be connected to the broader pattern of settler colonialism, which involves targeting the social and sexual reproduction of Indigenous peoples. In the long history of Anglo settlement, the US government has pursued various policies to "break the Indian"—that is, to dismantle Native peoples' capacity to reproduce their cultures. Such policies have included the prohibition of communal landholdings, the enforcement of nuclear family structures, the slaying of buffalo to eliminate Native peoples' control over their means of subsistence, the policing of Native languages and spiritual practices, the systemic practice of rape on Native reservations, and the boarding school system (for a comprehensive history, see Dunbar-Ortiz 2014). All of these policies and practices taken together speak to an element of settler colonialism that is directed against cultural reproduction and against the bodies of women and children. On the complex ways in which settler-colonial societies across the world police gender and reproduction, see "Karangatia: Calling Out Gender and Sexuality in Settler Societies" (2012). On the role of sexual violence in militarized border control, see Falcón (2001).

10. See Huang (2008) and Menjívar and Kil (2002) on nativist panic over Latina women's fertility and reproduction. As Martha Escobar argues, racial panic around Latina (im)migrants' reproduction rehashed the narrative of the poor Black woman as "welfare queen," a figure mobilized in the 1990s to shrink and restructure the welfare state. If criminality was "birthed by Black women" under the welfare queen narrative, Latina women were similarly construed as giving birth to racial invasion (Escobar 2016, 63). Outside the United States, racial panic related to the fertility of women of color also seems to play a role in anti-immigrant policies, suggesting a more general link between the control of immigration and the control of women's bodies (Fernando 2016).

11. See Franco (1985) on the tactics of terror in the US-sponsored dirty wars in Argentina, Chile, Guatemala, and El Salvador. Of course, as Anannya Bhattacharjee argues, the "sanctity of the family" is not a universally protected value; instead, it is "selectively respected by the nation-state." Bhattacharjee notes that, for immigrants, "the state is actively involved in determining the very existence of the family" (2006, 343).

12. For more on the ambivalent relationship among (im)migrant autonomy, surplus value, illegalization, and capital, see Mezzadra (2010) and De Genova (2012, 2013, 2016b).

13. See *In re Hutto—Settlement*, case no. 1:07-cv-00164-SS, filed August 26, 2007, https://www.aclu.org/legal-document/re-hutto-settlement?redirect=cpredirect /31504.

14. On the enduring construction of Black men as archetypal criminals in the aftermath of slavery, in US media portrayals, and in the contemporary criminal justice system, see Muhammad (2010) and Alexander (2012).

15. Although it may seem unprecedented, the home-like model of incarceration has a long history in the United States. Some have noted parallels between contemporary family detention and the Japanese internment camps of World War II, which also fused domesticity and punishment (Ina 2015). There are also clear connections to the violation of Native American families through incarceration, forced adoption, federal sterilization programs, and the boarding school system; see Lumsden (2016) for a powerful reading of these histories through an expanded framework of reproductive justice. The architectural specificity of the home-like prison is also reminiscent of the nineteenth-century women's prison reform movement, where reformers "called for architectural models that replaced cells with cottages and 'rooms' in a way that was supposed to infuse domesticity into prison life" (Davis 2003, 70).

16. Programa Frontera Sur was an agreement between the United States and Mexico initiated in 2014 to curtail the migration of Central Americans through Mexico's southern border. This program has led to an increase in the deportation of Central American (im)migrants from Mexico and an increase in crimes of extortion and kidnapping against these (im)migrants at the hands of private criminal networks and Mexican state officials (Arriola Vega 2017; Castillo 2016). Programa Frontera Sur is an example of a "source control" strategy that gained international prominence in the 1990s. In this type of arrangement, migrant-receiving countries broker military and security deals with other nations along migration routes in order to prevent (im)migrants from entering their national territory, thus avoiding the legal responsibilities that are triggered when an (im)migrant sets foot in the migrant-receiving country.

17. It is interesting to note that in its deal to run the "family residential center" at Dilley, the CCA negotiated a contract under which it receives a flat fee for 100 percent capacity, regardless of the number of "residents" actually incarcerated. In other prison contracts, payments rise and fall based on the number of beds filled (Harlan 2016). If immigration policy supposedly responds to unpredictable events at the border—such as the so-called surge—the Dilley contract speaks to the business logic that renders such unpredictability disadvantageous. The prison industry in fact seeks to insulate itself from volatility in the phenomenon of migration to which it purportedly responds. It goes without saying that this logic entirely contradicts the notion of "crisis," as well as the notion of prison construction as an emergency response.

18. Evidence provided by Lauren Martin (2012b) strongly suggests that the Hutto settlement sparked efforts within DHS to reconceptualize family detention under the terms of a shifting political terrain. In 2008, immediately following the Hutto lawsuit but well before the media-publicized surge, ICE requested bids from the private sector for the construction of new family prisons. In the document outlining that request, ICE provided clues that it was preparing to reengineer family detention in

the wake of the lawsuit. Against the recommendations of its critics, ICE envisioned these new family detention centers as secure, locked facilities. Yet the new models also addressed the scenographic emphasis of the Hutto settlement by specifically prohibiting the use of former prisons and incorporating domestic, humanitarian, recreational, and judicial themes. For instance, one proposal describes a "non-institutional, warm, welcoming" architecture that incorporates "gabled or sloped roofs for a more residential style/appeal" (quoted in Martin 2012b, 881). The original ICE documents are no longer accessible through its website, but Martin (2012b) reproduces several images from the "Family Residential Design Standards Manual."

19. According to a 2016 ICE publication, these detention centers are "residential, rather than restrictive, in nature. Interior spaces are not interrupted by security boundaries or check points, and residents are allowed to move freely through programming areas of the campus" (quoted in Gómez Cervantes, Menjívar, and Staples 2017, 277).

20. The Bush administration stymied detainees' ability to apply for asylum by denying legal advocacy organizations access to Hutto. The Obama administration continued this pattern of limiting access to counsel, while also promising an "aggressive deterrence strategy" that would deny political asylum to the "vast majority" of families (Johnson 2014). The fact that family detention was initially oriented toward deportation was especially apparent in Artesia, one of the three detention centers built following the 2014 surge. As attorney Stephen Manning (2014) explains in his report on the rise and eventual fall of Artesia, "the Administration's decision to deport [the detained families] was made before *any* of the women sent to Artesia had been interviewed [to determine their asylum status]." According to Manning, Artesia "was the Obama Administration's carefully orchestrated machine that had been efficiently built to effectuate 'waves' of deportations—massive incidents of deportations occurring at a high velocity."

21. See *R.I.L-R v. Johnson*, case no. 1:15-cv-00011-JEB, filed February 20, 2015, https://www.aclu.org/legal-document/rilr-v-johnson-memorandum-opinion?redirect=immigrants-rights/rilr-v-johnson-memorandum-opinion.

22. Although I presented a history of the "home-like" prison in the previous section of this chapter, I do not comment on that dimension of Dilley because my access to the center was strictly limited. In my role as a temporary volunteer with the legal advocacy organization I was permitted to enter only those areas of the detention center associated with my daily work: the visitation room, where we conducted preparatory meetings with detainees; the asylum offices, where detainees presented their cases; and the immigration court, where those who had failed an initial interview were given a second hearing. I was not allowed to enter the residential spaces or the areas associated with education, recreation, health, or food service. Thus, I could not directly observe how the rhetorics of "home" or "campus" were (or were not) manifested in the architecture and practices of the detention center.

23. As Loyd and Mountz (2018) show, many immigrant detention centers are built in "prison towns," which developed around the prison industry and often lack other viable forms of employment.

24. For a phenomenological account of the relationship between the prisoner's body and space, see Guenther (2013).

25. The issue of ankle monitors illustrates the urgency of abolitionist rather than reformist approaches. By branding ankle monitors an "alternative to detention," the prison and detention industries have actively co-opted criticisms of mass incarceration to introduce a burgeoning industry of "e-carceration" that extends surveillance and confinement into ex-offender and (im)migrant communities, extracts enormous sums from those who must wear the monitors, and expands the role of private, for-profit actors in the business of incarceration (see Pittman 2020; Takei 2017).

26. According to refugee law scholar Karen Musalo, the "refugee definition is understood to require proof of: (1) an objectively reasonable fear of a harm which is serious enough to be considered 'persecution,' (2) which is causally linked, or bears a 'nexus' to race, religion, nationality, membership in a particular social group, or political opinion" (2003, 781). According to Musalo, women and gender-based persecution cases have historically found it difficult to meet the "nexus" criterion in US asylum law.

27. In many spaces of women's culture, for instance, even women who are structurally oppressed are encouraged to feel a sense of control by fusing themselves to the idea of an empowering life story. Even if this does not materially change women's lives, the experience of "owning your story" is promoted as an end in itself to achieve a "desired relay from weakness to strength, aloneness to sociability, abandonment to recognition" (Berlant 2008, 11). Many theorists of contemporary neoliberal culture have focused on the irony that neoliberal subjects are supposed to identify their uniqueness as a market commodity at the same time that social guarantees are removed and individuals are placed in a field of intense competition, precariousness, and risk (W. Brown 1995; Hale 2006; Harvey 2007).

28. Here, I am broadly referencing the kind of liberal common sense that scholars have termed "postwar racial liberalism" (Murakawa 2014, 11). Predominant since the mid-twentieth century, this understanding of racism treats it as a psychological error that can be corrected by eliminating institutional bias and providing opportunities for minoritized individuals to achieve social recognition. In the area of arts and culture, liberal approaches to antiracism often focus on increasing the visibility of minoritized people and depicting them as complex individuals who defy stereotypes (Ybarra 2017, 29).

29. In the early 1980s, violence in Guatemala and El Salvador surged as a result of US-sponsored genocidal and counterinsurgency operations (see Joseph and Grandin

2010). On the genocide against Maya peoples in Guatemala in the early 1980s, see the official report of the Guatemalan Commission for Historical Clarification (available in English in Rothenberg 2012). As Guatemalans and Salvadorans fled to Mexico and the United States, President Reagan feared "opening the floodgates" and creating a "tidal wave" of what he considered an undesirable population (quoted in Gorman 2017, 1). The administration thus instructed the agencies responsible for administering asylum law to deny Guatemalan and Salvadoran asylum cases. Yet, Congress had recently passed landmark legislation protecting the right of individuals from all countries to apply for asylum. Thus, the immigration courts were not in a position to simply deny asylum to Salvadorans and Guatemalans based on their national origin. Instead, immigration judges had to figure out how to manipulate the technical interpretation of asylum and render negative determinations on a case-by-case basis. Some of the most common devices they employed included "challenging witnesses' credibility, requiring nonexistent or dangerous documentation (such as copies of death threats), delinking the decision to emigrate from the experience of violence, treating individual experiences as instances of generalized suffering, defining violence as criminal rather than political in nature, and defining 'indirect' threats, such as the assassination of neighbors or family members, as not rising to the level of persecution" (Coutin 2011, 576). The cumulative effect of these interpretive devices was to portray violence in Central America as too culturally ingrained, too generic, and (paradoxically) *too pervasive to be counted*. And because of the time-traveling nature of legal precedent, those depictions have endured, working themselves into the fabric of case law and morphing into seemingly technical artifacts such as the legal definition of "nexus" or "particular social group" (see Gorman 2017, 2019). Although the historical origins of these artifacts are largely forgotten, the artifacts themselves continue to perform the same depoliticizing function. They promote the idea that violence in Central America constitutes a kind of ingrained social dysfunction that fails to meet the technical requirements for asylum.

30. In medieval European law, church officials were considered *personae mixtae* (secular and spiritual) and *personae germinatae* (human by nature and divine by grace). Medieval bishops—from whom modern judges inherited both legal concepts and the practice of wearing robes—were understood as *christomimets*, doubles of the dual ontology of Christ (Kantorowicz 2016). Discussing the enduring influence of such concepts on modern courtroom ritual, legal theorist Peter Goodrich argues that it is "not a human being . . . but rather justice (jus) and law (lex)" that sit when the court is in session (1990, 191).

31. For some observers, the primary concern when using videoconference technology is that it disfigures the courtroom ritual. When participants in a trial participate virtually, they do not pass through the successive thresholds demarcating the mundane world from the semimystical house of law. For participants linked to a courtroom remotely, the "law comes, it goes, but it is constantly elsewhere" (Mulcahy 2008, 480).

Indeed, in the Dilley courtroom, those of us inside the prison in Texas were denied the experience of journeying into law's semisacred space. At the same time, the judge was denied the experience of journeying into prison space. Both parties greeted each other out of nowhere.

32. Judy Radul argues that when courtroom participants appear onscreen, the attention of those in the courtroom is drawn toward what might be happening out of the frame, "just beyond the cone of vision of the camera" (2011, 128). Radul's concern about the distracting effects of a potential out-of-frame event would be magnified in the architecture of prison, which, like a camera, delimits an abrupt divide between "inside" and "outside" worlds.

33. Andrea Gómez Cervantes and her colleagues report that areas within Dilley are referred to as "neighborhoods" and given animal names. These authors attribute this to a larger pattern of "feminized and infantilized language" within rebranded family detention centers (Gómez Cervantes, Menjívar, and Staples 2017, 278).

34. Although the historical contexts vary tremendously, some examples of this style of governance include the promotion of inverted truths and open secrets in the governing styles of neocolonial Latin American states (Taussig 1992), state practices of public manipulation in recent Guatemalan history (see, e.g., Goldman 2008 and Schirmer 1999), and Achille Mbembe's theorization of absurdist dynamics in the bureaucratic culture of postcolonial Cameroon. Mbembe argues that while the grotesque and the obscene are often theorized as tactics of popular resistance, they can also function as tactics of law—or, more specifically, the means by which "state power organizes the dramatization of its magnificence" (1992, 4).

35. K is under investigation, but he does not know why and does not understand how the courtroom functions. Every time K comes to a provisional understanding, something in the environment shifts. The book of law turns out to contain scribbles. Two lovers squeal at the edge of the courtroom. We suddenly learn how low the ceiling is. A group of people K thought were spectators turn out to be court employees. K adjusts to these changes and makes new inferences. But as soon as he does so, the room warps again.

36. For a small sample of the many works that employ a scenographic lens to study law, see Conquergood (2002), Enders (1999), Legendre (1997), and Thiong'o (1997). For a very useful summary of some prominent theories regarding the vexed relations between theater and law, see Peters (2008).

37. These contrasting forces are also the basis for Anthony Vidler's definition of mise-en-scène as "a product of subjective projection and introjection, as opposed to a stable container of objects and bodies" (2002, 1).

38. This is the basis for Eisenstein's theory of montage (see Eisenstein and Marshall 1987).

39. Indeed, in his analysis of the architectural designs of Giovanni Battista Piranesi, on which he bases a theory of cinematic space, Eisenstein specifically points to the fact that the experience of madness can be induced through the incoherent arrangement of concrete form: "The piling up of perspective recessions coincides with the madness of narcotic visions . . . , but each link of these generally dizzy perspectives 'in itself' is even naturalistic. The concrete reality of perspective, the real depictive quality of the objects themselves, are not destroyed anywhere" (Eisenstein and Marshall 1987, 135).

3. Bring Me the Room

1. Abolitionist immigration scholar Naomi Paik notes that religious congregations providing physical sanctuary to (im)migrants facing deportation favor those who can "perform the role of the 'good immigrant' and thereby expose US policy failures" (2017, 14). Paik cites a brief by the Unitarian Universalist Association of Congregations that summarizes how its member congregations can participate in the new sanctuary movement by hosting families in danger of deportation. The brief instructs congregations to choose "legal cases [that] clearly reveal the contradictions and moral injustice of our current immigration system." These families must have US citizen children, a "good work record," and a "viable case under current law" (quoted in Paik 2017, 14). Martha Escobar also discusses the pressures within the immigration justice and sanctuary movements to reproduce the good/bad immigrant binary. Writing of her experiences at the intersection of prison abolition and immigration advocacy, she cites examples of (im)migrants being encouraged to downplay their prison experiences in order to win acceptance from the mainstream immigration justice movement (Escobar 2016, 69–95). These examples demonstrate that not only US citizens but also (im)migrants in leadership positions can perform the surrogate sovereign role.

2. Puga's analysis builds on the work of scholars who have demonstrated the powerful role of a melodramatic imagination in US culture and politics (see, e.g., Anker 2014; Berlant 2008). These scholars define *melodrama* not just as a literary or theatrical genre but also as a political rationality. As film scholar Linda Williams puts it, this helps explain "why it is that in a democracy ruled by rights, we do not gain the moral upper hand by saying simply that rights have been infringed. We say, instead, much more powerfully: 'I have been victimized; I have suffered, therefore give me rights'" (2001, 9). The moral power of suffering is typically attributed to melodrama's origin in a Christian moral universe where suffering is linked to virtue, as theorized by Peter Brooks (1976).

3. Theater scholar Caroline Wake has analyzed this trend in Australia, where, in response to anti-immigrant policies, there has been a profusion of plays "made by, with, and about asylum seekers" (2013, 102). These plays vary in format and content,

but they frequently employ a "verbatim" structure in which actors reanimate texts from asylum hearings. Wake discusses some of the ways these plays reenact the interrogatory format of the asylum hearing. She quotes a writer-director discussing her method: "How do I know these people are genuine refugees? I thought I had to go through that—to convince an audience, I have to really convince myself. So I was rather forensic in my questioning" (2013, 114). In this instance, the director anticipates and naturalizes the involvement of a citizen audience in the sovereign scene of interrogation. In the United States, verbatim theater has also been employed to raise awareness of the injustice of immigration policies. For instance, the play *De Novo*, by Houses on the Moon, reanimates the transcript of an asylum hearing that went fatally wrong. The audience is invited to participate in a kind of theatrical retrial, conducting the asylum hearing de novo (over again).

4. This pattern arises in US immigration courts because of several mechanisms that provide visas, deportation relief, and other benefits based on (im)migrants' special value to US citizens. Some of the most obvious have to do with employment visas, which are contingent on an (im)migrant's value to a US employer, or (infamously) the various business and investor provisions that grant (im)migrant status to foreign nationals who invest in US companies or provide jobs. But the role of US citizens in mediating the value of (im)migrants also occurs in less explicit ways. For instance, (im)migrants facing deportation may apply for a "cancellation of removal" based on the argument that their deportation would cause "exceptional and extremely unusual hardship" to their US citizen relatives. In these instances, the law effectively suspends consideration of the harm caused by deportation to the person deported. Instead, the hardship of deportation is considered meaningful because it imposes a secondary hardship on a US citizen—thus requiring family members to defend and mediate each other's value.

5. See Noll (2005) for an analysis of the connections between asylum law and the liturgical act of grace.

6. Much of Fanon's work addresses the ruse of recognition that he witnessed in the struggle against French colonialism and the aftermath of slavery. He addresses Hegel head-on in a section of *Black Skin, White Masks* entitled "The Black Man and Hegel," arguing that the object-like status of Blacks under French colonial rule stimulates a drive for mutual recognition that is impossible to achieve (Fanon 2008, 191–97).

7. For the majority of US history, immigration authorities enacted overt policies against queer (im)migrants. This began to change in the 1990s, thanks to queer (im)migrant organizing, legal advocacy, and shifting public attitudes about sexual orientation and identity. Although barriers remain for particular groups of queer asylum seekers, and although many are critical of asylum law's sexual politics (see, e.g., Akbari and Vogler 2021; Lewis 2014; Luibhéid and Cantú 2005), claims based on sexual identity and orientation have emerged as an area of asylum law with a relatively high rate of success.

8. See chapter 2, note 28.

9. As attorney and immigration scholar Jacqueline Bhabha notes, the principle of *non-refoulement* "contains no obligation on a particular state to offer permanent asylum; it merely injuncts a state from sending a refugee back to a persecuting country. This obligation can be met by sending the refugee to another, safe country or by keeping the refugee in a temporary status until the risk of persecution ceases. According to the United States Supreme Court, considering the interdiction of Haitian refugees by the U.S. Coast Guard, it can even be met by forcibly preventing access to the host country's territory, so that no question of expulsion arises" (1996, 7).

10. This is what distinguishes the asylum system from the refugee system. Eligibility for both types of status is based on the same standard of "well-founded fear." However, asylum seekers apply for status from within the territory of the "host" country, and refugees do so while residing outside that territory.

11. According to the United Nations High Commissioner for Refugees (UNHCR) handbook, "A person is a refugee within the meaning of the 1951 Convention as soon as he fulfills the criteria contained in the definition. This would necessarily occur prior to the time at which his refugee status is formally determined. Recognition of his refugee status does not therefore make him a refugee but declares him to be one. He does not become a refugee because of recognition, but is recognized because he is a refugee" (quoted in Noll 2005, 206).

12. Political philosopher Giorgio Agamben theorizes the refugee in terms of a "scarto taboo"—the taboo of refugees' existence as "bare life," or life outside the authority of the nation-state system. Agamben writes that "by breaking the continuity between man and citizen, nativity and nationality, [refugees] put the originary fiction of modern sovereignty in crisis" (1998, 131). Agamben's theories of "bare life" and the "state of exception" have been highly influential in immigration studies and political theory more broadly. Yet, as many scholars have reminded us, Agamben's formulations tend to forget that the dynamics he theorizes in race-neutral terms are inextricable from histories of racialization in colonial modernity. For instance, the denial of legal personhood to groups of people, despite formal commitments to universal personhood; the diminished horizons of life produced in the wake of that denial; the invention of legal phantasms to demarcate persons excluded from personhood; and the foundational role of such exclusions in the development of liberal democracies are the histories of settler colonialism, transatlantic slavery, imperial warfare, and many other racializing assemblages of colonial modernity (Weheliye 2014).

13. On Central Americans' decades-long struggle for legal status, see Coutin (2003).

14. Indeed, one of the primary legal strategies employed by sanctuary participants was to argue at trial that their actions in support of Central American (im)migrants constituted a "civil initiative" rather than "civil disobedience" (Coutin 1993, 109). By acting to prevent the *refoulement* of genuine asylum seekers, sanctuary participants

argued that they were upholding rather than breaking the law: they were carrying out legal responsibilities the US government failed to enforce. This argument, however, relied on the exclusion of Central American (im)migrants who fell outside the asylum definition.

15. The colonial rescue politics of these scenes is also borne out by the manner in which the story of the 1980s sanctuary movement has been told. Most accounts place white US citizens at the center of the movement and minimize the contribution of Central Americans. Yet, as Perla (2008) argues, Central American revolutionaries both in the United States and in their countries of origin played a much larger role in the transnational sanctuary movement than is typically understood. See also Stuelke (2014) on the affective structures of solidarity in the sanctuary movement.

16. Raymond Williams traces the history by which tragic protagonists have descended the social ladder across history, from gods and royal families in antiquity to the "citizen" in modern times: "some deaths mattered more than others, and rank was the actual dividing line—the death of a slave or a retainer was no more than incidental and was certainly not tragic. Ironically, our own middle-class culture began by appearing to reject this view: the tragedy of a citizen could be as real as the tragedy of a prince. Often, in fact, this was not so much rejection of the real structure of feeling as an extension of the tragic category to a newly rising class" (2006, 73).

17. "Border imperialism" is a term conceived by Harsha Walia (2013), and it offers a comprehensive framework for conceptualizing how immigration law maintains colonial patterns on a global scale. Walia uses this term to refer to the many ways histories of colonization continue to dictate the legal parameters of migration. These histories influence not only the geographic "flows" of migration but also the differential manner in which human mobility is interpreted. Border imperialism denotes the basic hypocrisy of the fact that the relatively privileged and relatively white have historically been allowed to move around the world with few impediments, and when the terms of their mobility exceed the boundaries of the law, they are typically not subject to violent acts of incarceration and banishment nor labeled "illegals." Their mobility follows the imperial trajectory of capital, which routinely transgresses borders in search of raw materials, land, and cheap labor. The mobility of poor and racialized people, however, is legally interpreted very differently. Although such people are often displaced as a result of neocolonial processes, their mobility is often criminalized, and these processes of criminalization tend to be integrated into capitalism's ongoing drive to secure a disposable laboring class.

18. Undocumented laborers are notoriously subject to wage theft, and employers routinely abuse the threat of deportation to enforce substandard conditions (see, e.g., Bauer and Ramirez 2010; Taykhman 2016). As Nicholas De Genova puts it, "So-called illegal and officially unauthorized migrations are, to various extents, actively and deliberately imported and welcomed by prospective employers as a highly prized variety of labor-power" (2016b, 274). The role of the law in generating deportable

(im)migrants through policies of illegalization serves the US economy at many levels, from the industrial sites of agriculture and manufacturing to the intimate spaces of domestic labor. Martha Escobar notes that undocumented laborers became the ideal form of exploitable labor at a time when Black citizens ceased to fill that role. Legal and economic advances for Black citizens following the civil rights movement reduced their exploitability within the labor market. While Blacks were "constructed as neoliberal excess, undocumented (im)migrant labor assumed an essential function due to (im)migrants' limited abilities to make claims on the state and society" (Escobar 2016, 37).

19. The concept of retraumatization is often invoked in social scientific and clinical critiques of asylum law and in theater about the refugee condition. See Jeffers (2008), J. Rodríguez (2003, 93), and Wake (2013).

Coda

1. See Monk (2010). Monk stands up between 02:45 and 3:50. My deepest gratitude to Fred Moten for leading me to Monk's performance and Feld's research in a personal conversation about musical accompaniment.

2. The work of mapping disappearance is, of course, extremely important for loved ones struggling to find their disappeared relatives. As Jenny Edkins writes in her work on missing persons, it is the arduous process of reunifying "names without bodies and bodies without names" (2016, 359). Forensic activities and political mobilizations to reunite bodies, places, and names are central to the family-led campaigns taking place in the borderlands and throughout the wider region. If disappearance adds a loss of reality, chronology, and spatiality to the loss of a person, then the search for facts can work against these multiplying forms of loss and provide some degree of closure. Yet there are many situations in which bodies and names never come back together. The area of Texas where Honeyed Herb and Stone fainted is one where many (im)migrants crossing the US-Mexico border have died in recent years (see Délano Alonso and Nienass 2016). The improper handling of human remains, the factors that constrain relatives from initiating a search for their loved ones, the physical properties of the natural environment, and the culture of ungrievability around (im)migrant death mean that many of the dead have never been identified. Human rights and (im)migrant justice organizations nevertheless honor the unidentified bodies of the disappeared with a range of practices, including art installations, public processions, and small acts of care, such as writing messages or bringing flowers to the graves of the unidentified border crossers (Délano Alonso and Nienass 2016). These practices accompany the disappeared not in their individuality but as a collective—a collective of people whose liminal status saturates the borderlands, the land itself, with the resounding presence of unacknowledged loss. While borderlands communities work to honor the bodies without names, families

living in Mexico, Central America, the United States, and many other countries are searching across great physical distances for loved ones who disappeared while crossing the border. These families circulate the names of the lost through a thicket of information and misinformation, forming bonds with distant strangers willing to help (and sometimes, devastatingly, with distant strangers willing to exploit). Those who honor the bodies, those who honor the names, and those who are disappeared do not necessarily find one another; they do not necessarily touch, yet their collective activity adds up to something. As Ileana Diéguez writes on the work of searching for the disappeared: "I think about the *communitas* constituted not only by the explicit presence of those who search, but also by the present-absence of those who are searched for. I refer to this *communitas* sustained by the bonds and the bodies of the family members, who in their everyday spaces and in their journeys provide support for the presence/absence of their loved ones" (forthcoming; my translation). Here, Diéguez implies that loved ones, insofar as they continue to search, sustain their disappeared kin. What they sustain, in Diéguez's phrasing, is not their kin's presence but their kin's "presence/absence"—that is, their capacity to exert a radically destabilizing force. What Diéguez calls *communitas* I call the *chorus of that wish*, the synchronous but out-of-phase accompaniment where the searching and the searched-for call each other's names.

REFERENCES

Abrego, Leisy J., and Cecilia Menjívar. 2012. "Immigrant Latina Mothers as Targets of Legal Violence." *International Journal of Sociology of the Family* 37, no. 1: 9–26.

Agamben, Giorgio. 1998. *Homo Sacer: Sovereign Power and Bare Life.* Stanford, CA: Stanford University Press.

Ahmed, Sara. 2000. *Strange Encounters: Embodied Others in Post-Coloniality.* New York: Routledge.

Ahmed, Sara. 2014. *The Cultural Politics of Emotion.* Edinburgh: Edinburgh University Press.

Akbari, Roxana, and Stefan Vogler. 2021. "Intersectional Invisibility: Race, Gender, Sexuality, and the Erasure of Sexual Minority Women in US Asylum Law." *Law and Social Inquiry* 46, no. 4: 1062–91.

Alexander, Michelle. 2012. *The New Jim Crow: Mass Incarceration in the Age of Color-blindness.* New York: New Press.

American Immigration Council. 2021. "The Cost of Immigration Enforcement and Border Security." https://www.americanimmigrationcouncil.org/sites/default/files/research/the_cost_of_immigration_enforcement_and_border_security.pdf.

America's Voice. 2017. "The New Silent Raids: Check-in and Be Deported." Press release, May 11. https://americasvoice.org/press_releases/check-in-and-be-deported.

Anderson, Bridget, Nandita Sharma, and Cynthia Wright. 2009. "Editorial: Why No Borders?" *Refuge: Canada's Journal on Refugees* 26, no. 2: 5–18.

Anderson, Jill, and Nin Solis. 2014. *Los Otros Dreamers.* http://www.losotrosdreamersthebook.com/the-project-1.

Anker, Elisabeth Robin. 2014. *Orgies of Feeling: Melodrama and the Politics of Freedom.* Durham, NC: Duke University Press.

Arendt, Hannah. 1973. *The Origins of Totalitarianism*. New York: Houghton Mifflin Harcourt.

Arias, Arturo. 2003. "Central American-Americans: Invisibility, Power and Representation in the US Latino World." *Latino Studies* 1: 168–87.

Arriola Vega, Luis Alfredo. 2017. "Policy Adrift: Mexico's Southern Border Program." Houston: James A. Baker III Institute for Public Policy of Rice University. https://scholarship.rice.edu/bitstream/handle/1911/97772/MEX-pub -FronteraSur-062317.pdf?sequence=1&isAllowed=y.

Barthes, Roland. 1986. *The Rustle of Language*. New York: Hill and Wang.

Bauer, Mary, and Monica Ramirez. 2010. *Injustice on Our Plates: Immigrant Women in the U.S. Food Industry*. Montgomery, AL: Southern Poverty Law Center.

Benjamin, Walter. 1978. "Critique of Violence." In *Reflections: Essays, Aphorisms, Autobiographical Writings*, edited by Peter Demetz, 277–300. New York: Harcourt Brace Jovanovich.

Berlant, Lauren. 2008. *The Female Complaint: The Unfinished Business of Sentimentality in American Culture*. Durham, NC: Duke University Press.

Berlant, Lauren. 2011. *Cruel Optimism*. Durham, NC: Duke University Press.

Bernstein, Nina. 2017. "Waging Accountability: Why Investigative Journalism Is Both Necessary and Insufficient to Transforming Immigration Detention." In *Challenging Immigration Detention: Academics, Activists and Policymakers*, edited by Michael Flynn and Matthew Flynn, 11–27. Cheltenham, UK: Edward Elgar.

Bhabha, Jacqueline. 1996. "Embodied Rights: Gender Persecution, State Sovereignty, and Refugees." *Public Culture* 9: 3–32.

Bhattacharjee, Anannya. 2006. "The Public/Private Mirage: Mapping Homes and Undomesticating Violence Work in the South Asian Immigrant Community." In *The Anthropology of the State: A Reader*, edited by Aradhana Sharma and Akhil Gupta, 337–55. Oxford: John Wiley and Sons.

Bloom, Barbara E. 2015. *Meeting the Needs of Women in California's County Justice Systems: A Toolkit for Policymakers and Practitioners*. Oakland: Californians for Safety and Justice. https://safeandjust.org/wp-content/uploads /WomensToolkit_singles_5.5.15v1.pdf.

Boal, Augusto. 2008. *Theatre of the Oppressed*. London: Pluto Press.

Braz, Rose. 2006. "Kinder, Gentler, Gender Responsive Cages: Prison Expansion Is Not Prison Reform." *Women, Girls, and Criminal Justice* 7: 787–91.

Brecht, Bertolt. 1964. *Brecht on Theatre: The Development of an Aesthetic*. Edited by John Willet. New York: Hill and Wang.

Brooks, Peter. 1976. *The Melodramatic Imagination: Balzac, Henry James, Melodrama, and the Mode of Excess*. New Haven, CT: Yale University Press.

Brown, Adrienne Marie. 2017. *Emergent Strategy: Shaping Change, Changing Worlds*. Chico, CA: AK Press.

Brown, Michelle. 2014. "Visual Criminology and Carceral Studies: Counter-images in the Carceral Age." *Theoretical Criminology* 18, no. 2: 176–97.

Brown, Wendy. 1995. *States of Injury: Power and Freedom in Late Modernity*. Princeton, NJ: Princeton University Press.

Burch, Noël. 1969. *Praxis du Cinéma*. Paris: Éditions Gallimard.

Butler, Judith. 1997. *The Psychic Life of Power: Theories in Subjection*. Stanford, CA: Stanford University Press.

Butler, Judith. 2004. *Precarious Life: The Powers of Mourning and Violence*. New York: Verso.

Butler, Judith. 2014. "Wrong-Doing Truth-Telling." Lecture presented at European Graduate School, Saas-Fee, Switzerland, August. https://www.youtube.com /watch?v=nmoguMXPxCI&t=6s.

Butler, Judith. 2015. *Notes toward a Performative Theory of Assembly*. Cambridge, MA: Harvard University Press.

Butler, Judith. 2016. *Frames of War: When Is Life Grievable?* New York: Verso.

Butler, Judith, and Gayatri Chakravorty Spivak. 2007. *Who Sings the Nation-State? Language, Politics, Belonging*. Calcutta: Seagull Books.

Cacho, Lisa Marie. 2012. *Social Death: Racialized Rightlessness and the Criminalization of the Unprotected*. New York: New York University Press.

Camacho, Alicia Schmidt. 2008. *Migrant Imaginaries: Latino Cultural Politics in the US-Mexico Borderlands*. New York: New York University Press.

Camerini, Michael, and Shari Robertson, dirs. 2000. *A Well-Founded Fear*. DVD. New York: Epidavros Project.

Campt, Tina M. 2017. *Listening to Images*. Durham, NC: Duke University Press.

Carbado, Devon W. 2005. "Racial Naturalization." *American Quarterly* 57, no. 3: 633–58.

Cárdenas, Maritza E. 2018. *Constituting Central American-Americans: Transnational Identities and the Politics of Dislocation*. New Brunswick, NJ: Rutgers University Press.

Carmack, Robert M. 1981. *The Quiché Maya of Utatlán: The Evolution of a Highland Guatemala Kingdom*. Norman: University of Oklahoma Press.

Castillo, Alejandra. 2016. "The Mexican Government's Frontera Sur Program: An Inconsistent Immigration Policy." Washington, DC: Council on Hemispheric Affairs, October 25. http://www.coha.org/wp-content/uploads/2016/10/The -Mexican-Government%E2%80%99s-Frontera-Sur-Program-An-Inconsistent -Immigration-Policy.pdf.

Chacón, Jennifer M. 2013. "The Security Myth: Punishing Immigrants in the Name of National Security." In *Governing Immigration through Crime: A Reader*, edited by Julie A. Dowling and Jonathan Xavier Inda, 77–93. Palo Alto, CA: Stanford University Press.

Chaudhuri, Una. 1997. *Staging Place: The Geography of Modern Drama*. Ann Arbor: University of Michigan Press.

Chávez, Karma. 2012. "The Need to Shift from a Rhetoric of Security to a Rhetoric of Militarization." In *Border Rhetorics: Citizenship and Identity on the US-Mexico Frontier*, edited by Robert Dechaine, 48–62. Tuscaloosa: University of Alabama Press.

Chávez, Karma R. 2013. *Queer Migration Politics: Activist Rhetoric and Coalitional Possibilities*. Champaign: University of Illinois Press.

Chomsky, Aviva. 2021. *Central America's Forgotten History: Revolution, Violence, and the Roots of Migration*. Boston: Beacon Press.

Coleman, Mathew, and Austin Kocher. 2011. "Detention, Deportation, Devolution and Immigrant Incapacitation in the US, Post 9/11." *The Geographical Journal* 177, no. 3: 228–37.

Conquergood, Dwight. 2002. "Lethal Theatre: Performance, Punishment, and the Death Penalty." *Theatre Journal* 54, no. 3: 339–67.

Cornell Legal Information Institute. n.d. "Subsume." https://www.law.cornell.edu /wex/subsume. Accessed September 5, 2022.

Coulthard, Glen Sean. 2014. *Red Skin, White Masks: Rejecting the Colonial Politics of Recognition*. Minneapolis: University of Minnesota Press.

Coutin, Susan Bibler. 1993. *The Culture of Protest: Religious Activism and the U.S. Sanctuary Movement*. Boulder, CO: Westview Press.

Coutin, Susan Bibler. 2003. *Legalizing Moves: Salvadoran Immigrants' Struggle for US Residency*. Ann Arbor: University of Michigan Press.

Coutin, Susan Bibler. 2010. "Confined Within: National Territories as Zones of Confinement." *Political Geography* 29, no. 4: 200–208.

Coutin, Susan Bibler. 2011. "Falling Outside: Excavating the History of Central American Asylum Seekers." *Law and Social Inquiry* 36, no. 3: 569–96.

Cover, Robert M. 1985. "Violence and the Word." *Yale Law Journal* 95: 1601–29.

Cunningham, Hilary. 1995. *God and Caesar at the Rio Grande: Sanctuary and the Politics of Religion.* Minneapolis: University of Minnesota Press.

Davis, Angela. 2003. *Are Prisons Obsolete?* New York: Seven Stories Press.

Davis, Angela. 2011. *Abolition Democracy: Beyond Empire, Prisons, and Torture.* New York: Seven Stories Press.

De Genova, Nicholas. 2007. "The Production of Culprits: From Deportability to Detainability in the Aftermath of 'Homeland Security.'" In *Securitizations of Citizenship*, edited by Peter Nyers, 157–88. New York: Routledge.

De Genova, Nicholas. 2012. "Border, Scene and Obscene." In *A Companion to Border Studies*, edited by Thomas M. Wilson and Hastings Donnan, 492–504. Oxford: Wiley-Blackwell.

De Genova, Nicholas. 2013. "Spectacles of Migrant 'Illegality': The Scene of Exclusion, the Obscene of Inclusion." *Ethnic and Racial Studies* 36, no. 7: 1180–98.

De Genova, Nicholas. 2016a. "Detention, Deportation, and Waiting: Toward a Theory of Migrant Detainability." Global Detention Project Working Paper 18. Geneva, Switzerland: Global Detention Project. https://www .globaldetentionproject.org/detention-deportation-waiting-toward-theory -migrant-detainability-gdp-working-paper-no-18.

De Genova, Nicholas. 2016b. "The Incorrigible Subject: The Autonomy of Migration and the US Immigration Stalemate." In *Subjectivation in Political Theory and Contemporary Practices*, edited by Andreas Oberprantacher and Andrei Siclodi, 267–85. London: Palgrave Macmillan.

De Genova, Nicholas. 2017. "Introduction: The Borders of 'Europe' and the European Question." In *The Borders of "Europe": Autonomy of Migration, Tactics of Bordering*, edited by Nicholas De Genova, 1–36. Durham, NC: Duke University Press.

Délano Alonso, Alexandra, and Benjamin Nienass. 2016. "Deaths, Visibility, and Responsibility: The Politics of Mourning at the US-Mexico Border." *Social Research* 83, no. 2: 421–51.

De León, Jason. 2015. *The Land of Open Graves: Living and Dying on the Migrant Trail.* Oakland: University of California Press.

Deleuze, Gilles. 1983. *Cinema 1: The Movement-Image.* Translated by Hugh Tomlinson and Barbara Habberjam. Minneapolis: University of Minnesota Press.

Deleuze, Gilles. 1992. "Postscript on the Societies of Control." *October* 59: 3–7.

Department of Homeland Security. 2006. "DHS Closes Loophole by Expanding Expedited Removal to Cover Illegal Alien Families." Press release, May 15.

Diéguez, Ileana. Forthcoming. "Saberes y cuerpos liminales de las communitas en búsqueda." In *Las luchas por la memoria en Mexico*, edited by Alexandra Délano Alonso, Benjamin Nienass, Alicia de los Ríos Merino, and María De Vecchi Gerli.

Dixon, Ejeris, and Leah Lakshmi Piepzna-Samarasinha. 2020. *Beyond Survival: Strategies and Stories from the Transformative Justice Movement*. Chico, CA: AK Press.

Dunbar-Ortiz, Roxanne. 2014. *An Indigenous Peoples' History of the United States*. Boston: Beacon Press.

Eden, Kathy. 1986. *Legal and Poetic Fiction in the Aristotelian Tradition*. Princeton, NJ: Princeton University Press.

Edkins, Jenny. 2016. "Missing Migrants and the Politics of Naming: Names without Bodies, Bodies without Names." *Social Research* 83, no. 2: 359–89.

Eisenstein, Sergei, and Herbert Marshall. 1987. *Nonindifferent Nature*. Cambridge: Cambridge University Press.

Enders, Jody. 1999. *The Medieval Theater of Cruelty: Rhetoric, Memory, Violence*. Ithaca, NY: Cornell University Press.

Escobar, Martha D. 2016. *Captivity beyond Prisons: Criminalization Experiences of Latina (Im)migrants*. Austin: University of Texas Press.

Evans, David. 1999. "Theatre of Deferral: The Image of the Law and the Architecture of the Inns of Court." *Law and Critique* 10, no. 1: 1–25.

Falcón, Sylvanna. 2001. "Rape as a Weapon of War: Advancing Human Rights for Women at the U.S.-Mexico Border." *Social Justice* 28, no. 2: 31–50.

Fanon, Frantz. 2008. *Black Skin, White Masks*. New York: Grove Press.

Farmer, Paul. 2011. "Accompaniment as Policy." Speech, Kennedy School of Government, Harvard University, May 25. https://www.lessonsfromhaiti.org/press -and-media/transcripts/accompaniment-as-policy/.

Fassin, Didier. 2011. *Humanitarian Reason: A Moral History of the Present*. Berkeley: University of California Press.

Faudree, Paja. 2012. "How to Say Things with Wars: Performativity and Discursive Rupture in the Requerimiento of the Spanish Conquest." *Journal of Linguistic Anthropology* 22, no. 3: 182–200.

Feld, Steven. 1994. "From Ethnomusicology to Echo-muse-ecology: Reading R. Murray Schafer in the Papua New Guinea Rainforest." *The Soundscape Newsletter* 8, no. 6: 9–13.

Feltz, Renee. 2016. "Texas County Rejects Bid for New 'Hotel-like' Immigration Detention Center." *Guardian*, June 28. https://www.theguardian.com/us-news /2016/jun/28/texas-immigration-detention-center-family-rejected.

Fernandes, Sujatha. 2017. *Curated Stories: The Uses and Misuses of Storytelling.* New York: Oxford University Press.

Fernandez, Luis, and Joel Olson. 2011. "To Live, Love and Work Anywhere You Please." *Contemporary Political Theory* 10, no. 3: 412–19.

Fernando, Nilmini. 2016. "The Discursive Violence of Postcolonial Asylum in the Irish Republic." *Postcolonial Studies* 19, no. 4: 393–408.

Foster, Susan Leigh. 2003. "Choreographies of Protest." *Theatre Journal* 55, no. 3: 395–412.

Foster, Susan Leigh. 2010. *Choreographing Empathy: Kinesthesia in Performance.* New York: Routledge.

Foucault, Michel. 1986. "Of Other Spaces." *Diacritics* 16, no. 1: 22–27.

Foucault, Michel. 2001. "Truth and Juridical Forms." In *The Essential Works of Foucault, 1954–1984,* vol. 3, *Power,* edited by James D. Faubion, 1–90. New York: New Press.

Foucault, Michel. 2012. *Discipline and Punish: The Birth of the Prison.* New York: Vintage Books.

Franco, Jean. 1985. "Killing Priests, Nuns, Women, Children." In *On Signs,* edited by Marshall Blonsky, 414–20. Baltimore: Johns Hopkins University Press.

Freire, Paulo. 2014. *Pedagogy of the Oppressed.* 30th anniversary edition. New York: Bloomsbury.

Gebisa, Ebba. 2007. "Constitutional Concerns with the Enforcement and Expansion of Expedited Removal." *University of Chicago Legal Forum* 1: 565–89.

Genzlinger, Neil. 2000. "Television Review: Where Dreams of Asylum Can Come True or Die." *New York Times,* June 5. https://www.nytimes.com/2000/06/05/arts/television-review-where-dreams-of-asylum-can-come-true-or-die.html?sq=Where+Dreams+of+Asylum+Can+Come+True+or+Die&scp=1.

Gilmore, Ruth Wilson. 2007. *Golden Gulag: Prisons, Surplus, Crisis, and Opposition in Globalizing California.* Berkeley: University of California Press.

Gilmore, Ruth Wilson, and Craig Gilmore. 2007. "Restating the Obvious." In *Indefensible Space: The Architecture of the National Insecurity State,* edited by Michael Sorkin, 141–62. London: Taylor and Francis.

Gilmore, Ruth Wilson, and Jenna Loyd. 2012. "Race, Capitalist Crisis, and Abolitionist Organizing: An Interview with Ruth Wilson Gilmore, February 2010." In *Beyond Walls and Cages: Prisons, Borders, and Global Crisis,* edited by Jenna M. Loyd, Matt Mitchelson, and Andrew Burridge, 42–54. Athens: University of Georgia Press.

Goizueta, Roberto. 2003. *Caminemos con Jesus: Toward a Hispanic/Latino Theology of Accompaniment.* Maryknoll, NY: Orbis Books.

Golash-Boza, Tanya Maria. 2010a. "Structural Racism and Mass Deportation." *Racism Review*, June 24. http://www.racismreview.com/blog/2010/06/24/structural-racism-and-mass-deportation.

Golash-Boza, Tanya Maria. 2010b. "Targeting Jamaicans." Counter Punch, November 12. https://www.counterpunch.org/2010/11/12/targeting-jamaicans.

Golash-Boza, Tanya Maria. 2015. "The Racial Injustices of Mass Deportation." Counter Punch, March 20. https://www.counterpunch.org/2015/03/20/the-racial-injustices-of-mass-deportation.

Goldman, Francisco. 2008. *The Art of Political Murder: Who Killed the Bishop?* New York: Grove/Atlantic.

Gómez Cervantes, Andrea, Cecilia Menjívar, and William G. Staples. 2017. "'Humane' Immigration Enforcement and Latina Immigrants in the Detention Complex." *Feminist Criminology* 12, no. 3: 269–92.

Gonzales, Alfonso. 2013. *Reform without Justice: Latino Migrant Politics and the Homeland Security State*. Oxford: Oxford University Press.

Goodrich, Peter. 1990. *Languages of Law: From Logics of Memory to Nomadic Masks*. London: Weidenfeld and Nicolson.

Gorman, Cynthia S. 2017. "Redefining Refugees: Interpretive Control and the Bordering Work of Legal Categorization in U.S. Asylum Law." *Political Geography* 58: 36–45.

Gorman, Cynthia S. 2019. "Defined by the Flood: Alarmism and the Legal Thresholds of US Political Asylum." *Geopolitics* 26, no. 1: 215–35.

Guenther, Lisa. 2013. *Solitary Confinement: Social Death and Its Afterlives*. Minneapolis: University of Minnesota Press.

Hale, Charles R. 2006. *Más Que un Indio: Racial Ambivalence and Neoliberal Multiculturalism in Guatemala*. Santa Fe, NM: School of American Research Press.

Harlan, Chico. 2016. "Inside the Administration's $1 Billion Deal to Detain Central American Asylum Seekers." *Washington Post*, August 14. https://www.washingtonpost.com/business/economy/inside-the-administrations-1-billion-deal-to-detain-central-american-asylum-seekers/2016/08/14/e47f1960-5819-11e6-9aee-8075993d73a2_story.html?noredirect=on&utm_term=.0f7a1e162ec6.

Harney, Stefano, and Fred Moten. 2015. "Michael Brown." *boundary 2: An International Journal of Literature and Culture* 42, no. 4: 81–87.

Harris, Cheryl I. 1993. "Whiteness as Property." *Harvard Law Review* 106, no. 8: 1707–91.

Hartman, Saidiya. 1997. *Scenes of Subjection: Terror, Slavery, and Self-Making in Nineteenth-Century America*. Oxford: Oxford University Press.

Harvey, David. 2007. *A Brief History of Neoliberalism*. New York: Oxford University Press.

Hegel, Georg Wilhelm Friedrich. 1977. *Phenomenology of Spirit*. Oxford: Oxford University Press.

Henderson, Victoria. 2009. "Citizenship in the Line of Fire: Protective Accompaniment, Proxy Citizenship, and Pathways for Transnational Solidarity in Guatemala." *Annals of the Association of American Geographers* 99, no. 5: 969–76.

Hernández, César Cuauhtémoc García. 2013. "Invisible Spaces and Invisible Lives in Immigration Detention." *Howard Law Journal* 57: 869–98.

Hernández, César Cuauhtémoc García. 2017. "Abolishing Immigration Prisons." *Boston University Law Review* 97, no. 1: 245–300.

Hernández, David Manuel. 2019. "Carceral Shadows Entangled Lineages and Technologies of Migrant Detention." In *Caging Borders and Carceral States: Incarcerations, Immigration Detentions, and Resistance*, edited by Robert T. Chase, 57–92. Chapel Hill: University of North Carolina Press.

Hernández, Kelly Lytle. 2010. *Migra! A History of the US Border Patrol*. Berkeley: University of California Press.

Hernández, Kelly Lytle. 2017. *City of Inmates: Conquest, Rebellion, and the Rise of Human Caging in Los Angeles, 1771–1965*. Chapel Hill: University of North Carolina Press.

Herzing, Rachel. 2015. "Commentary: 'Tweaking Armageddon': The Potential and Limits of Conditions of Confinement Campaigns." *Social Justice* 41, no. 3: 190–95.

Hiemstra, Nancy. 2014. "Performing Homeland Security within the US Immigrant Detention System." *Environment and Planning D: Society and Space* 32, no. 4: 574–88.

Huang, Priscilla. 2008. "Anchor Babies, Over-breeders, and the Population Bomb: The Reemergence of Nativism and Population Control in Anti-immigration Policies." *Harvard Law and Policy Review* 2, no. 2: 385–406.

Hussain, Nasser. 2007. "Beyond Norm and Exception: Guantánamo." *Critical Inquiry* 33, no. 4: 734–53.

Ina, Satsuki. 2015. "I Know an American 'Internment' Camp When I See One." American Civil Liberties Union, May 27. https://www.aclu.org/blog/immigrants
-rights/immigrants-rights-and-detention/i-know-american-internment
-camp-when-i-see?redirect=blog/speak-freely/i-know-american-internment
-camp-when-i-see-one.

INCITE! Women of Color against Violence Staff, eds. 2007. *The Revolution Will Not Be Funded: Beyond the Non-profit Industrial Complex*. Cambridge, MA: South End Press.

Jeffers, Alison. 2008. "Dirty Truth: Personal Narrative, Victimhood and Participatory Theatre Work with People Seeking Asylum." *Research in Drama Education* 13, no. 2: 217–21.

Johnson, Jeh C. 2014. "Statement by Secretary of Homeland Security Jeh Johnson before the Senate Committee on Appropriations." Department of Homeland Security, July 10. https://www.dhs.gov/news/2014/07/10/statement-secretary -homeland-security-jeh-johnson-senate-committee-appropriations.

Johnson, Jeh C. 2015. "Statement on Family Residential Centers." Department of Homeland Security, June 24. www.dhs.gov/news/2015/06/24/statement -secretary-jeh-c-johnson-family-residential-centers.

Joseph, Gilbert M., and Greg Grandin, eds. 2010. *A Century of Revolution: Insurgent and Counterinsurgent Violence during Latin America's Long Cold War.* Durham, NC: Duke University Press.

Jubany, Olga. 2011. "Constructing Truths in a Culture of Disbelief: Understanding Asylum Screening from Within." *International Sociology* 26, no. 1: 74–94.

Kaba, Mariame. 2014. "Police 'Reforms' You Should Always Oppose." Truthout, December 7. https://truthout.org/articles/police-reforms-you-should-always-oppose.

Kafka, Franz. 2009. *The Trial.* Oxford: Oxford University Press.

Kanstroom, Daniel. 2007. *Deportation Nation: Outsiders in American History.* Cambridge, MA: Harvard University Press.

Kantorowicz, Ernst. 2016. *The King's Two Bodies: A Study in Medieval Political Theology.* Princeton, NJ: Princeton University Press.

Kaplan, Amy. 2003. "Homeland Insecurities: Reflections on Language and Space." *Radical History Review* 85: 82–93.

"Karangatia: Calling Out Gender and Sexuality in Settler Societies." 2012. *Settler Colonial Studies.* Special issue.

Koopman, Sara. 2008. "Imperialism Within: Can the Master's Tools Bring Down Empire?" *ACME: An International E-Journal for Critical Geographies* 7, no. 2: 283–307.

Legendre, Pierre. 1997. *Law and the Unconscious: A Legendre Reader.* New York: Springer.

Lepecki, André. 2013. "Choreopolice and Choreopolitics: Or, the Task of the Dancer." *TDR/The Drama Review* 57, no. 4: 13–27.

Lewis, Rachel. 2014. "Gay? Prove It: The Politics of Queer Anti-deportation Activism." *Sexualities* 17: 958–75.

Libal, Bob, Lauren Martin, and Nicole Porter. 2012. "'A Prison Is Not a Home': Notes from the Campaign to End Family Detention." In *Beyond Walls and Cages: Pris-*

ons, Borders, and Global Crisis, edited by Jenna M. Loyd, Matt Mitchelson, and Andrew Burridge, 253–65. Athens: University of Georgia Press.

Loyd, Jenna M., Matt Mitchelson, and Andrew Burridge, eds. 2012. *Beyond Walls and Cages: Prisons, Borders, and Global Crisis*. Athens: University of Georgia Press.

Loyd, Jenna M., and Alison Mountz. 2018. *Boats, Borders, and Bases: Race, the Cold War, and the Rise of Migration Detention in the United States*. Berkeley: University of California Press.

Ludwig, Mike. 2019. "ICE Is Monitoring and Targeting Immigration Activists." Truthout, April 30. https://truthout.org/articles/ice-is-monitoring-and -targeting-immigration-activists/.

Lugo-Lugo, Carmen R., and Mary K. Bloodsworth-Lugo. 2014. "'Anchor/Terror Babies' and Latina Bodies: Immigration Rhetoric in the 21st Century and the Feminization of Terrorism." *Journal of Interdisciplinary Feminist Thought* 8, no. 1: 1–21.

Luibhéid, Eithne, and Lionel Cantú Jr., eds. 2005. *Queer Migrations: Sexuality, US Citizenship, and Border Crossings*. Minneapolis: University of Minnesota Press.

Lumsden, Stephanie. 2016. "Reproductive Justice, Sovereignty, and Incarceration: Prison Abolition Politics and California Indians." *American Indian Culture and Research Journal* 40, no. 1: 33–46.

Lykes, M. Brinton, Erin Sibley, Kalina M. Brabeck, Cristina Hunter, and Yliana Johansen-Méndez. 2015. "Participatory Action Research with Transnational and Mixed-Status Families: Understanding and Responding to Post-9/11 Threats in Guatemala and the United States." In *The New Deportations Delirium: Interdisciplinary Responses*, edited by Daniel Kanstroom and M. Brinton Lykes, 193–225. New York: New York University Press.

Manning, Stephen. 2014. "The Artesia Report." Innovation Law Lab, January 13. https://perma.cc/4CU6-WBWY.

Markowitz, Peter. 2011. "Deportation Is Different." *Journal of Constitutional Law* 13, no. 5: 1299–1361.

Martin, Lauren L. 2012a. "'Catch and Remove': Detention, Deterrence, and Discipline in US Noncitizen Family Detention Practice." *Geopolitics* 17, no. 2: 312–34.

Martin, Lauren L. 2012b. "Governing through the Family: Struggles over US Noncitizen Family Detention Policy." *Environment and Planning A: Economy and Space* 44, no. 4: 866–88.

Martínez, Pedro Santiago, Claudia Muñoz, Mariela Nuñez-Janes, Stephan Pavey, Fidel Castro Rodriguez, and Marco Saavedra. 2020. *Eclipse of Dreams: The Undocumented-Led Struggle for Freedom*. Chico, CA: AK Press.

May, Michael. 2013. "Los Infiltradores: How Three Young Undocumented Activists Risked Everything to Expose the Injustices of Immigrant Detention—and Invented a New Form of Protest." *The American Prospect*, June 21.

Mbembe, Achille. 1992. "The Banality of Power and the Aesthetics of Vulgarity in the Postcolony." *Public Culture* 4, no. 2: 1–30.

McKinnon, Sara L. 2009. "Citizenship and the Performance of Credibility: Audiencing Gender-Based Asylum Seekers in US Immigration Courts." *Text and Performance Quarterly* 29, no. 3: 205–21.

Mena Robles, Jorge, and Ruth Gomberg-Muñoz. 2016. "Activism after DACA: Lessons from Chicago's Immigrant Youth Justice League." *North American Dialogue* 19, no. 1: 46–54.

Menjívar, Cecilia, and Sang H. Kil. 2002. "For Their Own Good: Benevolent Rhetoric and Exclusionary Language in Public Officials' Discourse on Immigrant-Related Issues." *Social Justice* 29, no. 1/2: 160–76.

Mezzadra, Sandro. 2010. "The Gaze of Autonomy: Capitalism, Migration and Social Struggles." In *The Contested Politics of Mobility*, edited by Vicki Squire, 141–62. New York: Routledge.

Milner, Clyde A., II. 1994. "National Initiatives." In *The Oxford History of the American West*, edited by Clyde A. Milner II, Carol A. O'Connor, and Martha A. Sandweiss, 155–95. New York: Oxford University Press.

Mingus, Mia. 2010. "Wherever You Are Is Where I Want to Be." May 3. https:// leavingevidence.wordpress.com/2010/05/03/where-ever-you-are-is-where-i -want-to-be-crip-solidarity/.

Monk, Thelonious. 2010. "Evidence." Posted by "wojciechkucha," February 6. https://www.youtube.com/watch?v=qweSlfP6BtI.

Moreton-Robinson, Aileen. 2015. *The White Possessive: Property, Power, and Indigenous Sovereignty*. Minneapolis: University of Minnesota Press.

Morgan-Trostle, Juliana, Kexin Zheng, and Carl Lipscombe. 2018. *The State of Black Immigrants*. New York: NYU Law Immigrant Rights Clinic/Black Alliance for Just Immigration. http://stateofblackimmigrants.com.

Morris, Julia. 2017. "In the Market of Morality International Human Rights Standards and the Immigration Detention 'Improvement' Complex." In *Intimate Economies of Immigrant Detention*, edited by Dierdre Conlon and Nancy Hiemstra, 51–69. New York: Routledge.

Moten, Fred. 2015. "Blackness and Non-Performance." Lecture, Museum of Modern Art, New York, September 25. https://www.youtube.com/watch?v =G2leiFByIIg.

Muhammad, Khalil Gibran. 2010. *The Condemnation of Blackness: Race, Crime, and the Making of Modern Urban America*. Cambridge, MA: Harvard University Press.

Mukpo, Ashoka. 2018. "ICE Is Targeting Activists in Vermont, and the State's DMV Has Been Helping Them." American Civil Liberties Union, November 16. https://www.aclu.org/blog/immigrants-rights/ice-targeting-activists-vermont-and-states-dmv-has-been-helping-them.

Mulcahy, Linda. 2008. "The Unbearable Lightness of Being? Shifts towards the Virtual Trial." *Journal of Law and Society* 35, no. 4: 464–89.

Murakawa, Naomi. 2014. *The First Civil Right: How Liberals Built Prison America*. Oxford: Oxford University Press.

Musalo, Karen. 2003. "Revisiting Social Group and Nexus in Gender Asylum Claims: A Unifying Rationale for Evolving Jurisprudence." *DePaul Law Review* 52: 777–808.

Myerhoff, Barbara. 1982. "Life History among the Elderly: Performance, Visibility, and Re-membering." In *A Crack in the Mirror: Reflexive Perspectives in Anthropology*, edited by Jay Ruby, 99–117. Philadelphia: University of Pennsylvania Press.

Nancy, Jean-Luc. 2000. *Being Singular Plural*. Palo Alto, CA: Stanford University Press.

Nevins, Joseph. 2010. *Operation Gatekeeper and Beyond: The War on "Illegals" and the Remaking of the US-Mexico Boundary*. New York: Routledge.

Ngai, Mae. 2013. *Impossible Subjects: Illegal Aliens and the Making of Modern America*. Princeton, NJ: Princeton University Press.

Nicholls, Walter J. 2013. *The DREAMers: How the Undocumented Youth Movement Transformed the Immigrant Rights Debate*. Palo Alto, CA: Stanford University Press.

Noland, Carrie. 2009. *Agency and Embodiment: Performing Gestures/Producing Culture*. Cambridge, MA: Harvard University Press.

Noll, Gregor. 2005. "Salvation by the Grace of State? Explaining Credibility Assessment in the Asylum Procedure." In *Proof, Evidentiary Assessment and Credibility in Asylum Procedures*, edited by Gregor Noll, 197–214. Leiden/Boston: Martinus Nijhoff/Brill.

Omi, Michael, and Howard Winant. 1986. *Racial Formation in the United States: From the 1960s to the 1990s*. New York: Routledge.

Paik, A. Naomi. 2017. "Abolitionist Futures and the US Sanctuary Movement." *Race and Class* 59, no. 2: 3–25.

Palmer, Breanne J. 2017. "The Crossroads: Being Black, Immigrant, and Undocumented in the Era of #BlackLivesMatter." *Georgetown Journal of Law and Critical Race Perspectives* 9: 99–121.

Paskey, Stephen. 2016. "Telling Refugee Stories: Trauma, Credibility, and the Adversarial Adjudication of Claims for Asylum." *Santa Clara Law Review* 56, no. 3: 457–530.

Perla, Héctor, Jr. 2008. "Si Nicaragua Venció, El Salvador Vencerá: Central American Agency in the Creation of the U.S. Central-American Peace and Solidarity Movement." *Latin American Research Review* 43, no. 2: 136–58.

Peters, Julie Stone. 2008. "Legal Performance Good and Bad." *Law, Culture and the Humanities* 4, no. 2: 179–200.

Peutz, Nathalie, and Nicholas De Genova. 2010. "Introduction." In *The Deportation Regime: Sovereignty, Space, and the Freedom of Movement*, edited by Nicholas De Genova and Nathalie Peutz, 1–29. Durham, NC: Duke University Press.

Phippen, J. Weston. 2016. "Is It an Immigration Detention Facility or a Child-Care Center?" *The Atlantic*, May 6. https://www.theatlantic.com/national/archive/2016/05/immigration-childcare/481509/.

Pittman, Julie. 2020. "Released into Shackles: The Rise of Immigrant e-Carceration." *California Law Review* 108: 587–618.

Preston, Julia. 2015. "Hope and Despair as Families Languish in Texas Immigration Centers." *New York Times*, June 14. https://www.nytimes.com/2015/06/15/us/texas-detention-center-takes-toll-on-immigrants-languishing-there.html.

Puga, Ana Elena. 2012. "Migrant Melodrama and Elvira Arellano." *Latino Studies* 10, no. 3: 355–84.

Puga, Ana Elena. 2013. "Migrant Melodrama, Human Rights, and Elvira Arellano." In *Imagining Human Rights in Twenty-First-Century Theater*, edited by Brenda Werth, 155–76. New York: Palgrave Macmillan.

Puga, Ana Elena. 2016. "Migrant Melodrama and the Political Economy of Suffering." *Women and Performance: A Journal of Feminist Theory* 26, no. 1: 72–93.

Radul, Judy. 2011. "Video Chamber." In *A Thousand Eyes: Media Technology, Law, and Aesthetics*, edited by Marit Paasche and Judy Radul, 117–42. Berlin: Sternberg Press.

Razack, Sherene. 1998. *Looking White People in the Eye: Gender, Race, and Culture in Courtrooms and Classrooms*. Toronto: University of Toronto Press.

Reiman, Jeffrey. 2007. *The Rich Get Richer and the Poor Get Prison*. 8th ed. Boston: Allyn and Bacon.

Ricoeur, Paul. 1984. *Time and Narrative*. Vol. 1. Chicago: University of Chicago Press.

Roach, Joseph R. 1996. *Cities of the Dead: Circum-Atlantic Performance*. New York: Columbia University Press.

Robbins, Liz. 2017. "Once Routine, Immigration Check-ins Are Now High Stakes." *New York Times*, April 11. https://www.nytimes.com/2017/04/11/nyregion/ice-immigration-check-in-deportation.html?_r=0.

Rodríguez, Dylan. 2017. "The Political Logic of the Non-profit Industrial Complex." In *The Revolution Will Not Be Funded: Beyond the Non-profit Industrial Complex*, edited by INCITE! Women of Color against Violence Staff, 21–40. Cambridge, MA: South End Press.

Rodríguez, Juana María. 2003. *Queer Latinidad: Identity Practices, Discursive Spaces*. New York: New York University Press.

Rodríguez, Nestor, and Cecilia Menjívar. 2009. "Central American Immigration in the 'Post'–Civil Rights Era." In *How the United States Racializes Latinos: White Hegemony and Its Consequences*, edited by Jose Cobas, Jorge Duany, and Joe Feagin, 183–99. Kent, WA: Paradigm Press.

Rosas, Gilberto. 2006. "The Managed Violences of the Borderlands: Treacherous Geographies, Policeability, and the Politics of Race." *Latino Studies* 4, no. 4: 401–18.

Rosenbaum, Carrie. 2018. "Immigration Law's Due Process Deficit and the Persistence of Plenary Power." *Berkeley La Raza Law Journal* 28: 118–56.

Rothenberg, Daniel, ed. 2012. *Memory of Silence: The Guatemalan Truth Commission Report*. New York: Palgrave Macmillan.

Rutgers School of Law and Newark Immigrant Rights Clinic in conjunction with American Friends Service Committee. 2012. *Freed but Not Free: A Report Examining the Current Use of Alternatives to Immigrant Detention*. Newark, NJ: Rutgers School of Law.

Sack, Daniel, ed. 2017. *Imagined Theatres: Writing for a Theoretical Stage*. London: Taylor and Francis.

Saldaña-Portillo, María Josefina. 2016. *Indian Given: Racial Geographies across Mexico and the United States*. Durham, NC: Duke University Press.

Santa Ana, Otto. 2002. *Brown Tide Rising: Metaphors of Latinos in Contemporary American Public Discourse*. Austin: University of Texas Press.

Schechner, Richard. 1985. *Between Theater and Anthropology*. Philadelphia: University of Pennsylvania Press.

Schechner, Richard. 2003. *Performance Theory*. New York: Routledge.

Schenwar, Maya, and Victoria Law. 2020. *Prison by Any Other Name: The Harmful Consequences of Popular Reforms*. New York: New Press.

Schept, Judah. 2014a. "Prison Re-form: The Continuation of the Carceral State." Tennessee Students and Educators for Social Justice, July 15. https://tnsocialjustice

.wordpress.com/2014/07/15/prison-re-form-the-continuation-of-the-carceral -state/#more-640.

Schept, Judah. 2014b. "(Un)seeing Like a Prison: Counter-visual Ethnography of the Carceral State." *Theoretical Criminology* 18, no. 2: 198–223.

Schirmer, Jennifer. 1999. *The Guatemalan Military Project: A Violence Called Democracy.* Philadelphia: University of Pennsylvania Press.

Schneider, Rebecca. 2008. "Solo solo solo." In *After Criticism: New Responses to Art and Performance,* edited by Gavin Butt, 23–48. Hoboken, NJ: John Wiley and Sons.

Schneider, Rebecca. 2011. *Performing Remains: Art and War in Times of Theatrical Reenactment.* New York: Routledge.

Schriro, Dora. 2017. "Women and Children First: An Inside Look at the Challenges to Reforming Family Detention in the United States." In *Challenging Immigration Detention: Academics, Activists and Policy-makers,* edited by Michael Flynn and Matthew Flynn, 28–51. Cheltenham, UK: Edward Edgar.

Sekula, Allan. 1986. "The Body and the Archive." *October* 39: 3–64.

Sexton, Jared, and Elizabeth Lee. 2006. "Figuring the Prison: Prerequisites of Torture at Abu Ghraib." *Antipode* 38, no. 5: 1005–22.

Silva, Denise Ferreira da. 2009. "No-bodies: Law, Raciality and Violence." *Griffith Law Review* 18, no. 2: 212–36.

Simon, Jonathan. 2007. *Governing through Crime: How the War on Crime Transformed American Democracy and Created a Culture of Fear.* Oxford: Oxford University Press.

Simpson, Audra. 2014. *Mohawk Interruptus: Political Life across the Borders of Settler States.* Durham, NC: Duke University Press.

Smith, Andrea. 2013. "The Problem with Privilege." *Andrea Smith's Blog,* August 14. https://andrea366.wordpress.com/2013/08/14/the-problem-with-privilege-by -andrea-smith.

Speed, Shannon. 2019. *Incarcerated Stories: Indigenous Women Migrants and Violence in the Settler-Capitalist State.* Chapel Hill: University of North Carolina Press.

States, Bert O. 1985. *Great Reckonings in Little Rooms: On the Phenomenology of Theater.* Berkeley: University of California Press.

Stemen, Don. 2017. *The Prison Paradox: More Incarceration Will Not Make Us Safer.* New York: Vera Institute of Justice.

Story, Brett. 2017. "Against a 'Humanizing' Prison Cinema: *The Prison in Twelve Landscapes* and the Politics of Abolition Imagery." In *Routledge International Handbook of Visual Criminology,* edited by Michelle Brown and Eamonn Carrabine, 455–65. London: Taylor and Francis.

Stuelke, Patricia. 2014. "The Reparative Politics of Central America Solidarity Movement Culture." *American Quarterly* 66, no. 3: 767–90.

Stumpf, Juliet. 2006. "The Crimmigration Crisis: Immigrants, Crime, and Sovereign Power." *American University Law Review* 56, no. 2: 367–419.

Takei, Carl. 2017. "From Mass Incarceration to Mass Control, and Back Again: How Bipartisan Criminal Justice Reform May Lead to a For-Profit Nightmare." *University of Pennsylvania Journal of Law and Social Change* 20: 125–83.

TallBear, Kim. 2014. "Standing with and Speaking as Faith: A Feminist-Indigenous Approach to Inquiry." *Journal of Research Practice* 10, no. 2: 17. http://jrp.icaap .org/index.php/jrp/article/view/405/371.

Tamez, Margo. 2012. "The Texas-Mexico Border Wall and Ndé Memory." In *Beyond Walls and Cages: Prisons, Borders, and Global Crisis*, edited by Jenna M. Loyd, Matt Mitchelson, and Andrew Burridge, 56–69. Athens: University of Georgia Press.

Taussig, Michael. 1992. *The Nervous System*. New York: Routledge.

Taykhman, Nicole. 2016. "Defying Silence: Immigrant Women Workers, Wage Theft, and Anti-retaliation Policy in the States." *Columbia Journal of Gender and Law* 32: 96–144.

Taylor, Diana. 1997. *Disappearing Acts: Spectacles of Gender and Nationalism in Argentina's "Dirty War."* Durham, NC: Duke University Press.

Taylor, Diana. 2003. *The Archive and the Repertoire: Performing Cultural Memory in the Americas*. Durham, NC: Duke University Press.

Tazzioli, Martina, Glenda Garelli, and Nicholas De Genova. 2018. "Autonomy of Asylum? The Autonomy of Migration Undoing the Refugee Crisis Script." *South Atlantic Quarterly* 117, no. 2: 239–65.

Thiong'o, Ngũgĩ wa. 1997. "Enactments of Power: The Politics of Performance Space." *TDR/The Drama Review* 41, no. 3: 11–30.

Ticktin, Miriam. 2017. "A World without Innocence." *American Ethnologist* 44, no. 4: 577–90.

Vidler, Anthony. 2002. *Warped Space: Art, Architecture, and Anxiety in Modern Culture*. Cambridge, MA: MIT Press.

Vitale, Alex S. 2017. *The End of Policing*. New York: Verso.

Volpp, Leti. 2013. "Imaginings of Space in Immigration Law." *Law, Culture and the Humanities* 9, no. 3: 456–74.

Wake, Caroline. 2013. "To Witness Mimesis: The Politics, Ethics, and Aesthetics of Testimonial Theatre in *Through the Wire.*" *Modern Drama* 56, no. 1: 102–25.

Walia, Harsha. 2013. *Undoing Border Imperialism*. Chico, CA: AK Press.

Weheliye, Alexander. 2014. *Habeas Viscus: Racializing Assemblages, Biopolitics, and Black Feminist Theories of the Human*. Durham, NC: Duke University Press.

Williams, Jill. 2014. "The Spatial Paradoxes of 'Radical' Activism." *Antipode*, January 13. https://antipodeonline.org/2014/01/13/the-spatial-paradoxes-of-radical -activism.

Williams, Linda. 2001. *Playing the Race Card: Melodramas of Black and White from Uncle Tom to O. J. Simpson*. Princeton, NJ: Princeton University Press.

Williams, Raymond. 2006. *Modern Tragedy*. Peterborough, Canada: Broadview Press.

Ybarra, Patricia. 2017. *Latinx Theater in the Times of Neoliberalism*. Chicago: Northwestern University Press.

Zaman, Jawziya F. 2017. "Why I Left Immigration Law." *Dissent Magazine*, July 12. https://www.dissentmagazine.org/online_articles/left-immigration-law.

Note: Page numbers in *italics* indicate figures.

concrete form, as staging ground for surreal, 87–89
constitutional protections, 24, 26, 68,
142n8
"contaminated reality," 7
"continual state of emergency," 36
Corrections Corporation of America
(CCA), 62
Coulthard, Glen, 97, 98, 115
courtrooms, medieval, 80–81, 150n30.
See also immigration courtrooms
Crabapple, Molly, 9–10, 12
"crazy-making," 33–34
credible fear interviews, 72, 75, 85, 125–28
"criminal immigrant," figure of, 23, 25, 39
criminalization, 137n8; "aggravated felony,"
legal invention of, 24–25, 141–42n5; of
Black people, 67, 142n6; increase in,
4–5; of Latinxs, 25; of mobility, 155n17;
population-based logic of, 22; sidestepping of, 22–23
crimmigration, 23–27, 98

decolonial perspectives, 4, 7, 96–98, 115
Deferred Action for Childhood Arrivals
(DACA), 138n9
De Genova, Nicholas, 21, 135n3
Deleuze, Gilles, 16, 143n15
Department of Homeland Security (DHS),
35–37, 62–63, 68, 107
deportation: buses used for, 72–73, 73;
"cancellation of removal" application,
153n4; dramatization of, 11; family
detention as gateway to, 68; from
New York City, 21; noncitizens' lack of
protections, 24, 26, 68, 142n8; shielded
from view, 14–15; white supremacist
origin of, 24, 141n4. *See also* removal
derealization, 59, 87–89
detention, as term, 26. *See also* family
detention
deterrence, rhetoric of, 63, 68, 145n3, 145n7
Development, Relief, and Education for
Alien Minors (DREAM) Act, 137n8,
137–38n9

Dilley. *See* South Texas Family Residential
Center (Dilley)
disappearance, 86; dependence on spectacles, 38; as "deserved," 38, 137n8, 142n5;
destruction of factuality of, 34, 45; fragility of, 39, 40, 44; geographical location
not determined, 17, 129–33; historical
context of, 26–27, 34, 45; invisibility as,
34; loss of reality through, 27, 33–34, 59,
156n2; paradigm of state violence, 20;
and physical barriers, 31; as planned, 27;
psychological component of, 64; staging
of, 37–39; as state kidnapping, 26; as
state project, 33, 34; state's attempt to
manufacture fear of, 45; theater of, 15, 32
disappeared, as term, 26–27
Disappearing Acts (Taylor), 32
disappearing rooms, 3–4, 129
documentary theater, 94
dominance, 119–20, 124
doubling, 47, 88
due process protections, 24, 26, 68

"economic migrants," 102
Eden, Kathy, 117
Eisenstein, Sergei, 87–88, 152n39
empathy, 60, 92; kinesthetic, 44–46
emplacement, 80, 81
enemy of the state: concept of, 35–36;
dramatization of, 37–38, 113; image of,
10, 10; and population-based criminalization, 22
enforcement, 98
"Evidence" (Monk), 132
exceptionality, 5–6, 16
"expedited" removal, 62–63, 145n6, 148n20

fairness, critique of, 24, 91–92, 94
faith leaders, 30, 32, 52
families: detention of on US-Mexican
border, 62–64; innocence, targeting of,
64; kinship, attacks on, 30–31, 47, 62–63;
permanent separation, rehearsal for, 31;
and Removal Room, 30–31; separation
of, 62–63, 66. *See also* children

"illegal surrealism," 46

(im)migrants: Central American, role of in US society, 76–77; classification of, 16; deliberate funneling of to dangerous routes, 5, 131, 137n7; "economic," 102; as never really arrived, 11, 139n18; racialized as exploitable workforce, 3–4, 36, 78, 85, 135n3, 136n5, 156n18, 155n17; as "removable," 20, 23, 38, 43; required to participate in own exclusion, 11; as term, 135n1; treated as supplicants, 10, *10*, 16, 78, 85. *See also* noncitizens

immigration: crimmigration, 23–27, 98; floodgates metaphor for, 67, 99, 150n29; as racial justice issue, 6–7

Immigration and Customs Enforcement (ICE), 5; check-ins, 14–15, 19–22, 38, 141n2; humiliation, engineered spectacle of, 37–38; isolation tactics, 13, 30–31, 44, 47; shadow zone of law, 39; under Trump administration, 23–24. *See also* Border Patrol, US

Immigration and Customs Enforcement (ICE) officials: "the body" as term used by, 32; brutality of, 31–32, 39, 76–77; deportation officer, as job title, 40; impact of accompaniment teams on, 52–53; as petty sovereigns, 31. *See also* asylum officers

Immigration and Naturalization Service (INS), 107

immigration courtrooms: at Dilley, 81–86; elevation of judge, simulation of, 83–84; imagined as safe spaces, 80–81; inside detention centers, 15, 68–69, 81–86; migrant melodrama in, 94; spatial elements of, 80–84, *83*; as theaters, 1–2; trailer-courtroom image, *56*; virtual events, 15, 54, 56, 81–86, 88–89, 150–51n31, 151n32. *See also* judge; Removal Room

"immigration detention improvement complex," 15

immigration enforcement agencies: increase in criminalization, detention, deportation, and raids, 4–5

immigration justice movement, 1, 4–7; "allyship," asymmetry of, 93–94; Black-led, 6–7; challenges to family detention, 68; "inside-outside" strategy, 6; youth-led, 5. *See also* accompaniment; human rights regime

immigration law: contradictions of, 3; hypocrisy of, 4–5; 1980s as start of increase in, 24, 97, 136–37n6; opportunities to challenge, 40, 43, 46; racialized workforce manufactured by, 3–4, 36, 65, 78, 85, 135n3, 155n17, 155–56n18; reimagination of from (im)migrant's point of view, 12, *12*; rightlessness produced by, 26; as "second war," 26; spiritual poverty of, 13; split character of, 2–4; twin structure of, 101–3, 105–6, 115. *See also* asylum law; law

impossibility represented by gestures, *10*, 10–11

impunity, broadcasting of, 84

inadequacy, sensation of, 95

Indigenous peoples, 64; Native Americans, 7, 146n9, 147n15; and settler colonialism, 1–3, 145–46n8, 146n9

individual: vs. collective realities, 75–77, 92, 99, 113, 124; and recognition, 75–77, 92, 104–6, 113, 124; and tragic frame of asylum, 104–6, 113, 124

industrial development, 144n2

infiltration of detention centers, 55, 143–44n19

innocence, targeting of, 64

interfaith organizations, 46–47. *See also* sanctuary movement

intergenerational memories, 45

invisibility, 13–14, 26, 30, 33–35, 39, 118

Ionesco, Eugène, 84

Islamophobia, 36–37

Jubany, Olga, 104

judge: broadcast on screen, as no-show, 15, 56, 70, 82–85, *83*; as ecclesiastical figure, 81, 86, 150n30; elevation of, simulated, 83–84; engineering of spectacle by, *10*, 11–12. *See also* immigration courtrooms justice, 6–7, 98, 105; no-show, 56, 82; ob-*scene* iteration of, 81; staging of, 84, 87

Kafka, Franz, 84, 89, 151n35
Kaluli people, 132
kidnapping-detention-asylum, 77–78
kinesthetic empathy, 44–46

Las Casas, Bartolomé de, 2
Latin America, disappearance in, 26–27, 34
law: abstract normative principles of, 87; colonial as cruel and strange theater, 3; contradiction dispensed by, 84–85; criminal-law production frenzy, 24; embarrassment to, 84; founded on hopeless contradictions, 2; fragility of, 11, 39, 40, 44; impunity broadcasted by, 84; shadow zone of, 39; and subsumption, 123, 125–26. *See also* immigration law
Lee, Elizabeth, 71, 73
legal permanent residents (LPRS), 25
Lepecki, André, 43
liberal law-and-order discourse, 22
liberal tragedy, 104–5
linear chronology, legal and literary art of, 75–77
love, 6, 11, 52, 64, 98, 114–15

master-slave dialectic, 96
material form, 87
melodrama, migrant, 16, 94, 101–3, 114, 152n2
Mexico, 145–46n8; militarized immigration-containment partnership (Programa Frontera Sur), 67–68, 147n16; networks of deported people, 55, 143n18
mise-en-scène, 102–3, 129, 139n14, 140n23, 151n37; and asylum officials, 16; of immigration courtrooms, 1–2; as method, 7–14; plasticity of lived experience awakened by, 9, 13; racial boundaries redrawn by, 39; of Removal Room, 20, 23; of Requerimiento, 2; staging of abstract principles and concrete form,

87–89. *See also* scenographic detail; staging; theater
mobility: autonomy of, 6, 16–17, 77–79, 92, 100, 124, 140n22; border imperialism, 106, 155n17; designated as migration, 140n22; limited class of people recognized, 99; refugees, international definition of, 100–101, 154nn10–11; as threat to sovereignty, 100, 113; unsanctioned, 6, 16–17, 77–78, 100–103; US capital dependent on, 65. *See also* movement
Modern Tragedy (Williams), 104
Monk, Thelonious, 132
Moten, Fred, 46
movement, 42–44; battling of impulses, 45; choreography of accompaniment, 47, 53; doubling, 47; freedom of, 92, 124–25; kinesthetic gestures, 84; and policing, 43–44, 143n15. *See also* mobility
Myerhoff, Barbara, 38

Nancy, Jean-Luc, 88
national crisis rhetoric, 67
National Immigration Youth Alliance (NIYA), 143–44n19
nation-state system, 6, 65, 94, 103, 110, 118, 139n17, 140n22, 146n11, 154n12; and changes in humanitarian rights regime, 99–101
Ndé Lipan Apache, 7
neoliberalism, 54, 72, 75, 101, 104, 149n27
nervousness, 86–90
New Sanctuary Coalition of New York, 15, 20–21, 41–53; NGO model adopted by, 54
New York City, deportations in, 21
New York Field Office Enforcement and Removal Operations, 35
"nexus," 75–76
Ngai, Mae, 3
"ninth floor," 19. *See also* Removal Room
nobodies and somebodies, 11, 139n17
noncitizens: and constitutional protections, 24, 26, 68, 142n8; harsher punish-

ments for, 25, 141–42n5; as nonexistent, 35; as "removable," 20. *See also* (im)migrants

non-refoulement, 99–100, 154n9

Obama, Barack, 67
Obama administration, 5, 24, 67–69, 148n20; Border Patrol militarized by, 67–68
Online Detainee Locator, 129
open illusions, 31–32, 72–73
open secrets, 84, 151n34
order of release on recognizance/order of supervision, 21

pale, the, 139n17
personhood, legal, 8, 154n12
plausibility, 117–18
Poetics (Aristotle), 105, 117
police: anti-Black character of, 25, 37, 142n6; in Benjamin's theory, 40; "security" extended into new domains by, 40
policing: choreopolicing, 43, 143n15; function of recognition, 106; infrastructures of preceded targets, 37; movement, control over, 43–44, 143n15
positionality, questions of, 41–42, 45–46, 49
postwar racial liberalism, 149n28
power: asymmetry of, 91–96, 101, 115, 119; attempts at horizontal structures, 101; prison as spatial and temporal vector of, 80; and uncertainty, 21–23, 112, 141n2; unfair distribution of, 91–92
Preston, Julia, 69–70
prison-industrial complex: for-profit detention centers, 62; funding of, 67, 147n17; reemergence of under new terms, 68, 144n2
prison reform, 60–61; baiting of observers into acceptance of, 69–71, 88; exceptionalizing of negative elements, 71; family detention centers presented as, 58, 68; refusal to participate in, 79–80, 89–90, 91, 93; staging of, 61, 71; as staying power, 68, 75

prisons: body of, 80; as commodified captivity, 67, 85, 88; confinement as forgettable, 82–83, 88–89; crisis of form, 59, 89–90; "failures" of, 61; in film, 141n3; harm amplified by, 145n3; as heterotopias, 58–59, 61, 69–70, 80; as prerequisite of torture, 73–74; rebranded as "family residential centers," 59; as solutions to ambivalence, 65; as spatial and temporal vector of power, 80; visual asymmetry of, 72
Programa Frontera Sur, 67–68, 147n16
property, 54, 142n7
Puga, Ana Elena, 94, 102
punishment, 8, 22–23, 26; and shadow zone of law, 39; of transnational life, 74, 78–79
"purity" of asylum narrative, 7, 109, 111, 113, 124

racial elimination, 78, 87; family detention centers as spaces of, 15–16, 58, 63–64, 69; incarceration as, 63–64; in language of Requerimiento, 1, 3, 15–16; and politics of recognition, 58, 61; women's reproduction targeted, 63–64, 67, 146nn9–11
racial hunting, 36, 63
racialization, 142n12; of the removed, 38–39; whiteness used to dismantle, 41; workforce manufactured by immigration law, 3–4, 36, 65, 78, 85, 135n3, 155n17, 155–56n18
"racial naturalization," 136n5
racial profiling, 25
Ragbir, Ravi, 20–21, 48, 53
reality, 103, 116–17; concrete, 87–89, 152n39; "contaminated," 7, 124; false, 27; loss of through disappearance, 27, 33–34, 59, 156n2; planes of, 121–22, 126–28; as set of spatial and temporal relations, 14
"reality effect," 116–17
recognition: as act of grace, 95; asylum officers' moral attachment to act of, 112, 114; as benevolent, 95, 98, 105; coloniality of, 4–7; and colonial project, 96–97;

recognition (continued)
    as developmental stage, 96; fairness,
    critique of, 91–92; individualized, 75–77,
    92, 104–6, 113, 124; mutuality of, 96, 115,
    153n6; policing function of, 106; politics
    of asylum, 96–106; and psychological
    attachment, 97, 114–15; refusal to seek,
    17, 79, 85–90, 93, 114–15; right not to tell
    your story, 92, 124–28, 149n27; and self-
    overcoming, 124; and settler colonial-
    ism, 98, 135–36n4; and sovereignty, 95;
    and state violence, 98; symbolic award-
    ing of by audience, 94; tragic, 104–5, 118,
    124; universal human need for assumed,
    92, 97; as unsustainable, 124
reform, concept of, 60–61
refugees, 154n9, 154n12; international
    definition of, 100–101, 154nn10–11
"refugee theater," 94
refusal, 20–21; as act of accompaniment,
    93; to adopt sovereign position, 93–94;
    to participate in prison reform, 79–80,
    89–90, 91, 93; right not to tell your
    story, 92, 124–28, 149n27; to seek rec-
    ognition, 17, 79, 85–90, 93, 114–15; of
    sovereignty, 93
rehearsal, 9, 13–14, 16, 96; of compassion,
    118–20; of permanent separation, 31;
    practice independent of object, 84; and
    repetition, 107, 108
removability: of brown bodies, 37; drama-
    tization of, 37–38; racial production of,
    38–39; visibility of, 15
removal: "catch and remove" initiative,
    63; "expedited," 62–63, 145n6, 148n20;
    as physical and perceptual project, 20;
    step-by-step, 30–31. See also deportation
Removal Room, 17; accompaniment teams
    banned from, 48–53, 51; any sphere
    of existence as, 20; check-ins, 14–15,
    19–20, 38, 141n2; circulation, displays of,
    43–44; graded series of access to offices,
    30–31; image of, 28–29; invisibility of
    physical environment, 34; mise-en-
    scène of, 20, 23; physical environment

of, 27–40, 51–52; rearrangement of,
    50–53, 51; as rehearsal for permanent
    separation, 31; sense of danger in, 30;
    spatial elements of, 20, 30–31, 65, 74.
    See also immigration courtrooms
repetition, 53; in asylum process, 107, 108,
    116, 121, 124–26
representation, 13–14, 140n23, 141n3
Requerimiento, 1–3, 11, 15, 139n17
retraumatization, 126, 156n19
Ricoeur, Paul, 75
"right to have rights," 48–49
Robertson, Shari, 107
"roundup," 71
Rouse, Charlie, 132
Ruiz, Juan Carlos, 46

safety: and citizenship privileges, 41, 45,
    49, 93; detainee fear of US, 76–79, 88,
    89; and white privilege, 45, 54–55
Saldaña-Portillo, María Josefina, 64
sanctuary, physical, 21, 94, 152n1
sanctuary movement: asymmetry
    reproduced by, 93–94; churches, 48;
    horizontal structure attempted, 54, 101;
    new (2000s), 93–94, 101, 152n1; original
    (1980s), 101–2, 155n15; screening within,
    94, 102, 152n1. See also accompaniment
    teams; New Sanctuary Coalition of
    New York
scenographic detail, 8–11, 94, 136n5,
    141n1; and accompaniment, 15, 23; and
    criminalization, 23; families not allowed
    to say goodbye, 31; incoherence of, 58;
    and institutional arrangements of bod-
    ies in space, 138–39n14; persistence or
    "insistence" of, 16; and Removal Room,
    20; terror, arrangement of, 34. See also
    mise-en-scène; theater
Schept, Judah, 60
security guards, 34, 39, 50–51, 82, 85
self-restraint, 23, 42–43
September 11, 2001, 36, 62, 142n7
settler colonialism, 64–65, 146n9; Indig-
    enous critiques of, 7; Latina women

and children, stereotypes of, 63–64, 67; and recognition, 98, 135–36n4; unfinished conquest on border, 78. *See also* coloniality

Sexton, Jared, 71, 73

"showing doing," 11

sidestepping, 22–23

silence, 23; required for accompaniment, 41–43

silencing of autonomy, 78–79

"silent raids," 30, 34

Simpson, Audra, 97, 98

Smith, Andrea, 80

social movements, 7, 48–49, 54

solidarity, true, 129

South Texas Family Residential Center (Dilley), 15, 56–58, 147n17; immigration courtroom at, 81–86; nervous accompaniment at, 86–90; structure and processes, 72–86; visitation trailer, 74–81. *See also* family detention; family detention centers

sovereignty: citizen-judge as personification of, 95; mobility as threat to, 100, 113; and recognition, 95; refusal of, 93; universalist principles as challenge to, 99

Spanish conquistadors, 1–3, 11

spatial logics: family detention as spatial fix, 65, 78; irreconcilable, 87–88; of Removal Room, 20, 30–31, 65, 74; of "silent raids," 30, 34

spirit, promiscuity of, 46–47

staging: concrete form, as staging ground for surreal, 87–89; of death penalty, 139n16; of derealization, 87–89; of disappearance, 37–39; of justice, 84, 87; of prison reform, 61, 71; of "refugee theater," 94. *See also* theater

state: belief in virtuous core of, 49; disappearance as project of, 33–34. *See also* nation-state system

stateless people, 21

state theater, 15, 27, 78

state violence, 20, 49, 98, 105; escalation of under Trump administration, 23–24;

and recognition, 98; as structural and systemic, 49

Story, Brett, 60

storytelling, 76, 117–18

subject-object relations, 14

supplicants, (im)migrants treated as, 10, 10, 16, 78, 85

surrealism, 87–89

surveillance, 25, 43, 72, 138n9, 142n7, 143n15; ankle monitors, 37, 75, 149n25

swearing in, ritual of, 7–9; reimagination of, 12, 12

Taussig, Michael, 33, 45

Taylor, Diana, 27, 32, 38, 114

T. Don Hutto Family Detention Center, 62, 65–68, 144n2, 147–48n18, 148n20

terror: objective project of, 45; proxy work of, 32; recognition thrown into crisis by, 79, 89–90, 92–93; regional zone of, 79; scenographic arrangement of, 34; state's attempt to manufacture, 45, 72–73

Texas Rangers, 36

theater: absurdism and surrealism, 84–85, 88–89; asylum hearing as, 113–14; Brechtian tradition, 140n23; of criminalization, 23; disappearance as, 15, 32; experimentation process, 8–9, 14; gesture in, 8, 84; legal absurdity as, 84–85; open illusions, 31–32, 72–73; performance expected of detainees, 76–79, 86–90, 91; social status, dramatization of, 38; spatial elements of, 8, 14, 87–88, 103. *See also* scenographic detail; staging

theater of the oppressed, 8–9

theatricality: of nonsense, 2–3; of Requerimiento, 2–3

Ticktin, Miriam, 124

Tohono O'odham nation, 7

tragic frame of asylum, 103–6, 113, 117–19, 124

transnational accompaniment networks, 55, 143n18, 155n15

transnational life, 6, 7, 17; punishment of, 74, 78–79; and undocumented status, 111